D0572407

just tell me HOW it works

Practical Help for Adults on All-Things-Digital

Paul Lance

Just Tell Me How It Works: *Practical Help for Adults on All-Things-Digital*

Published by:
Grandview Press
13930 Old Harbor Lane, Suite 105
Marina del Rey, CA 90292

Author photo by Amy Cantrell Photography
Company logo designed by Khaos Digital

For general information on our products and services, please contact Customer Service, Grandview Press, 13930 Old Harbor Lane, Suite 105, Marina del Rey, CA 90292.

Books may be purchased for educational, business or sales promotional use. For information please write: Special Markets Department, Grandview Press, 13930 Old Harbor Lane, Suite 105, Marina del Rey, CA 90292

To contact the author for further information about workshops, presentations, seminars, and educational materials, write to: Paul A. Lance, % Grandview Press, 13930 Old Harbor Lane, Suite 105, Marina del Rey, CA 90292

You may also e-mail the author at Paul.Lance@JustTellMeHowItWorks.com.
Visit the author's website: www.justtellmehowitworks.com.

Library of Congress Control Number: 2013944692
Grandview Press, Marina del Rey, CA

ISBN-13: 9780615842332
ISBN-10: 061584233X

10 9 8 7 6 5 4 3 2 1

Author's Acknowledgments

First and foremost, I would like to dedicate this book to my wife, Ellen Klugman Lance, whose support, encouragement, and editorial comments have made this adventure possible.

I would also like to thank the people who helped make this book a reality. In no particular order (and with apologies for anyone I may have missed): Steven Lance, Tom Ruffner, Tom Cavanaugh, Carol Mitch, Sasha Ruocco, Suzanne Wickham, Rion Dugan, Jerry and Ellen Hirschberg, Bill Bradford, Eric Doctorow, David Lewine, Jeffrey Cole, Ph.D., Mark Marcum, Simon Knights, Burk Sauls, Tricia Stewart Shui, Scott Millward, Gerald Alcantar, Ivo Gerscovich, Lucy Hood, Doug Korte, Craig Renwick, Doug Goetz, Ken LaCorte, Jennifer Pooley, David Catzel, Mike Mataraza, Marc Sacher, Max Lance, Dan Bienenfeld, Mildred Lewis, Adam Fox, Dennis DeMeyere, John Flores, Nancy McCabe, Gabriel Gornell, Angela Gardner, Stephen Hanselman, Frank Fochetta, Cathy Hemming, John Silbersack, Steven Sammons.

And finally: many thanks to the Wikipedians – those faceless, nameless people from all around the world – whose contributions have made the online encyclopedia Wikipedia possible. Also to the myriad of bloggers and online correspondents who helped clarify for me concepts and issues on all-things-digital.

Our Promise

Digital technology changes at an astonishing rate. As a result, many books of this nature become obsolete quickly.

Our promise is that the material and information you're reading within **Just Tell Me How It Works**: *Practical Help for Adults on All-Things-Digital* is current and up-to-date.

How can we make this promise? Well, our book is printed **on-demand**. In English, this means that every copy of the book is fresh-off-the-press. As a result, our publisher has promised it can turn-around changes to this book within two short weeks.

What this means to you, the reader, is this book will always be at the forefront of technology. We'll not just include the latest digital device or service; but we'll continually scan the future of technology and offer up what's about to enter the marketplace and what's 5-10 years down the road (just peruse Chapters 24 and 25 for a look into the future).

So just relax; enjoy the book; and be reassured you're on the cutting-edge!

Preface

Welcome to the adult guide to the digital world.

- Are you feeling overwhelmed by all the new technology?

- Afraid of what you don't know?

- Worried that you're being left behind?

- Exasperated by a world in which everything is turning "digital"?

- Intimidated by the constant change?

You're not alone in these feelings. Millions of highly competent adults find themselves nearly paralyzed at the thought of operating in an increasingly digital universe.

Just Tell Me How It Works believes you don't have to feel overwhelmed or afraid or intimidated. More to the point, we believe you should be in charge of this technology, not the other way around. This book will offer what you need to know in order to participate more confidently in this new **digital world**.

Embarking on the Journey

Just Tell Me How It Works will guide you – gently and effortlessly – through every facet of this **digital universe**, which, for our purposes, we'll broadly define as those devices and services that can store, copy, edit, move or exchange information.

We will address neophytes as well as any of you whose off-the-cuff learning has left you frustrated and stymied by gaps in understanding.

We'll start with the basics of computers. Don't panic…it's not as complicated as you've been led to believe. (And for those of you already using a computer, we'll help plug in the holes that might still be on your mind.)

We'll show you the fundamental hardware and accessories that make up a computer. We'll explain – in ways you can easily comprehend – what each item does, and, more importantly, how you can use it.

Whether you're a first time driver or have already taken it out for a spin, we'll demystify the Internet while sharing tricks and tips on how to navigate this informational super-highway with ease.

We'll then turn your attention to entertainment. Whether you've been lingering at the edge of the pool or have already gotten your feet wet, **Just Tell Me How It Works** will make you comfortable with taking the plunge in two areas: the new digital generation of devices which you may be familiar with; and newly invented devices with which you may not be familiar.

We'll focus on televisions, recorders, music players, DVD players, reading devices, iPads and tablets, and even your telephone – since, as you've seen on the news and from younger generations, phones are morphing into mini-entertainment centers.

Additionally, this book will explore how devices can enhance your basic entertainment needs such as reading and music and photography. We'll even show you ways to find new hobbies (or even improve your existing ones). After all, the original intent of technology has always been to provide you with added pleasures in life.

We'll also help you navigate through the tangled mess known as "**social networking**".

You have undoubtedly heard about Facebook, YouTube, Twitter, and, perhaps, Skype or Facetime. Some of you may have already gotten a jump-start and are already connected. Social networking has become one of the most popular forms of online communication; and this book will help you learn about social networking venues in order to connect more closely to family and friends.

And finally, we'll offer up a peek into the future.

We'll show you a glimpse of what you might expect in this ever-evolving digital universe. By the end of the book, we want you to feel comfortable not only with what is already out there; but also with what is coming in the years ahead.

We know some things about you

We know you're much smarter than the digital society gives you credit for.

We know that while you might not understand how a device works – or even what it looks like – once something is explained to you, you're smart enough to try it out; and, if it works for you, you're clever enough to incorporate it into your daily life.

We know you're capable, practical and effective – let's be honest, you've been that way all your adult life – and we know you are more than up to the challenge and adventure of whatever life can offer you.

A word about change

You may have heard the quotation *"The only thing constant in life is change."*

You're probably muttering: "Yeah, and whoever said that didn't ever have to put up with the barrage of new electronic devices, new upgrades, new manuals" – the digital list of changes goes on and on.

Just relax. Take a deep breath.

Yes, changes will continue – especially in the digital marketplace.

But is the rash of technology any different from car manufacturers putting out new model cars every fall or the prospect of new movies being released every week? Not really.

What's more, once you take the plunge and learn something once, chances are any changes that come along will just be a variation from those basics – so the learning curve isn't as steep as you might imagine. (Think of it as riding a bicycle: once you learn the basics, the rest is simple and you'll never forget how to ride).

About this book

Here's what you can expect to find inside this book:

Up-to-Date

The information in this book is completely up-to-date. Since the publisher allows us to add any new changes or innovations in technology (with only a two week turnaround), what you're reading is cutting-edge material.

Simplicity

We plan to make everything simple. After all, that's the whole point of this book. Yet even as we give you the simple steps-by-steps, the book won't be "talking down" to you. (You don't deserve to be condescended to).

Skip around

While we've grouped the content into basic categories, we don't recommend you read the book from cover to cover. Quite the opposite. Instead, flip to the Table of Content then jump to the sections that interest you.

Do you love to read and want to know about electronic book readers? Skip ahead to that section.

Are you planning to purchase a new television or camera and are a little overwhelmed by the choices? Go right to the appropriate section.

You get the idea – make this your book, your entry into what interests you most.

Definitions

You'll find definitions highlighted throughout the book. We know, we know – boring. You want a book that helps you understand technology…not a dictionary. But try not to skip over these highlighted words.

Technology has its own lingo and understanding that technology is lingo-dependent. In many cases, you'll probably encounter the same words again and again. Skipping over the words (or having the wrong definition) results in gaps in understanding. Better to learn them the first time around than to keep asking 'what did that mean?'

The basics: How does it work?

We'll always start off each section by answering some straightforward questions:

- What is it?

- What does it do?

- How do I use it?

- How does it fit into my life?

- Is this right for me?

And we'll summarize each section with:

The pros

We'll explain the advantages of a particular device. This will become especially helpful when you want to compare two or more pieces of technology and ascertain which one is right for you.

The cons

Every piece of technology has its downside. Just as some people enjoy jazz music, while others prefer rock-and-roll or rhythm and blues; so, too, there are pros and cons within any digital device.

We'll navigate these "cons" as objectively as possible in order to help you make informed decisions on what works best for you.

The hidden costs

We'll also provide you with the "hidden costs" behind any digital device. Sometimes, these hidden costs are financial; while other times the hidden costs might involve your time (or might heighten your frustration level). We'll guide you through these waters.

And now...

We promised you simplicity, so let's just dive right in:

Contents

Contents:

CONTENTS

CONTENTS

Section 1: The Device

Chapter 1

Computers: The Basics

Who should read this section

Digital age newbies; or anyone who already uses a computer but feels ill-at-ease because of gaps in his or her basic understanding about computers and computer lingo.

If you're planning to buy a new computer and are uncertain whether you should purchase a desktop or a laptop; a Windows computer or an Apple Mac, we'll explain in easy terms what each choice means and has to offer.

Who should skip this section

If you already own a computer and feel comfortable using it, you might just want to skim through the next few chapters until we hit upon a topic that catches your attention and interest.

Understanding computers

We understand that many of you might already own and operate a computer.

For those who feel sufficiently computer-savvy, just skip ahead until you find the section(s) you're interested in learning more about.

For those who are afraid of computers – or just want a refresher course – we'll offer a basic explanation in our hope to take away any hesitancy, confusion, or pre-conceptions you might have:

Quite simply: The computer is a **box**.

Normally, people think of computers as their monitor and keyboard, but, in actuality, the computer is a big clunky box (see above image on left as one example).

Laptops are also boxes, albeit not big and clunky. We'll get to those sleek and thin computers (see above image on right) in just a little bit.

You already have plenty of "boxes" around your home or apartment. Your refrigerator and stove are "boxes". Your television is a "box". Your radio or stereo or microwave ovens are all "boxes".

You get the idea…

Most of our modern conveniences come in box-like shapes. Inside, they are a mass of wires and electrical components, all arranged to accomplish certain tasks and all designed to make your life easier.

The same holds true for a computer.

Inside the **box** are a jumble of wires and electronics.

> The "**box**" is also referred to by a variety of names: "housing unit", "tower", "box", "cabinet", or "computer case". They all serve to describe the computer itself.

We'll list just a few of the essentials, but you really don't need to understand what's inside. (In the same way you don't need to understand what the electronics are for inside a refrigerator – you just need to know that it works.)

Hopefully, having this basic lingo will help make trips to the computer store – or conversations with computer repair geeks or even a friend or family member – a little easier.

Motherboard

The heart-and-soul of the computer. Essentially, the motherboard is a flat panel (a circuit board) that is usually **affixed to one side** of the computer box interior. All the other electronics are plugged into the motherboard. (Hence the name!)

See figure below for an image of a **motherboard**.

Imagine this image as taking up one entire side of the computer box.

Central Processing Unit (often called the "CPU" or "processor")

Simply: this is the "brains" of the computer and the most important element of the computer system. The CPU is plugged into the Motherboard.

Memory

This is the internal storage area in the computer. The term "**memory**" is appropriate as these are actually computer chips that hold information. These chips are expandable, meaning you can always add more chips / memory to your existing computer, without having to buy a new one.

Memory is also what allows you and the computer to **multi-task**.

> "**Multi-task**" means the ability to allow you to perform more than one task at the same time.
>
> As an example, you can run more than one computer program simultaneously: You can be typing in a word processing document; switch to sending an e-mail; then switch to a game of Solitaire.
>
> In this example all three programs would be up-and-running at the same time.

Mass storage (also known as the "hard drive")

The hard drive is a device that stores large amounts of data, which could include photos, music, personal correspondence and much more. The hard drive is also plugged into the Motherboard.

> A quick distinction between Memory and Mass Storage…
>
> "**Memory**" refers to the storage area within the computer. This storage, however, is temporary – when the computer is turned off, nothing is retained in the memory.
>
> In "**mass storage**" or your "**hard drive**", information is retained even when the computer is turned off. This enables you to save pictures, documents, files, e-mails and so-forth in permanent storage within your computer.

Ports

This is just another way to describe the "**slots**" or "**outlets**" that are found along the back of the **computer**.

> In most new computers, you'll also find these **ports / slots** located along the front panel of the computer (for easy access).

These ports / slots allow you to plug in a myriad of **devices** such as a monitor, keyboard, mouse, printer and so-forth.

> All these **devices** will be discussed later in this (and the following) chapter.

There are two common types of ports / plugs:

USB Ports / Plugs

Most ports / slots are known as "**USB ports**" and they accommodate what are called "**USB plugs**" (see below).

USB is short for *Universal Serial Bus*, a standard term the computer industry uses to describe cables and their connections.

At the end of most keyboards and the mouse, you'll find a USB plug (similar to the plug above). The USB plug is inserted into the port / slot on the computer itself.

On some devices – such as (say) a printer – you'll attach one end of the USB plug into the computer (as per our example above). The other end of the USB plug attaches directly into the printer (into a USB plug that's nearly identical to the image above).

In short: If you want a device – such as a printer or keyboard or mouse – to work, you have to plug it into one of these ports, just as you'd plug a lamp into an outlet in order to make it work.

HDMI Ports / Plugs

A second type of port / plug is known as an "**HDMI port**" and they accommodate what are called "**HDMI plugs**" (**See figures below – the figure on the left is the port; the figure on the right is the plug**).

> **HDMI** stands for *High Definition Multimedia Interface*. In English: these cables allow for easy transfer of high-definition information.
>
> These cables are especially handy – and have become the current standard – for most modern televisions and computer monitors.

The HDMI port / plug is often used to accommodate most modern monitors. You insert one end into the HDMI port (left image in our graphic above); the other end is inserted into the monitor (usually at the very back).

DVD drive

Computers come equipped with a **DVD drive**, located on the front panel of the computer.

> The **DVD drive** is a "**tray**" which allows you to insert a CD or DVD disc.
>
> Some newer model computers come with a Blu-ray drive. Same principle as the DVD drive with the added bonus of being able to play high-definition Blu-ray discs as well. (See Chapter 9 for additional details on DVD and Blu-ray).
>
> The upshot of high-definition: you get a sharper picture with crystal-clear resolution.

Quick instructions to operate the DVD drive:

1. There is a small button just below (and to the right) of the drive.

2. Push the button, and the tray to the DVD drive opens.

3. You then insert a disc – all boxed (packaged) software comes with a disc or, if you're so inclined, you can even insert a DVD movie to watch on your computer. (See Chapter 3 on Software for a more in-depth explanation).

4. Once the disc sets properly in the tray – with the top side upward (shiny side down) – you push the small button just below the drive to close the tray.

5. Once the tray is closed, the computer will automatically load the program (or movie) you've inserted.

By now, you may be muttering to yourself: "Enough of the nuts-and-bolts, how do I pick the right computer?"

Fair enough…let's move on. We'll make picking the right computer very, very simple:

Picking the right computer

In order for computers to work, they must contain an **operating system**.

> An "**operating system**" (OS) is a pre-installed set of software programs that manages the computer and its various pieces of hardware and peripheral devices (such a keyboard, mouse, printer and so forth).

While there are many "manufacturers", there are only **two types** of computers you can buy.

> Okay, we lied…
>
> Technically, there are **<u>four</u> types of operating systems** for most computers: Microsoft Windows, Apple's OS, Linux and Google's OS.
>
> Since Linux is such a small percentage of the marketplace – and, if you're interested in Linux, you probably already way overqualified for this material – we've decided not to cover it in this book.
>
> Google's Android and Chrome are also, technically, operating systems, but are used primarily with cell phones and online tablets, so, again, we won't be covering them here.
>
> You might, however, look at Chapter15 on Cell Phones for more information on the Android.

One type of computer – and by far the most popular – runs on Microsoft Windows.

The second type of computer is the **Mac** which runs on Apple's operating system.

> **Mac** is short for "**Macintosh**" (the apple / fruit).
>
> For trivia fans, the forerunner to the Mac was named the Lisa. Aimed at the corporate market, the name "Lisa" was (mercifully) switched to the Mac.

That's it. That's all you need to know. Either you buy a Window-based computer or an Apple-based computer.

How simple is that!

> So simple it's worth repeating a second time:
>
> You can only buy **one of two types of computers**:
>
> Either a <u>Window</u>-based computer; or
>
> An <u>Apple</u>-based Mac computer.

> Again, our apology to Google's **Chrome** and the **Linux** computers, neither of which have made any sizable dent in the marketplace.

Comparing Windows with the Mac

Let's start with similarities – and there are lots of similarities between these two types of **computers**.

> We're actually talking about two types of **operating systems**, but to make life simple, we're calling them two types of **computers**.

For a start:

Both utilize a monitor, keyboard and a mouse.

Both automatize certain essential functions. For example, when you click on an image or load a disc into the computer tray, the associated programs will load up automatically. (Makes sense since the basic purpose of a computer is to make everything simple.)

Both allow the user (you) to interface with the computer using symbols and images rather than straight text.

If you look at the **images above**, you'll see examples of the **desktops** for Windows (on the left) and the Mac (on the right).

"**Desktop**" refers to the main screen that appears whenever you start up your computer.

As you can see, they look surprisingly alike – especially when you realize that the background image can be changed to suit your individual tastes.

In these graphics, both contain images – along the side and bottom of the desktop – that you click on in order to activate the respective program.

So if they're basically the same, how do I choose one type of computer over the other?

Here's the general rule-of-thumb:

- Windows focuses on office / business functions while Mac focuses on graphics and multimedia.

- Mac is considered preferable for visual arts or entertainment purposes while Windows is best suited for business use.

- Mac is popularly used for photo editing and for playing video and music.

- While Windows is universally used by different computer manufacturers (Dell, Gateway, Hewlett-Packard), the Mac is used only with Apple's hardware and software.

- Windows is used by a majority of computer users, but is more vulnerable to being **hacked**. Mac is considered a (reasonably) more secure operating system.

The term "**hacked**" refers to someone's malicious ability to tap into your computer – usually from another computer – and infect your computer with viruses and so forth. Very nasty stuff.

We'll discuss how to protect yourself in Chapter 3 on Software (in the section on Protecting your Computer).

Desktop versus laptop: Which is right for you?

Let's make sure you're with us so far.

Essentially, there are two types of computers you can purchase – either a Mac with an Apple operating system or a computer with a Windows operating system.

Next thing you need to decide: do I want a desktop or a laptop?

Okay, what's a "**desktop**" and what's a "**laptop**"?

As the names imply, a desktop is a larger computer – especially when you also factor in the monitor, keyboard and mouse – that tends to fit on…well, on your desk.

A laptop computer is a **portable** computer. The screen (monitor), keyboard and mouse are all built into the laptop. And, as you can imagine, the laptop is small enough and portable enough to comfortably fit on…well, on your lap.

> And we do mean "**portable**". You can take the laptop wherever you go – whether traveling, visiting or just going to the local coffee shop.
>
> Because of its long-lasting battery life, you can turn on and run your laptop computer wherever you might be, without the need to plug it in.

That's it in a nutshell:

A desktop computer takes up space – you'll certainly need a desk or table top space to set up your desktop computer. The desktop computer is considered stationary – once you've set it up, **chances are it will stay there**.

> You <u>can</u> move the **desktop**, but that means disassembling the plugs, wires and connections. It's often not really worth the effort.

A laptop computer is portable; takes up very little space; and you can take it whenever you're on the go.

Ultrabook – Touch Screen - Tablet

A new variation of the traditional laptop called an "Ultrabook" has recently hit the marketplace and will only increase in functionality and gain further popularity over the next few years.

Manufacturers may invent new names for the Ultrabook to try to carve out their own brand identity. Regardless of brand differences, this kind of laptop has many of the following key features:

- Super thin

- Extremely lightweight

- Has a touch screen (where you interact directly with the laptop by tapping or swiping your fingers on the screen)

- Many have (or will soon have) a 180 degree hinge that rotates the touch screen to form into a tablet.

Consider the Ultrabook the wave of the future for computers.

This laptop is a three-in-one hybrid with the full power of a traditional laptop; the flexibility of a touch screen device; and the portability of an iPad / Tablet.

We'll discuss this hybrid further in Chapter 14 on iPads and Tablets; and certainly recommend you peruse that chapter if the Ultrabook catches your fancy.

What's the catch?

The laptop or Ultrabook computers sound ideal – what's the catch?

There really isn't a catch.

In years past, you needed the bigger, chunkier desktop computer in order to hold all the pieces necessary to run the computer and its assorted programs.

As technology evolved and computer parts became miniaturized, manufacturers were able to compress powerful electronics into the laptop computer.

Today, laptop computers are as powerful as most desktop computers and the prices are comparable.

If there are any potential trade-offs: the size of a laptop screen is usually quite small. Desktop monitors are usually double the size of a portable laptop, making it easier to see what's on the screen. Additionally, the compact size of laptops can make them more ergonomically challenging (and some people find the touch pad annoying).

Still, given the laptop's power and portability, their squished keyboards might be a small price to pay.

Bridging both worlds: A docking station

If you decide on a laptop or Ultrabook, you have the additional option to purchase what is known as a "**docking station**".

Somewhat self-explanatory, this is a small device (or "**station**") into which your portable computer nests (or "**docks**"); and which contains ample connections to plug in a printer, monitor, mouse and keyboard and so forth.

Essentially, your docking station can be set up as a "home base" – with all of the size and functionality of a desktop computer – yet when you're ready to travel or just head out to the local coffee shop, you simply remove your laptop or Ultrabook and away you go.

Okay, so now what? Steps to set up your computer

So you've mulled all the options and you've gone out and bought a (Mac or Windows) computer as a (desktop or laptop). Now what?

Again, very simple. **Here's the basic step-by-step**:

1. Purchase your computer.

    - You can buy a computer at any number of retail outlets including Costco, Best Buy, the Apple Store and so forth.

    - You can also buy a computer online – but this is a Catch-22 / trick comment, since this pre-supposes you already have a computer and can go onto the Internet to buy a computer.

        Still, you can always call Information on your telephone for companies like Apple, Dell, Hewlett-Packard – all of whom will be happy to sell you their computers over the phone.

    - Many places will offer to set up your computer (for a fee); but why spend the extra money when it's easy enough to do it yourself:

2. Your purchased desktop computer will generally come in one or two large boxes. While this will obviously vary based on manufacturer, you should find inside the box:

    - The computer "box" – yes, that big boxy thing that takes up all that space – see our description in the first few paragraphs of this chapter.

    - A monitor

    - A keyboard

    - A mouse

    - Accessories (that includes cords, plugs, some software and more).

Setup for your laptop

In the case of setting up your laptop, the steps are so much easier.

Since the monitor, keyboard and mouse are all self-contained within the laptop computer, all you need to do is plug it in and push the start button.

(Yes, the laptop computer can function solely on its battery, but in the beginning we recommend you plug the laptop into an electrical outlet in order to familiarize yourself with the laptop features and to give you a chance to charge the battery fully.)

3. All packaged computers come with an easy start-up brochure. We suggest you follow their step-by-steps. In essence, however, the next steps should be:

    •   Find a secure place to set-up your computer – ideally, one that will allow you easy access to both the front and back of the computer.

    •   You'll also need to set up an area your monitor, keyboard and mouse – preferably on a desk or table space – with a chair to sit and work at the computer.

    •   Finally, make sure you have an Internet connection available – your telephone or cable / satellite company can handle this, but **you'll need to call them to install it**.

        (We recommend you do this before you unpack your computer in order to save time and needless aggravation.)

You might want to take a moment to **skim Chapter 4** on the Internet before you call for service.

In that chapter, we'll give you an overview of the options your service provider can offer.

"**Service Provider**" is just another way of identifying your telephone, cable or satellite company.

- Plug your monitor into the back of the computer. Cords (and instructions) are included.

- Plug your keyboard and mouse into the back of the computer. Again, the cords and directions are included.

  Chances are these plugs will either be a USB or HDMI plug which we discussed earlier in this chapter. If you're a little confused by the manufacturer's directions, you might want to review that portion referred to earlier in this chapter.

- Plug your computer into the Internet.

  You'll need a special cord to connect your computer to the Internet. Called an "**Ethernet cord**" – which is just a fancy type of telephone cord – this special cord is given to you by your telephone or cable / satellite company upon installation.

- One end of the Ethernet cord goes into the space designed by the telephone or cable company; the other end will go into the Ethernet port in the back of the computer (see figures below).

 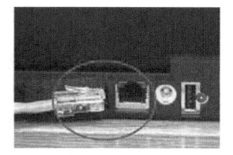

- Alternately, you can create a "**wireless**" connection. You'll still need an Ethernet cord; however, instead of plugging directly into your computer, you'll be plugging the cord into a box known as a "**router**". This "**router**" will then allow you to interact wirelessly to your computer and all your accessories.

  (If this "**wireless**" connection has any appeal, we suggest you browse Chapter 4 on the Internet for more specifics).

- Finally, just plug in the main black computer cord. One end goes into the back of the computer; the other end goes into the electrical wall socket.

4. You're done. Just turn on the power switch on the computer and it will automatically start right up.

Hey, my computer's not working – what's up?

Occasionally, you've followed all the directions – ours as well as the manufacturer – and yet the computer doesn't seem to be working.

Here are questions to ask yourself (along with a few easy troubleshooting tips):

Did you turn on the computer?

The way to turn on any computer is to locate the "**power button**"; then press the button.

Quite often, the **power button** can be identified by the logo of a circle with a single line coming out of it. As one example, see our jacket cover and the logo inside the word "**How**".

For most desktop computers, the power button is located on the front panel of the tower unit, usually at the very center or near the top.

For most laptop computers, first open the lid to the laptop. The power button is located above the keyboard, most often at the upper right.

The power button can be the single-most bewildering element of any computer!

Sometimes the power button is at the top; sometimes the bottom; sometimes to the right; sometimes the left – we've even seen the power button along the side, which really befuddles things.

Just know that the power button is there. Every computer has one – honest!

(If in doubt, go to the "**getting started**" paperwork which comes with all computers. You'll find the manufacturer has tried their best to label and identify where the power button is located.)

So you pushed the power button, but the computer still isn't working.

Did you plug in the computer?

Check that everything is properly plugged in.

Make sure to double-check the main black computer cord. One end should be plugged into the rear of the desktop computer (or plugged along the side in most laptop computers) while the other end should be plugged into your electrical outlet. If in doubt, re-plug.

Ironically, not plugging in this black computer cord – or not plugging it in properly – is one of the most common errors that computer technicians encounter.

Still not working? Is the electricity on?

Another common error that computer technicians encounter is that electricity for the room is controlled by a switch on the wall…and the switch is off! (You may have everything plugged in properly, but have just forgotten to turn on the wall switch.)

These troubleshooting tips should handle most set-up issues. Remember: your computer manufacturer – or the store where you purchased your computer – will be more-than-happy to help you with your computer set-up. If you have the slightest doubt, just pick up the phone and ask for their help.

One final word: Shutting down your computer

Logic would dictate that when you're ready to shut down the computer, you simply push the power button "**off**".

Logical, yes. The way it *really* works – no.

Computers must be turned off (or "**shut down**") from inside the computer – not literally "inside" the physically box, but rather from within the main computer program).

Here are steps to shut down your computer.

1. Close any programs you have been working on (see Chapter 3 for specifics).

2. Make sure to save any information or documents, and then close the program. (For most Window-based programs, click on "File" in the upper left of the program; then select / click "Exit". For Mac, just click on the red circle / dot in the upper left of the program – this action will shut down the program.

3. Once you've closed all your programs, you're ready to shut down the computer.

4. For Windows:

    In early Windows versions, you click on the Windows icon on the bottom left of your screen. This will bring up your programs and where – at the bottom right – you'll see the "Shut Down" button.

    Just click the "Shut Down" button and the computer will automatically turn itself off.

    For Windows 8: Move your mouse to the far right, which will reveal a menu of options (referred to as a **menu bar**). Select "Settings"; click on the "Power" button; then choose "Shut Down".

5. For Mac:

    Click the Apple icon on the upper left of the screen.

Select and click on "Shut Down".

You'll be asked if you're sure you want to shut down.

Select "Shut Down" and the computer will automatically turn itself off.

Microsoft / Windows computers: At a glance

The Pros

- The most popular operating system, Windows can be found in the majority of computers. You also have a greater range of price points in purchasing a Windows computer system.

- Because of its popularity, Windows supports a wide-range of computer programs.

- Windows is the ideal choice if you're planning to conduct business on your computer – anything from writing (word processing) to accounting (spreadsheets) to presentations.

- Because Windows is so widely used, you are more likely to get help and tips from family members and friends.

The Cons

- Windows is more likely to be targeted with online "**attacks**".

> The more widespread the technology, the more likely there are individuals who will attempt mischief and malice.
>
> These "**attacks**" usually take the form of viruses or spyware.

Microsoft tries its best to send out free updates to prevent these attacks, but, again, because of its global popularity, Windows is more susceptible to such violations.

(We recommend you flip to Chapter 3 on Software and read through the section on Protecting your Computer.)

- Microsoft tends to front-load its Windows operating system with a host of internal programs. Most of the time, that's never a problem. Unfortunately, the end-result is the time it takes to initially start-up a Windows computer is extremely slow, especially when compared with the Apple Mac computers.

The Hidden Costs

- If your computer does experience difficulties – usually quite rare, but it happens nonetheless –trying to troubleshoot the problem can be **exasperating**.

> Particularly when it comes to your personal time and emotional stress.

- Also, if you need to call for advice (or hire computer experts like Best Buy's Geek Squad), there can be costs involved.

Apple / Mac computers: At a glance

The Pros

- If your purpose in using a computer is focused primarily on **entertainment** rather than business needs; and if you only plan to send e-mails or write an occasional letter, consider getting a Mac.

> By "**entertainment**" we mean accessing the Internet; watching movies or video on your computer; listening to music; and so forth.

This is equally true if you're planning to use your computer for graphics. Say, for instance, if you want to edit your digital photographs; or someone in your household is a budding Steven Spielberg and plans to edit a movie.

- Apple's operating system is quite secure. As such, Mac computers rarely experience online attacks.

- Apple's service is quite good. In fact, if you live near an Apple store, they offer free classes on their products.

The Cons

- Because Mac computers are not as prevalent as Window computers, **not all programs are available for the Mac.**

True, although not quite as true as in years past.

Once you're hooked on a Mac, however, you probably won't even know what you're missing.

- You're locked into Apple hardware for the Mac computer itself. This isn't too big an issue as Apple produces good-quality products.

- You generally pay a higher price for a Mac computer – you're often paying extra for the Apple brand name. Also, Apple doesn't offer any ultra-budget line of computers or products.

The Hidden Costs

- Apple computer users swear by the Mac. Unfortunately, they're not a widespread bunch. If you run into a problem on your Mac, getting help isn't always easy.

Chapter 2

Computers: Handy Accessories

Who should read this section

If you are about to purchase or upgrade to a new computer – you should check out this section for handy accessories.

If you'd like to see what accessories are available for your computer – some essential, some handy, some just fun bells-and-whistles – you might give this section a look.

Who should skip this section

If you've decided not to buy a computer – ever – then just skip over this chapter.

(If, however, you have an interest to see what peripheral accessories are available and how they can enrich your computer experience, we recommend looking through this chapter.)

While we're calling this chapter "**Handy Accessories**," several of these devices are an integral part of your computer set-up.

Let's start with a few of the basic necessities:

The Monitor

Although laptop computers and a few of the packaged desktop computers come with built-in monitors, most computers will require a monitor (see below).

The monitor functions much like your television screen; in that, images from the computer are projected outward (via a cable) from your computer box onto the monitor.

> **Monitors** are so much like television sets that we recommend skimming through Chapter 7 on Televisions for a basic overview.

Like current television sets, computers monitors are flat-screen. Gone are the clunky tubed monitors from the past. In their place are **LCD or LED** flat-screen monitors. They're extremely lightweight and very adaptable for just about any space.

LCD stands for "**Liquid Crystal Display**" and **LED** stands for "**Light-Emitting Diode**". Both horrible names, hence the acronyms.

Again, we recommend our chapter on Televisions (Chapter 7) for more detail.

For those who have read the Television chapter and are curious whether you can purchase a Plasma monitor – the short answer is "no".

Plasma sets only come in sizes 42" or greater, which is far too large for a computer monitor.

In addition to being flat-screen, today's computer monitors are also high-definition, offering a sharper image with crystal-clear resolution.

To take advantage of the clarity of pictures, graphics and videos, we recommend you attach your computer monitor to your computer box using an **HDMI cable**.

Most new computer monitors have something called an **HDMI** (High-Definition Multimedia Interface) input.

You simply purchase an HDMI cable and insert one end into the monitor and the other end into the computer for crystal-clear viewing.

Honest, it's as simple as that!

Another item about monitors worth mentioning concerns their **size**.

The **size** of computer monitors – and televisions for that matter – are measured in inches (from one corner of the screen diagonally to the opposite corner below).

Obviously, your office or desk space will dictate the size of your computer monitor. See our notes in the box below:

The sizes of computer monitors are much like "Goldilocks and the Three Bears"

The "small" sizes are traditionally the 17" or 19" monitors. In addition to being small, they are also the least expensive.

The "large" sizes range from 27" to 30". If you're planning to set up your monitor on a traditional desk configuration, you may find these monitors to be too large (and you'll find yourself overwhelmed by the images).

The "just right" size for most people should be the 20" to 22" monitors. These monitors are reasonably price; offer a large viewing screen; yet aren't so overwhelming in size.

Obviously (where possible), we recommend you stop by a computer or retail store and look at the various sizes. Like Goldilocks, you should be able to pick out the size that's just right for you.

A quick summation about computer monitors:

- You'll find they are generally sold as LCD or LED flat-screen monitors (see Chapter 7 on Television for the differences). The short answer in case you don't want to skip around, there's very little difference between them, so just choose the monitor that feels right for you.

- The On/Off Power Button is usually located on the far right hand side, near the bottom. Make sure you locate the right one before putting it on or off, as computer monitors have an array of buttons. No harm if you hit the wrong button as they're mostly just for fine-tuning.

- Make sure both the monitor and computer box are HDMI compatible. If so, purchase an HDMI cable so that you can obtain the highest quality picture available.

- Finally, pick the right size monitor for your office or desk space. We'd recommend 20" to 22" monitors but each person's tastes and needs will obviously vary.

- That said, just about any manufacturer brand will do.

  If you'd like to do some additional research, we recommend checking the ratings in *Consumer Reports* magazine which offers a comprehensive, non-biased list of features, sizes, prices and so forth.

Consumer Reports magazines are certainly easily available at your public library.

The Mouse and Keyboard

Two other basic necessities for your computer are the **mouse and keyboard** (see below).

Keyboards are fairly standard. Most come available in standard 101-key sizes. Here are a few items of note:

- Laptop computers come with a built-in keyboard, and, as such, are slightly smaller in size.

- If you're purchasing an Apple Mac, you'll probably want an Apple keyboard. This keyboard – while resembling the standard keyboard in many ways – also includes **features unique to the Mac.**

Truth is, you can also **utilize just about any standard keyboard** that has a USB connection to connect with your Mac.

(Double-check the compatibility to make sure the keyboard works with a Mac. You can usually find that written on the keyboard's packaging description).

However, since the **Apple keyboard** has features unique to the Mac, in this case you might want to go with the brand name.

- Some keyboards feature an ergonomic design. If you have trouble typing or if you have wrist problems, you might want to check out these types of keyboard configurations.

- Traditional keyboards often include a pad of numbers on the far right. This can be very useful if you're inputting a large quantity of numbers – for example, during tax season – but otherwise just take up space on the keyboard.

- You'll also find keyboards with "**function**" keys. These keys – usually marked F1 through F12 – are designed for one-touch tasks.

  You can, for example, tap the F1 key and you'll automatically be taken to the Help feature. Additional function keys can automatically save a document, take you directly to the Internet; and so forth.

  Depending on the type of keyboard you purchase, many of these function keys can be reconfigured for the tasks you most often use.

- Finally, you can also purchase keyboards with a variety of bells-and-whistles. For example, some keyboards will allow you to control your music or check your e-mail, all with a single tap of a button.

Much like the keyboard, the **mouse** is also a fairly standard device. Again, a few items of note:

- Laptop computers feature a built-in mouse, usually in the form of a small button the size of an eraser tip or a finger-controlled pad.

  Many people find these built-in devices annoying and hard-to-maneuver. If you're one such person, know that you can purchase a standard mouse for your laptop – just plug it in and you're good to go.

- If you're purchasing an Apple Mac, you're not tied to an Apple mouse. Unlike the Apple keyboard which has features unique to the Mac, the mouse is just a mouse (and any with a standard USB connection will do).

- Some mouse – dare we say "mice" – feature an ergonomic design. If you have wrist problems, you might want to check out these types of mouse configurations.

- By in large, each mouse contains **three essential ingredients**:

  1. A left mouse button.

     This is the button you traditionally use to click (or double-click) on an icon or program. When you're asked to **"click"** on something, you'll be using the left mouse button.

  2. A right mouse button.

     By clicking the right mouse button, you will usually find a list of program possibilities – with some of the most frequent tasks such as **"cut"** or **"copy"** or **"paste"**.

     We can't stress enough the 'magical wonders' of the right mouse button. If you're ever lost or confused, try clicking on the right mouse button and you might be surprised to find that the task you're looking for is **"right"** there.

3. Finally, the mouse usually contains a "**wheel**". The wheel is often located at the center of the mouse (usually between the left and right buttons).

   If you're reading a document or are accessing a lengthy web page, the wheel will allow you to "spin" **up and down** the document or page as fast or as slow as you'd like.

> If you're paging through the Internet, using the "**space bar**" key on your keyboard will serve the very same purpose as the **wheel** on your mouse.

- Finally, you can actually purchase a mouse with a variety of bells-and-whistles. Unlike certain keyboards where the bells-and-whistles are handy, additional features on the mouse take a lot of getting used to and aren't suited for everyone's taste.

To "click" or "double-click"? that is the question…

One of the more baffling quandaries – second only to the erratic place-ment of the computer's "power" button – is when to "click" or "double-click" the mouse. Here are a few suggestions:

- When you're asked to "click" or "double-click", always use the left mouse button.

- When you "double-click", make sure to click twice in rapid succession. (Don't click; grab a cup of coffee; then return to click a second time.)

- As a rule of thumb, we suggest you "single click" (click once). If that doesn't produce the result you're looking for, then try to "double-click" (click twice).

- If you're planning to move items, "click" once; hold down the mouse button; then drag it to the desired folder or location with your finger still pressed down. Lift your finger when the desired folder or location is reached.

- If you're planning to open a program – which we'll explain in more detail in Chapter 3 – "double-click" on the desired icon on your desktop.

- If you're inside a web browser and want to navigate the Internet – which we cover in Chapter 5 – you only need to single click to move around.

We trust this information will help!

Before we leave this section on the mouse and keyboard, we'd like to talk about one more piece of technology: the "**wireless mouse and keyboard**".

Traditionally, when you obtain a mouse and keyboard – again, remembering that they usually come pre-packaged with the computer you purchase – each has cords which tether it to the computer box / tower.

You also have the option of **purchasing a wireless mouse and keyboard**.

> You won't find the **wireless mouse and keyboard** as a pre-packaged option, although most computer manufacturers will offer to include them as part of the shipment (with an additional charge, naturally).

The advantage of a wireless mouse and keyboard is that you won't have all those cords and cables running across your desk.

Just remember: If you do purchase a wireless mouse and keyboard, make sure to keep spare batteries handy. There's nothing more frustrating than to be working on your computer, only to find the batteries for your mouse and keyboard have **drained**.

> **A quick tip:**
>
> After you've purchased your wireless set, don't throw away the old corded mouse and keyboard.
>
> In case of an emergency – like your batteries have **drained** and you've run out of spares – just hook up your old corded mouse and keyboard and you're all set.

What is "Plug and Play"?

A quick word about "Plug and Play"…

Both the Mac and Windows computers come equipped with a built-in feature called "Plug and Play".

What this means quite simply is that anytime you purchase and plug in a new device – (say) a specific monitor – the computer searches internally for that device (both the make and model), then automatically installs it. Handy!

There's nothing else you have to do – just "**plug**" in the device and it automatically "**plays**".

Printer

Along with the monitor, keyboard and mouse, there is one other accessory that is important to have with your computer: **a printer**.

The reasoning should be clear. As you begin to receive e-mails and visit websites on your computer, you will undoubtedly find information, discover articles or most-likely receive letters or photos that you'd like to print. Hence, the need for a printer (**see below**).

There are **two basic types of popular printers** on the marketplace:

1. The first type of printer is what's known as a toner-based printer. These printers are also referred to as laser printers. The toner that is used in these types of printers is dry ink / powder.

   A few items of note about laser printers:

   - Laser printers are available both in black-and-white and color.

   - They produce high quality text and graphics.

   - They are very productive printers, especially where speed and the volume of copies are important.

2. The second type of popular printer is known as the inkjet printers. Like the name implied, they use solid sticks of colored ink – similar in consistence to candle wax – that are melted, then heat-transferred to the printed page.

    A few items of note about inkjet printers:

    - Inkjet printers are generally less expensive than laser printers.

    - The quality and graphics from inkjet printers are generally inferior to laser printers.

    - Lower-end inkjet printers may actually take a few minutes for the ink to fully dry on the paper.

The expense is all in the cartridges

Both laser and inkjet printers have cartridges that need to be replaced. The frequency of changing cartridges clearly depends on how often you plan to print.

The toner cartridges for laser printers tend to last longer than the cartridges for inkjet printers.

On the other hand, the cost for laser printer cartridges is more expensive than inkjet cartridges. Additionally, the cost for color laser printer cartridges is far more expensive than black-and-white toner cartridges.

Both types of cartridges have an expiration date. Make sure you check the dates on the cartridges you purchase and think carefully before keeping an array of extra cartridges on hand.

Although a printer is a handy accessory, remember to factor in the costs of cartridges and paper when making your purchase.

A variation to the standard printer is the all-in-one device that combines a printer with a copier and a scanner.

Since we've just covered printers, let's say a quick word about **copiers and scanners**.

Copier

You've undoubtedly seen (and used) copy machines in offices, at copy center outlets, and through brand names like Xerox.

All **copiers** work in the same general fashion:

1. Lift the top lid on the machine.

2. Place what you want to copy face down on the glass plate, and then close the top lid.

3. Choose the number of copies you want to make.

4. Press the Start or Copy button.

5. Voila! The copy is printed and delivered from the machine's tray.

6. You can also feed a number of pages through the machine's feeder – usually located on the top (above the lid).

   Same process as above. Just load and hit the Start or Copy button.

   Make sure that your pages are loaded in the proper fashion. Some copiers require face up; while others ask for the pages to be placed in a face down position. Your enclosed manual will tell you which way and there's usually a graphic indicator etched onto the feeder.

   Also, copiers will vary in the amount of paper you can put in the feeder. Some will only allow as many as 5-10 pages as a time; while sturdier models will allow you to feed more pages at a time.

Scanner

Scanners operate in the same way as copiers, except instead of printing out onto a paper, they allow you to convert your paper into a digital file.

Why would I want to do that?

Well, by making a digital copy – of a document or photo – you could then attach the digital copy to your e-mail and send it to an associate or friend or family anywhere in the world.

You can also ditch your file cabinets by converting your most important documents into electronic ones.

We grant you, the process is somewhat cumbersome, but, at times, it has its advantages.

All-In-One

We've started by describing copiers and scanners because there is one handy accessory on the marketplace that is worth taking note: An **all-in-one** combination of **printer, copier and scanner** (see image below).

In addition to printer, copier and scanner, most **all-in-one devices** also include a fax machine. Many even have the ability to print photos directly from your camera!

As you can see from the above graphic, the all-in-one device is larger than the traditional printer. Nevertheless, if you have the space, this might be just the ticket.

In years past, the quality of these all-in-one devices was questionable. Yet as technology has improved, the quality of these all-in-one machines now rivals most of the individual printers, copiers and scanners. They're certainly worth the look.

Webcam

A webcam is a video camera that feeds its images in real time from **your computer** to another computer (that, likewise, is set up with a webcam of its own).

The webcam is quite small, inexpensive, lightweight and portable (**see below as one example**).

> Some of the newer model computers, notably laptops, come equipped with a **built-in camera**. Make sure you check first before going out to buy a **webcam**.

The webcam is easy to set-up: one end hooks to the very top or side of the computer monitor (as in our graphic above); while the other end connects as a USB plug into the computer itself.

> Note that most new monitors have USB
> ports – usually located at the rear – which
> save having to run cables all over the place.

If you've been paying attention, however, you've already noticed two snags. We'll cover both. The first snag is obvious; the second snag we'll show you…

1. You can only place a video call to someone who also has a video webcam on the other end.

    Tricky! I mean, how many people do you know who have webcams? You'd actually be surprised by the number, but it's certainly not common.

    So why even bother?

    The webcam is an excellent device if you want to communicate visually with friends or **family** who live at the other end of the country (or even elsewhere around the globe).

> This is especially handy if you want to see a
> newborn in the family (but don't want to get
> roped into babysitting chores).

    Using a webcam under these circumstances is a terrific way of keep up face-to-face, so to speak. (And it's certainly a lot cheaper than flying long distances to visit.)

2. The second snag isn't quite so obvious.

    In addition to the webcam, you'll also need to connect via an Internet program.

Don't despair. These programs – such as Skype, Facetime, Yahoo! Messenger and MSN Messenger – are often free and easy to **set up**.

> Essentially, you hook up your **webcam** to your computer; then sign up for an online program such as **Skype**.
>
> If the person you're trying to reach does the same thing at the opposite end, you both will be able to connect.
>
> We'll discuss these programs (and how to sign up) in depth in our section on video calls in Chapter 23.

Again, while we understand the webcam isn't for everyone; consider this device essential if you want to communicate visually with friends or family.

External drives / USB drives

There is one final accessory for your computer that you might want to consider getting: an external hard drive (which is also referred to as an "**USB drive**", "**flash drive**", "**flash stick**", "**thumb drive**", and even, internationally, as a "**pen drive**"). Many names all used to describe the same storage drives. (See the images below for two kinds of examples.)

Most external drives are quite small. Some – like the image on the left – can contain twice or three times the storage capacity of a regular computer. Others – like the images above on the right – are as small as a stick of gum and can be slipped into your pocket.

How do external hard drives / USB drives work?

Easy! Just plug one end of the drive into your USB port (see the section on ports and plugs in Chapter 1 for additional information).

External hard drives / USB drives will automatically be identified by your computer (see "**Plug and Play**" earlier in this chapter).

That's it. Your computer will identify the drive and you're ready to go.

But my computer already has a built-in hard drive, why do I need an extra portable one?

Two good reasons:

1. One of best pieces of advice you'll receive – usually, again and again – is to "**back up**" your computer.

    What this means in English: You'll want to store an extra (safe) copy of your documents, photos and so forth.

    Usually, all your documents are stored in the same place.

    In Windows, for example, you click on Windows Explorer where you find a section marked "**Librarie**s".

    Under "**Libraries**" you'll find four folders: "**Documents**", "**Music**", "**Pictures**" and "**Video**". All of your personal information should be stored in those four folders.

    Using your mouse button, if you "**drag**" these four folders into a new external hard drive, all your personal information will be saved as copies and you've effectively "**backed up**" your computer.

Don't worry – your original folders and their content will still remain on your hard drive.

When you "**drag**" these folders using your left mouse button, all the content are automatically copied.

When you "**drag**" these folders using your right mouse button, you have a choice to either "**copy**" or "**move**" the content.

Obviously, we suggest "**copying**" these folders onto the portable USB drive, since the very term "backed up" implies retaining a second copy of your files.

Once you've finished backing up (or copying) your information, simply tuck the external drive in a safe space.

Backing up your computer

We've just given you the steps to "**back up**" your computer.

We suggest you back up – essentially make a second (safe) copy of all your files – once every month.

Backing up your computer shouldn't take longer than 10-15 minutes, but it guarantees you'll always have a spare copy of your important documents and photographs in case something goes wrong with your computer (or in case of an electrical blackout or some natural disaster).

---

2. A second reason for purchasing an external hard drive / USB drive – as if backing up your computer isn't a good enough reason – concerns the amount of space photographs, videos and so forth take up on your internal hard drive (the one that's built-in to your computer).

    While photos and videos abound, they come at a price: storage space. You'll soon find that stored pictures of your family take up a lot of space on your computer (and will start to slow down the computer's performance).

    A simple solution: Purchase an external hard drive / USB drive and you'll be able to store all your pictures and videos on a safe, separate drive.

    Because of technology advancements, these drives are extremely inexpensive and can store a ton of stuff.

While not a necessity, owning one or two of these drives for **storage and safekeeping** makes a lot of sense.

> You might also consider **storing** one of these drives somewhere apart from your home – say with a family member. That way, if some disaster strikes, you'll have an extra copy somewhere safe.

Computer Accessories: At a glance

The Pros

- Certain accessories are a must for computers. While a mouse and keyboard always come pre-packaged with any computer, you'll certainly need a monitor (and you'll find owning a printer to be a necessity).

- Most computer accessories are quite inexpensive and aren't designed to break your budget.

- Some accessories – such as the external hard drive / USB drive – are very handy in securing your valuable documents, photos, music and videos.

- Because of the computer's ability to **"plug and play"** (discussed earlier in this chapter), setting up these accessories is just a matter of plugging it in.

The Cons

- We would be less than honest if we said that every one of these accessories is always easy to set up.

  For example, while a webcam is easy to set up, signing up for a service like Skype can be difficult (not intimidating, but somewhat irksome at times).

- Too many accessories and you'll find your computer workspace to be overcrowded. You might be selective in what accessories you purchase (for example, purchasing an all-in-one instead of an individual printer, copier and scanner).

The Hidden Costs

- As mentioned, one of the biggest expenses – and usually a "hidden cost" until you actually need to purchase them – are printer cartridges.

Inkjet cartridges are the least expensive, followed by black toner cartridges for laser printers (with the cost of color toner cartridges guaranteed to make your eyebrows lift in astonishment).

Chapter 3

Computers: Software and Protecting your Computer

Who should read this section

First-time computer users, because computers run on software.

People who already own a computer, but who aren't taking advantage of its range and scope.

This section will help de-mystify software programs and will provide you with a clearer understanding of what they are (and how they work).

We'll also be covering how to protect your computer in this section, so we highly recommend you take a look.

Who should skip this section

If you already have a solid understanding of software; or if you have no interest in ever owning a computer, this section isn't for you.

(For that matter, if you're never planning to own a computer, you can probably skip directly to the Entertainment section, beginning with Chapter 7.)

What is software?

Simply put: **software programs** (or just plain "**software**") are a unified collection of computer programs and data that tells your computer what to do (and how to do it).

When you first purchase and turn on your computer, for example, the computer comes pre-equipped with a variety of software programs. Chances are you will never come in direct contact with any of this software. These programs run in the background and give your computer instructions on when to open files, print and so much more.

But these aren't the types of software programs we're planning to tell you about.

There are thousands and thousands of computer software programs, all designed to help you with work or play or personal enjoyment.

We'll cover those areas specifically in a moment, but first let us explain the basic steps needed to set up just about <u>any</u> software program.

You can purchase software in one of two ways: Either in a pre-packaged box; or via a direct Internet download. It doesn't matter which way you buy it. They both contain the same software, although in the pre-packaged box, you have an actual disc to load the software; while downloading from the Internet, you save the software to the computer, and then run the information.

Here are the basic steps to **load your software program**:

> **Loading software** is a very easy process – software developers do their best to make it that way.

1. As mentioned, you can purchase particular software – say, a program to help you with your taxes, or a program to help you touch up your photographs – from either a store (boxed) or you can download directly from a dealer's website.

2. Assuming you purchase software in a pre-packaged box, inside you'll find a DVD in a jewel-case box (and, usually, a set of **instructions**).

> The **process** is so easy and straight-forward (as you shall see) that some boxes just come with the DVD and no instructions.

3. Just insert the DVD into the computer tray and the **installation will automatically initiate**.

> This installation is usually called "**the setup**".

4. This process will probably take a few minutes as the software loads files and self-contained directions onto your computer. Again, it does so automatically.

    You'll probably have to click "Next" and "Yes" a few times – but in the end the software loads onto your computer.

    The software will usually pause in its set-up to ask you to add a Registration Code.

    The **Registration Code** is included within the box, often on the back side of the jewel-case box which contained the DVD. The code is a series of letters and numbers – sometimes, quite lengthy – that you type into the computer in the space where indicated.

    If you download the software directly from a website – see Step 9 below – you'll receive a confirming e-mail from the dealer with the registration code prominent within the body of the e-mail.

The software company might also ask you to "**register**" your software. Here, the company asks for your e-mail address and contact information.

In exchange for this information, the company promises to alert you to software updates and promises to provide you with valuable company information.

Registering your software is a rather shameless way for the company to acquire your e-mail address (and for them to send you an endless barrage of advertisements).

Note that "**registering**" your software is different from the "**Registration Code**" mentioned in the previous step.

It's sometimes helpful to register your product, but not really necessary, especially if you have concerns about privacy or needlessly giving out your e-mail address and contact information.

5. Once the software has finished loading – you'll know this since you will either have to click "End" or "Finish" or will be asked to **reboot your computer** – you can then put away the DVD and you're now ready to run your software program.

"**Reboot**" is just a computer term meaning to "restart" your computer.

Again, you don't have to do anything beyond clicking "yes" when the software program asks you to reboot. The program automatically restarts your computer and then you're good-to-go.

---

6. After the software program installs, you'll find a small graphic icon with the name and picture of the software located on your **computer desktop**.

> Your "**computer desktop**" is that open space –
> often with a fancy background and a series of
> graphic icons – into which your computer opens
> every time you "**start-up**" your computer.
>
> "**Start-up**" is simply the term used every time
> you turn on your computer (pushing the "on"
> switch when you're ready to begin).

7. Any time you're ready to use the software program, just *double*-click on the icon – again, the program usually sets this icon (with the name and picture of the software) onto your computer desktop. By double-clicking the icon, the computer will automatically start that program.

8. Since the content of each software program is different, just follow the easy-to-use instructions found in the directions / manual (again, usually contained within the box).

9. You may also choose to download the software program directly from the online manufacturer.

If this is the case, you would go to the online site and then **purchase** the program.

> In this case, you'll be asked to provide the
> company with your contact information and
> credit card information.

After you've purchased the software program, you'll be given instructions to "**run**" the program.

To "**run**" the program often involves clicking on a series of "yes" or "okay" as the program automatically downloads and installs.

From here, go to step #4 above and continue in the same manner.

As mentioned, if a Registration Code is needed, the company provides that information as part of the e-mail receipt they send to you upon your credit card approval.

("**Registering your e-mail and contact information**" is rarely necessary since the company has already retained all that information once you've purchased the software).

A quick lesson on computer files

All computer files have a three letter extension at the end. These letter extensions are preceded by a dot or period – in other word "**.doc**", "**.txt**" and so forth – and are known as a "**file extension**".

These file extensions help the computer identify (and categorize) the types of program associated with each file.

Consider them like a telephone area code. When calling someone, you enter the area code (i.e. 212) before the actual number. With a computer file, you have (say) ".doc" at the end of the file name to identify the type of program associated with that file.

Chances are you will never see those three letters on your file name, since Windows and Mac keep those extensions "hidden" (as they don't want you changing these extensions as it confuses the computer).

Among the more common file extensions:

".doc"	Refers to Microsoft word processing files.
".wav" or ".mp3"	Refers to music files.
".bak"	Refers to backup files.
".txt"	Refers to text files.
".pdf"	Refers to portable document files (also called Adobe files).
".zip"	Refers to compressed files.

We could go on, but as you can see the names and initials were compiled by computer geeks (with no particular logic and far too much time on their hands).

You're probably asking: "So if we don't see the file extensions, why should we bother reading this?"

Unfortunately, the same computer geeks – remember them, the ones with no logic and far too much time on their hands? – are also the same geeks who write the manuals for your computer.

So…if you pick up any kind of manual, you might run across some of these extensions.

We just wanted to give you a little background so you can be better informed.

Different types of software

We understand we're doing this in reverse (by giving you "how to" instructions before we explain the types of software); but, as we mentioned, once you know how to load one software program, you can apply this process to any software program.

That said; let's look at the various types of software (which we've broken down for you by **category headings**):

Remember, there are thousands and thousands of software programs, so this isn't the proper forum to include them all.

Instead, we'll try to give you some generic "**category headings**: to help you narrow your search for the software that's right for you.

Software: For work

A giant industry has been created out of software programs for the workplace. Take Microsoft as a perfect example. While Microsoft's operating system dominates most of today's computers, one of the company's strengths lies in its seamless integration of work-related software.

Microsoft's all-inclusive work software – known as Microsoft Office – includes word processing (Word), e-mail (Outlook), spreadsheets (Excel), office presentations (PowerPoint), databases (Access) and even more.

The advantage to Microsoft's all-inclusive software is that these programs function seamlessly together. You can take portions of one program and insert it into another. Very handy, as millions of users can attest.

Apple's Mac computers have a similar all-inclusive software program called iWork. iWork includes word processing (Pages), office presentations (Keynote) and spreadsheets (Numbers). While not as expansive as **Microsoft Office**, iWork nonetheless integrates these programs seamlessly within the Mac computer.

> If you're intrigued by **Microsoft Office**, but have purchased a Mac computer, there's good news. Microsoft Office comes available for use on the Mac as well.

Another popular software program for the work environment is QuickBooks. QuickBooks helps you organize your business finances – such as creating invoices, tracking sales and expenses and so forth – all in one place. You can get QuickBooks for both Windows and the Mac.

As mentioned, there are thousands of software programs – some free, although most at a cost – and, since this isn't the proper place to list them all, we have one handy suggestion:

1. Determine what work function(s) you most often engage in. For example, if you're a writer, you'd certainly need a word processing program; if you're an accountant or own your own business, spreadsheets and programs like QuickBooks are a necessity.

2. Using your **Internet search engine**, enter a phrase like "Bestselling word processing software" or "Top accounting software".

> We have a whole chapter in this book devoted to **Search Engines** (Chapter 5), so you might start there if you're unfamiliar with how to search.

You can also tailor the search to your specific needs. For example, you can enter a phrase such as "Top word processing software for non-fiction authors" or the like.

In the end, you'll find more-than-enough results to ascertain which program is right for your needs.

3. Finally, make sure the software you purchase is compatible to your computer. Remember what we said earlier about QuickBooks? It has one version that is for Windows and another version for your Apple Mac. Make sure you purchase the right one.

Software: For home

The distinction between software for home and software for work is a fine line.

Many people will find they frequently utilize a word processing program – for example, Microsoft's "Word" or Apple's "Pages" – for composing personal letters, creating "to do" lists and so forth.

Another example of this fine line distinction comes with finances. You might not need a powerful program like QuickBooks to run a business, but you certainly may find that a software program like Quicken can manage your personal finances while software programs such as TurboTax can help when tax time rolls around.

There are a myriad of software programs designed for home activity. For example, there are programs that are specific to landscape design; nutrition; cooking; exercise; even software programs specifically geared to legal matters such as wills and estate planning.

We'll reiterate our suggestion made earlier:

- Determine what areas of the home you'd like to enhance. For example, you might be interested in food preparation or physical exercise or organization for your closets.

- No matter what your interests, you can use your Internet search engine – again, we have devoted a whole chapter in this book to Search Engines (Chapter 5) – to locate a software program to help you with your tasks.

Software: Educational

If large companies have made a cottage industry of software programs for work and at home, the same can also be said for educational software.

By "**educational**" software, we're not just talking about dry school subjects. Falling into this category are hobbies and personal interest.

Here are some general examples to get your thoughts humming about the possibilities:

If you're interested in **photography**, a variety of software programs, such as Adobe Photoshop Elements, will help you edit your pictures (or even your videos). You can create slideshows and special effects with just a few clicks of your mouse.

> If you're interested in **photography**, make sure to look at Chapter 13 on Digital Cameras.

- Interested in learning a new language? There are a host of language software programs available – such as Rosetta Stone, Berlitz and more – that will help you learn a foreign language efficiently and effectively.

- Is genealogy / family history your favorite pastime? Software programs such as Family Tree Maker, Legacy Family Tree and more can help you research and organize every branch of your family tree.

- Encyclopedias are now available as software programs, often with video links to bring the various topics to life.

- In addition, you'll find software that will teach you math, history, science, how to play chess, learn about animals and wildlife, how to study for the SAT, real estate, and other exams, how to play a musical instrument.

The list of available software to help enrich your life just goes on and on.

Software: For play

We're just going to touch briefly on software programs for play since we've actually devoted an entire chapter on Video Games (Chapter 16).

Why an entire chapter on video games?

For a start, software for play – which we're also calling video games – has grossed billions of dollars. In fact, the release of popular new video games even exceeds (monetarily) many top motion picture box office films.

Need more convincing? Over 67% of households in the United States play video games.

But if you think video games are simply shoot-em-ups or cartoon characters scurrying around, you're vastly mistaken.

The quality of video software graphics is extraordinary. What's more, certain video software / games can be educational or informative in nature. For example, there are games which focus on railroad management, along with a number of games which focus on empire building or even city planning.

You'll be surprised at the wide variety of games available – all designed to tweak your interest or pastime.

A word about software programs...

Whether you download software directly from the Internet or purchase software packed in a pretty-looking box, each program works inherently the same: you click on the main file to launch the "executable" program.

For example, you might be downloading a sports program that is called "SportsProgram.exe". Note that the **".exe"** file extension identifies this as an **"executable"** program.

When you install a program from a box, chances are you'll never see that file. Once you insert the CD or DVD you're your drive, the program does all the installation in the background.

If you download a program directly from the Internet, you'll be asked to either **"Run"** or **"Save"** the program to your computer. At that point, you'll notice that the file to be run or saved is identified as an **"exe"** file.

A word of caution...

Never open an executable file (.exe file) unless you're absolute certain of the source. If you've gone to a website (which you trust) and have decided to download their software, then by all means proceed.

If, however, you receive an .exe file – via e-mail is the most notorious culprit – never open the file unless you can verify (and trust) the source.

Software: Protecting your computer (FBI guidelines)

"**Protect your computer**" is the best advice you can be given.

This is such an important topic, that we're actually going to offer the following guidelines directly from the FBI's online website:

Keep Your Firewall Turned On:

A **firewall** helps protect your computer from hackers who might try to gain access to crash it, delete information, or even steal passwords or other sensitive information.

> A "**firewall**" is a security system that helps protect your computer from unauthorized access.
>
> Remember: While firewalls are generally incorporated as part of Windows and Mac computers, they still need to be turned on.
>
> You're usually given this option when you first set-up your computer, so make sure to say "yes" to this security protection.

Software firewalls are widely recommended for single computers. The software is pre-packaged on some operating systems or can be purchased for individual computers.

> Both Microsoft Windows and Apple's Mac operating system come equipped with **firewall protection**.
>
> You can also easily purchase firewall software programs such as ZoneAlarm, Kaspersky and others.

Install or Update Your Antivirus Software:

Antivirus software provides a different function than software firewalls. Antivirus software is designed to prevent malicious software programs from embedding onto your computer. If it detects malicious code, like a virus, it works to disarm or remove it. Viruses can infect computers without users' knowledge. Most types of antivirus software can be set up to update automatically.

> Top **antivirus software** includes Symantec's Norton Antivirus, McAfee, Kaspersky, Webroot and more.

Install or Update Your Antispyware Technology:

Spyware is just what it sounds like—software that is surreptitiously installed on your computer to let others peer into your activities on the computer. Some spyware collects information about you without your consent or produces unwanted pop-up ads on your **web browser**.

> See our section on web browsers and search engines (Chapter 5) for more details.
>
> Until you get there, know that a "**web browser**" is the term used for the program that allows your computer to connect to the Internet.
>
> (You might also have heard these web browsers referred to as Internet Explorer on your Windows, or Safari on your Mac computers).

Some operating systems – including Microsoft Windows and Apple's Mac operating system – offer free spyware protection. Inexpensive software is also readily available for download on the Internet or to purchase at your local computer store.

Be wary of ads on the Internet offering downloadable antispyware – in some cases these products may be fake and may actually contain spyware or other malicious code. It's like buying groceries – shop where you trust.

Keep Your Operating System Up to Date:

Computer operating systems are periodically updated to stay in tune with technology advances or to fix security holes. Be sure to install these updates to ensure your computer has the latest protection.

> By "**computer operating systems**", the FBI is referring to your Windows or Apple Mac computer.

Be Careful What You Download:

Carelessly downloading e-mail attachments can circumvent even the most vigilant anti-virus software. Never open an e-mail attachment from someone you don't know, and be wary of forwarded attachments (or links) from people you do know. They may have unwittingly advanced malicious code.

Turn Off Your Computer:

With the growth of high-speed Internet connections, many opt to leave their computers on and ready for action. The downside is that being "always on" renders computers more susceptible.

Beyond firewall protection, which is designed to fend off unwanted attacks, turning the computer off effectively severs an attacker's connection – be it **spyware or a botnet** that employs your computer's resources to reach out to other unwitting users.

A "**botnet**" is a number of private computers infected with malicious software and controlled as a group without the owners' knowledge (i.e. to send spam).

"**Spyware**" and "**botnet**" are just some of the terms for malicious software that could "infect" your computer.

The most common phrase you'll hear is "**computer virus**". You might also hear the terms "**Trojan Horse**", "**adware**" and even "**worms**". Not too pleasant, but that's the general idea.

Protecting your computer: Our general advice

- Both Microsoft Windows and Apple's Mac operating systems come with pre-installed firewalls, anti-virus, and spyware protection, They are quite reliable and very handy, so we suggest you "agree" to use them – you'll be asked when you first set-up your computer or laptop.

  Sometime these pre-installed software protection programs – notably, anti-virus software – are for a free-trial period only. Don't be surprised if you're asked to pay a yearly fee after the trial period is over. Again, usually worth the cost.

- If you're thinking of adding two anti-viruses or spyware programs for 'double-protection' – think again.

  Multiple anti-virus and spyware programs often run at-odds with each other and can cause conflicts within your computer. Decide on the best protective program you'd like to run and stick with it.

- Both Windows and the Mac operating systems provide **automatic updates** for your computer. When you come across a prompt asking whether you want to au-tomatize these updates, we suggest that you click "okay / agree" to the request!
- Heed the FBI warning about taking precaution in opening e-mail attachments. You may receive an e-mail from someone named "Helen", but that person might not be the "Aunt Helen" you know (or your Aunt Helen's e-mail account may have been hijacked by someone else).

  When in doubt, contact the person whom you think sent the e-mail and make sure that the contents are safe (and that they, indeed, did send you the e-mail).

- Don't panic or grow paranoid.

  Although you want to take care to protect your computer, there is no need to grow anxious or paranoid in this regard.

  Even if your computer gets "infected", there are a number of ways of ridding yourself of the virus or spyware problem.

  (We recommend you follow the earlier FBI guidelines so you won't even need to worry about infections.)

  Relax; take proper precautions; then go ahead and enjoy your computer.

Software: At a glance

The Pros

- There are a myriad of enriching computer software programs.

- Software programs make using your computer fun.

- Think of software programs as reading a good book or magazine: There are an endless variety of topics, all designed to take you on enjoyable adventures or provide you with a wealth of information.

The Cons

- Too much of a good thing. Even on a single topic (say, "preparing nutritional meals" or "learning how to play chess"), there can be a large number of computer software programs available.

  Sifting through the software programs to find the one that's just right for you can take a bit of time and research.

- Loading too many software programs onto your computer can cause your computer to act sluggishly.

  Don't load software randomly onto your computer.

  If you're not certain whether you'll ever use a software program on "how to speak Finnish", wait until the urge comes upon you. If you've already installed it and no longer have an interest, such programs are easy enough to "**uninstall**" (remove).

The Hidden Costs

- As mentioned earlier, sometimes competing software programs can become at-odds with one another.

Identifying which programs are "at-odds" requires some lengthy research; and removing the offending program can be irksome and time-intensive.

Chapter 4

Computers: The Internet

Who should read this section

If you own – or are thinking of owning – any device referenced in this book, you should read this chapter on the Internet. Quite simply, "connecting via the Internet" has become the way in which most-if-not-all digital devices update themselves; connect with one another; and provide you with information.

If you want to stay informed and "remain connected" with friends and family, the Internet is the way to go.

If you use the Internet but feel you lack grounding in the basics of doing so.

Who should skip this section

If you've become a hermit or never intend to enter the digital era, there's no reason to read further. (For that matter, there was no real reason to purchase this book!)

Even so, reading about the Internet will provide you with a broader (albeit simplified) understanding of the infrastructure of our new digital universe.

The Internet: A quick overview

The **Internet** – often referred to as the World Wide Web (shortcut "**WWW**" or just the "**Web**") – consists of a global system of interconnected computer networks that use a standard protocol to provide information to billions of users worldwide.

The "**Internet**" is actually a shortened form of the technical term: "**Internetwor**k".

"**Internetwork**" was derived as a combination of the word "**inter**" ("between") and "**network**" (from the collection of computers components known as a computer "network").

The origins of the Internet date back to the 1960s and was commissioned by the United States government (in conjunction with private commercial groups) to link millions of private, public, academic, business and government networks into one cohesive information resource service.

In 50 short years, more than 2.4 billion people – nearly a third of the Earth's population – now utilize the services of the Internet.

This giant linking of networks carries information and services such as electronic mail, on-line chat, **interlinking Web pages** and much more. The information is received in a variety of forms such as documents or music or video and so forth.

What this means in English: You can easily move from one "website" (or web page) to another with just a click of the mouse.

This **interlinking** is achieved through a process known as "**hyperlink**" wherein a web page, file or document is "**linked**" to another location or file.

This link is activated by clicking on a highlighted word or image on the screen. In most websites, these links can be found in words colored blue.

Here are some fun user **facts**:

The **statistics below** were gleaned a year or so ago, so you can actually increase the number substantially.

- If you looked up the word "Internet" on your computer, you'd find over 5.6 <u>billion</u> results to your search.

- There are approximately 3 billion searches performed every day on Google which – while the largest – is just one of several search engines available.

- Over 3 billion videos are viewed on the website YouTube every day – that's just one video site available among many more.

- After English (27%), the most requested languages on the Web are Chinese (23%), Spanish (8%), Japanese (5%) and so forth.

- 42% of the world's Internet users are based in Asia; 24% in Europe and 14% in North America.

Connecting to the Internet

In very simple terms, you connect to the Internet via **telecommunication** (which, by-in-large, is handled by telephone, cable and satellite companies).

> **"Telecommunication"** is the transmission of information over significant distances.

There are two basic ways you **connect your computer to the Internet**:

> This connection is often referred to as going **"online"**.

Wired connection

"**Wired**" is obviously a catch-all phrase we're using. This is the **easiest way** to connect to the Internet.

You'll probably hear the term "**broadband**" which simply refers to the telecommunication signal to allow all this data and images to flow to your computer.

You might also hear terms like "**DSL**" or "**Cable line**" or "**Fiber Optics**" which are the various types of connections that allow for the signals to access your computer.

We wouldn't spend much time worrying about these terms. Chances are you won't be given a choice when you sign up!

Your telephone company will probably offer DSL; your cable company will provide a cable line; and, if you're lucky enough, you might be one of the few places in the country capable of receiving fiber optics.

Access to the Internet comes from a wire: One end of the wire is plugged into your telephone, cable or satellite outlet; while the other end of the wire connects directly into the rear of your **computer**.

You can actually **wire up** multiple computers in one household.

In this instance, you'll need a device called a "**router**" (which the telecommunication company provides).

The router has a number of outlets (called "**ports**") from which you can connect a wire from this outlet directly into each individual computer in your household.

All you need to get going is to sign up:

Chances are, you already have service with one of these companies. For example, you might have telephone service with ATT, Verizon, Sprint or the like; and you might have cable or satellite service for your television through DirecTV, Comcast, Time-Warner or similar services.

Just call the company (**service provider**) you already are using and ask them about how to connect your computer to the Internet. They'll be happy to help you out. (They will probably also offer you a discount at the opportunity to "bundle" more-than-one service.)

What's more, when you call your telephone, cable or satellite company to order Internet access, they will also be happy to install everything – including providing the necessary connection into your computer.

(If not, perhaps it's time to switch your service provider!)

Wireless connection

Here, too, we're using "**wireless**" as a catch-all phrase. You might already be familiar with the term, since one variation of "**wireless**" is the cellular service you utilize for your cell phone.

Wireless access to the Internet comes '**over the airwaves**' so to speak – in short, without any cables or wires.

> This concept of '**over the airwaves**"
> is known as the **Wireless Local Area
> Network** (or **WLAN** for short).

Actually, technically, that's not exactly true.

In order to distribute this wireless connection to your computer – or a number of computers and / or wireless-compatible devices in your household – you'll need a '**wireless access point**' which is a device that connects directly to the Internet via a router (see "Wired connection" above).

So we're back to the plug-in router and you're probably asking yourself "why bother?"

Well, in the "**wired**" scenario, you have a router, but then must connect each extra computer or device one by one using a wire / cable. Before long, you have wires-cables all over the place.

With a "**wireless scenario**", yes, you have a router, but from that point forward, every extra computer or device around your household can be connected (**synchronized**) wirelessly. Just one router…no other wires or cables.

What are wireless "hotspots"?

If you've purchased a **laptop** and can connect wirelessly, you should be aware that there are many free ways to access the Internet while you're on the go.

> This is also true for other **wireless devices** such as iPads, tablets and smartphones.

Many public and private companies have created access points (which are termed "**hotspots**") within their facilities to allow you to connect to the Internet.

You'll find these hotspots in libraries, colleges and universities, coffee shops, hotels, airports and more: generally, most places where large numbers of people tend to congregate.

Here are some general observations:

- As a rule, most of these hotspots are "free".

- Some companies, such as hotels and airports, are likely to charge a fee to access their hotspots. The fee is usually nominal, but it is a fee nonetheless.

- Many hotspots – including those hotspots that are "free" – **are likely to ask for your e-mail address before giving you access**.

> Hence the quotations around "**free**". While access to the hotspot is free, providing the company with your e-mail address usually allows them to send you (often-unwanted) promotional material.
>
> You have a way to opt-out of receiving any promotional material, but the usual two-step process is just plain annoying.

Using computer outside your home

On occasion, you'll find certain facilities or organization – libraries and business conferences are typical examples – will actually provide you with a computer to use. (The information below also hold true for use of a friend's computer outside your home.)

Most often you can use these computers for free, sometimes for a nominal fee.

For your personal security, we strongly recommend:

- Limit your use on these computers, especially work-related computers. There's a good chance wherever you "surf" on the Internet can be tracked by the facility or organization.

- Never allow an outside computer to "remember" your password!

  Any time you sign into a website – as an example, signing into your Amazon or Apple account – you will automatically be asked whether you want the computer to "save" your password. Don't do it! It is very easy for some stranger to use this same computer and access your "saved" password.

- Finally, always make sure to **"sign out"** from this kind of computer after you've used it. Never – ever! – leave the computer up-and-running without signing out.

The need for speed?

We've tossed some words around: wired, wireless, broadband, DLS, cable line, fiber optics to name a few.

No matter which term is used, they're all designed to provide you access to the content that's available on the Internet.

Some services are faster than others, while other services charge you a premium for faster (and faster) speeds.

Unless you're planning to watch videos (say, on YouTube) every time you go online, there really isn't as much need for as much speed as you might think.

You'll probably be more-than-satisfied with just enough speed to load any website without any delay or glitch.

As a general guideline: Speed on the Internet is usually measured via a data transfer rate referred to as "**megabits per second**" (or "**mbps**").

The average speed that most companies offer in the United States is between 6-10 mbps. Even the lower end, say 3-6 mbps, should be more-than-adequate for most people's needs.

Just one more thing and you're ready to "surf the 'Net"

In order to access the Internet, you need an **Internet Service Provider** (known as "**ISP**") for your computer (in the same way you would need a cable or satellite provider to get all the channels for your television).

Just as you can't plug in your television and get all the channels that are available; but rather need to access them from somewhere (your cable or satellite provider), so, too, you need an ISP in order to access the Internet.

- Screwy? Yes.

- Designed to get extra money for the telecommunication companies? Yes.

- Necessary? Unfortunately, "yes" as well.

The good news is many telecommunication companies – the ones who you'll be calling to help install the wired or wireless service for your computer – are also Internet Service Providers (ISPs).

If for some reason the telecommunication company that is hooking you up cannot provide you Internet service, you can always sign up for popular Internet services such as AOL, MSN, Earthlink, Yahoo and so forth.

Deciding on your Home Page

The very first time you sign onto your **ISP** and are "welcomed", you'll be automatically transferred to the ISP's home page.

> Again**, ISP** stands for **Internet Service Provider**, such as AOL, MSN, Earthlink and Yahoo referred to above.

Unfortunately, most ISP home pages look like a cluttered closet. On the home page, you'll find news headlines and weather and sports and shopping tips and money tips and auto tips and… The list of topics just goes on and on.

While you can configure their home page to suit your needs – in other words, only pick the topics that are of interest to you – that task is often cumbersome and, frankly, not worth the effort.

Just because you need to sign up for an ISP, doesn't mean you're locked into their home page.

Most people access the Internet via a web browser: the most popular being Microsoft's Internet Explorer or Apple's Safari.

You can actually choose which page (or pages) you'd like to see every time you open your web browser.

(We'll cover this option in more detail in our next chapter – Chapter 5 on Search Engines. We'll also show you how to use your web browser and search engines when exploring the Internet.)

"ISP", "web browser", "search engines" huh?

We've thrown a few terms at you; now let's see if we can offer up an appropriate analogue:

Suppose you want to watch a television show…

Think of "**ISP**" as the electricity that causes the television to run.

Think of "**web browser**" as the actual television set itself.

Finally, think of "**search engines**" – the subject of our next chapter – as the remote that allows you to find and access the various television channels.

We trust you get the idea.

The Internet: At a glance

The Pros

- Accessing the Internet is your doorway into an unbelievable array of information, videos, pictures, and data.

- The Internet is the foundation upon which all computers and most digital technology resides.

- In addition to being informative, the Internet is surprisingly fun to use.

- Shopping via the Internet means you don't have to get into your car and drive around town looking for what you want. If the yen to purchase something strikes in the middle of the night, there are no "closed" signs on Internet stores: they're open 24 hours a day, 7 days a week.

The Cons

- You can easily find yourself spending a great deal of time "wandering" the Internet.

  (Access to so much information can often become hypnotic. You can spend hours on a simple task – say, for example, purchasing a new pair of shoes – by visiting the vast array of shoe websites and the equally-large quantity of shoes that are available.)

- Additionally, it is very easy to spend vast amounts of time engaging in the array of games and "eye-candy" available on the Web.

The Hidden Costs

- Shopping on the Internet can become extremely addictive. Here are two precautionary tips:

  First: By-in-large, most Internet sites are safe and secure. Make sure to use a credit card when purchasing any item to minimize any risk of damaged goods or fraud.

Second: If you decide to return an item, remember that the initial cost of shipping the item will probably not be refunded back to you.

Chapter 5

Computers: Search Engines

Who should read this section

If you have a computer (with access to the Internet) and are ready to begin exploring the 'informational highway', we expect this chapter will be very useful to you.

If you're already "searching the 'Net" and are frustrated at how infrequently you find exactly what you're looking for, our tips and suggestions should be quite helpful.

Who should skip this section

If you have a computer but don't plan to use the Internet a great deal, this might not be a worthwhile section for you.

(On the other hand, if you want to search the Internet effectively – even during the limited time you use it – you might want to review this section!)

A few simple terms you should know

We've already defined some of these terms, but here's a quick synopsis:

Internet

The global system of interconnected computer networks that utilizes a standard protocol to allow billions of users – this, of course, includes you! – in order to access text, video, images, and other information.

The **Internet** is also referred to as the **World Wide Web** (or **www**) or even the **'Net**, for short.

Website

A website is a connected group of **pages**, usually maintained by one person or organization / company and is traditionally devoted to a single topic or several closely related topics.

> These connected pages are often referred to as "**web pages**".

Navigating

Navigating around the Internet – which means, simply, moving from one website to another – is often referred to as "**surfing the Web**" or "**surfing the 'Net.**"

http://

https://

This phrase – known as **HyperText Transfer Protocol** – begins each web entry and defines how messages are formatted and transmitted.

> These double lines -- // -- are known as **"hash marks"**. They're located on the bottom right side of the keyboard (right next to the comma and period).

Normally, we'd just let this slip by since it is automatically inserted into the search and isn't something you have to enter.

Notice, however, the second phrase – **https://** -- if you see the "s" added to that phrase, it designates a **"Secure"** layer. For example, you'll find this coding at the start of all bank / financial institution websites.

While the majority of websites simply begin with http:// and are, by-in-large, secure, the added level of encryption used within sites that begin https:// is a solid guarantee that your information – contained on the site and transmitted to your computer – is extremely secure.

http://www

Notice the phrase **"www"** after http:// (or https://). This, as we've mentioned, stands for **World Wide Web**. This short phrase – http://www – designates the beginning of every website entry.

Good news. Since it begins every entry, you don't need to type any of it when searching or trying to bring up a website.

If you were trying to type in our website: Just Tell Me How It Works, you could just type in: www.JustTellMeHowItWorks.com or just plain JustTellMeHowitWorks.com.

Understanding web browsers and search engines

Although that's it on the simple terms, we do need to make one final distinction: a "**web browser**" and a "**search engine**" are two different things.

A "**web browser**" is a software program that allows you to display (and interact) with text, video, images and other information typically located on the pages of a website on the Internet.

A "**search engine**" is a computer program that allows you to…well, *search*.

The two most popular **web browsers** are Microsoft's Internet Explorer and Apple's Safari.

> You can also obtain / download other **web browsers** like Mozilla Firefox, Google Chrome, Netscape, Opera and more.
>
> For our purposes, we'll stick to the two most popular (and commonly used) browser: Internet Explorer and Safari.

Luckily for everyone, these web browsers come pre-installed on either a Microsoft Windows or Apple Mac computer – which, if you've been reading sequentially, you know are the primary types of computer systems you can buy.

As you can see from the **two images below** – which are both loaded onto the Google Home Page – there is very little to differentiate between the two. (Internet Explorer is the web browser on the left; while Safari is the web browser on the right.)

Think of a web browser like the <u>shell</u> of the television set – with the search engine and various websites as the pictures / television shows.

The mass of white space with the Google logo – which takes up over the bottom 3/4 of the image – is actually the Google Home Page. Again, using our analogy, this would represent the **television show**.

> In this instance, we've done double-duty since the Google site is <u>both</u> a **Home Page** as well as a **search engine** site.

Web browser: The address bar

Located at the upper / center portion of web browsers is a space known as the **address bar**. Simply, this is where you can type the address for any website you want to visit.

In the two images below, you can see the Internet Explorer address bar (circled on the left); and the Safari image (circled on the right).

As an example of how it works, you can type in www.JustTellMeHowItWorks.com; then hit the "Enter" or "Search" key; and – voila! – the address bar will automatically take you to the website you're looking for.

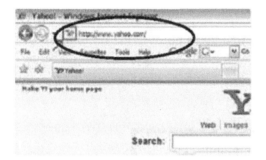
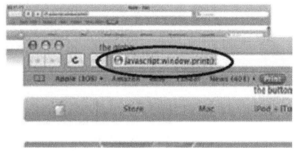

Search Engines: A brief overview

A **search engine** is a program designed to help you find information stored on the World Wide Web. The search engine allows you to ask for specific content – typically, you ask for some criteria by providing a "search" word or phrase or question – and the search engine retrieves a list of sites and references that match those criteria.

While the percentage of use fluctuates somewhat, the most recent figures for these five most popular search engines are:

- Google   66.4%

- Microsoft / Bing   15.3%

- Yahoo   13.7%

- Ask   3.0%

- AOL   1.5%

As you can see, **Google** dominates the marketplace measurably as the most used search engine.

> This market dominance is why **"Google"** has become a catch-all search phrase in our lexicon. (Much like Xerox was synonymous for "copier" years ago).

Market share aside, there's not much to distinguish the various search engines. Still, Google is the #1 search engine for many nuanced reasons, so if you're looking to attach yourself to one particular search engine, this is probably the one to use.

Everything we've told you about web browsers and search engines isn't quite true

While we've given you the basics, technology is ever changing…ever reinventing and tweaking itself.

Both major web browsers – Internet Explorer and Safari – allow you to use the address bar (see section above) to make Internet searches. They both seamlessly utilize Google, Bing or the search engine of your choice to serve the dual function of web browser and search engine.

In English, this means that you don't need to absorb the last 3-4 pages.

Just know that your computer – whether an Apple Mac or Microsoft Windows operating system – comes pre-equipped with a web browser, which can also function as a search engine.

(Just review the above section on the address bar to see where to type in your addresses or search terms / criteria.)

How to search: Some basic facts

We're now down to the heart of the matter: what is the best way(s) to search the Internet.

Every word matters. All the words you put into the search will be used. Obviously, if you search for "Newman", you'll get far more results than if you search "Paul Newman".

Searches are not case sensitive. If you're searching for New York Times or new york times, it makes no difference.

Generally, punctuation is ignored in searches; as are common words such as "a", "an", "the", and so forth.

Narrowing your search

We tried an experiment. We typed in the word **birds** into the search field; pressed "Enter" (or "Search") and discovered over 597 <u>million</u> results (or "hits" as these results are usually called).

We decided to narrow our search to **bluebirds**. Again, we typed that word in the search file and pressed "Enter" and we now discovered over 650,000 results / hits. Better, but over a half-million possible websites/ pages is still too much.

Again, we narrowed our search. This time, we typed in and searched for **bluebirds in Connecticut**. Again, we're narrowing the results; but we still have over 260,000 hits.

Finally, we used one of the search engine's not-easily-remembered tricks: If you use quotation marks around the phrase you're searching for, the search engine will look for that <u>specific</u> phrase.

Since we only want to know about bluebirds in Connecticut, we put quotation marks into the search field: "bluebirds in Connecticut". Now, we're getting somewhere – the search resulted in only 22 website / pages. Certainly, much more manageable…and a distinct improvement from our initial 597 million hits.

You get the idea: The more specific your search inquiry, the more likely that you'll find exactly what you're looking for.

Sometimes, you might go overboard in trying to narrow your search. Instead of millions of hits, your search might produce **no hits whatsoever**. In this instance, try "broadening" your search or "rephrasing" your search using some other key words.

> **"No hits whatsoever"** is highly unlikely given the amount of information on the Internet, but most people who frequent the Web have come across this scenario.

Some tips and tricks

- If you use a minus sign ("-") in front of a word, the search engine will look for everything except what has a minus in front of it.

- For example: If you look for "Brad Pitt" – "Angelina Jolie" in your search, you should receive websites or articles about Brad Pitt **without** reference to Angelina Jolie.

> Life should be so simple. Unfortunately, **searches on the Internet** are often tricky, so don't be surprised if what you're trying to eliminate appears anyway.

- If you start the search with **define,** the search will automatically look for a dictionary definition of the word. (As example: **define prototype** in your search box will send you to a definition of the word "prototype").

- Additionally, if you use **weather** in front of your zip code, the search will automatically produce weather for your area. (As example: **weather 90292**).

- Often using the word "popular" or "favorite" in your search, might give you some helpful websites or information. If you search for "popular shopping websites" or "favorite James Patterson novels", you're likely to get interesting suggestions or recommendations.

- Hopefully, you get the idea. We recommend you search the phrase "Google Tips and Tricks" for additional helpful hints.

Obviously, what we're giving you here is just the "tip" to the proverbial iceberg. The more imaginative or focused your search words, the more specific your results – all very helpful when you're trying to narrow down what you're looking for.

And with that: have fun searching the Internet!

Google Alerts

Now that you're armed with information and tips about searching the Internet, we'd like to mention one final – and worthwhile – service: **Google Alerts**.

You can access Google Alerts by typing "Google Alerts" into your search engine or just by typing in www.google.com/alerts.

As the name of this service implies, Google "alerts" you to new content on the Internet. This content could be news, websites, blogs, video, even discussion groups.

You simply indicate the subject you're interested in; then "Create an Alert". Google will then notify you by e-mail or on your Google page when new content or information is available.

You can also receive this information as a web feed – usually referred to as an **RSS Feed** ("**Really Simple Syndication**") – by which you subscribe to a news service or blog and receive updates.

Moreover with Google Alerts, you can check for new content in three ways: "once a day", "once a week" or "as it happens".

As an example, if you're following a particular 'hot button' political issue or are intrigued by the ne'er-to-well goings-on of some infamous celebrity, you can receive updates as frequently as you'd like.

All-in-all, a handy compliment to the Internet and its searches!

Search Engines: At a glance

The Pros

- A web browser and search engine are a necessity if you want to find information on the Internet. Fortunately, access to and use of most are free.

- There are numerous tips and tricks to help with your search – for example, using quotation marks between words you want to be considered as a phrase ("2016 Summer Olympics") or using a minus sign to eliminate words from a search ("2012 Summer Olympics" -swimming).

- Once you feel comfortable searching the Internet, a new world of information is available at your fingertips (or, mouse and keyboard, if you will).

The Cons

- Your search is only as good as the criteria you provide.

  It's like the Goldilocks motif in a way: if your search is too general, you'll receive too many possible answers; if your search is too narrow, you won't receive many (if any) answers. Instead, you need to find the right word (or combination of words) to achieve the proper search balance.

- Access to so much information can become hypnotic; you can also easily find yourself spending a great deal of time "lost" in the Internet.

The Hidden Costs

- There are few hidden costs associated with the search engine, per se.

  As we mentioned earlier, however, shopping on the Internet can become extremely addictive; and so, in that sense, you might look at compulsive Internet shopping as a hidden cost by-product.

The same holds true with certain websites that "charge" for access to information. For example, many newspapers and magazines have erected a **"paywall"** on their website (in which access is only granted with subscriptions or for a fee).

We can appreciate a newspaper or magazine's financial survival instincts by erecting a **paywall**,

Still, paying for news (read: information) on the Internet seems silly, since the very foundation of the Internet allows for free exchange of news and ideas (Huffington Post, CNN, ABC, Drudge Report to name just a few).

Chapter 6

Computers: E-mail

Who should read this section

Anyone with a computer.

E-mail messages are received nearly instantaneously; and they can send digital "attachments". As such, e-mails are certain worth understanding if you want to communicate with friends and family on a daily or frequent basis.

E-mails outnumber "**snail mail**" (mail sent via the post office) well over 81 to 1.

Even "texting" from your mobile cell phone is just a variation of e-mail messaging. Hence, the need to give this chapter a once over.

Who should skip this section

If you – and your friends and family – are content with sending and receiving letters via the post office; and you feel there is no need for "digital" mail – just pass over this chapter.

(As a personal aside: if you have exquisite penmanship, we certainly hope you mail letters periodically, whether you use e-mail or not. We love receiving letters with flowery penmanship…which is fast becoming a dying art.)

> **E-mail** is short for **Electronic Mail**.
>
> The acceptable spelling is either e-mail or email.
>
> Dictionaries seem split on which is the proper spelling; and people who write about technology are equally divided in its proper spelling.
>
> So, at the moment…your choice.

Understanding the components of any e-mail address

Let's start with the basic components of any e-mail address. Understanding how an e-mail address is divided can be helpful – especially when you sign up for an e-mail address of your own.

The e-mail address is divided into three parts:

Name @ Website

1. The first part is your "user name".

When you sign up for an e-mail account – see the next section below – you'll be asked to provide a "**User Name**". The user name is the name you'll be given in the first part of the e-mail address.

If you're lucky and your name is (say) Jonathan Grabowinsky, there's a very good chance that if you select "**JonathanGrabowinsky**" you'll be granted that user name.

Take note that there are **no spaces in an e-mail user name**. So the name would not be Jonathan (space) Grabowinsky; but rather, JonathanGrabowinsky (no spaces).

While spaces aren't allowed, most e-mail companies will let you to use a period ("**.**") between your first and last name. If "JonathanGrabowinsky" is taken, perhaps "Jonathan. Grabowinsky" is available.

If, however, your name is (say) John Doe or Jane Smith, you'll undoubtedly find that the name is taken – even your name with a period between them. In this case, you're left with two options:

- You can add a number after your name. (For example, you can try your user name as "JohnDoe2014" or "JohnDoe1234". Remember, there are no spaces in your user name, so the name would not be "John (space) Doe (space) 2014".

- You can also pick a phrase or nickname to use as your user name. (For example, you can try "basketballfan" or "myapplepiesaregreat". Somehow – whether using numbers or a phrase or nickname – you'll find the right combination).

Some e-mail "rules of thumb"

If you're planning to use your e-mail address for any business purpose, we recommend creating an e-mail user name that utilizes a variation of your name (and avoids any nicknames).

(For example: "JaneSmith2013" is preferable to "iamthegreatestmom" when sending e-mails connected to any business e-mail.)

Additionally:

Try to create an e-mail that you're likely to remember. (Otherwise, you'll find yourself scrambling for the notes to yourself about your user name).

2. The second part of any e-mail address is the "at" symbol. You'll find the @ symbol as part of the "2" on your keyboard.

You get the "**@**" symbol by holding down the "**Shift**" key as you hit the number "**2**".

Some new keyboards recognize the importance of the **@** symbol and have it positioned as one of the keys on the keyboard. (Just check to see if it's there or not.)

3. Finally, the last part of the e-mail address is the website name. In your case, this will be the name of the e-mail company you have signed up with (see next section below).

If, for example, you sign up for (free) e-mail service with Yahoo, **Hotmail / Outlook** or Gmail – the three most popular e-mail services.

> Currently, Microsoft has launched **Outlook.com**, a free e-mail online e-mail service that is designed to replace **Hotmail**.
>
> We're guessing that Outlook is more recognizable than Hotmail, although we suspect both names might co-exist for a while.
>
> We'll refer to Microsoft's e-mail service as Hotmail / Outlook.

Your e-mail address will look something like:

- JohnDoe123@yahoo.com

- Jonathan.Grabowinsky@hotmail.com or Jonathan.Grabowinsky@outlook.com

- worldsbestmom@gmail.com

How to sign up for an e-mail account

The first thing you need to do in order to send and receive e-mails is to **sign up for an e-mail account.**

> Yes, it <u>does</u> seem to us that everywhere you turn on the Internet, you need to **sign up** for something.
>
> On the plus side, almost every e-mail account is available for free.

Among the most popular free e-mail accounts:

Yahoo! Mail (www.mail.yahoo.com)
Hotmail / Outlook (Windows Live Hotmail) (www.hotmail.com or
(www.outlook.com)

G-mail (from Google) (www.mail.google.com)
AOL mail (www.webmail.aol.com)
iCloud Mail (from Apple) (www.icloud.com)

Chances are you already have an e-mail account (but may not know it)

When you signed up with an **ISP (Internet Service Provider)** to access the Internet – this is the telephone, cable or satellite company that hooked you up – you might not realize that most ISPs provide free e-mail service free (as part of the package).

You'll still need to register for an e-mail *address* (see directly below), but you won't have to join one of the online e-mail companies.

Here's the easy process to sign up for an e-mail account:

1. Go online and find the appropriate e-mail site (see the list of 'most popular free e-mail accounts' directly above).

2. Click on the button that says "Sign Up", "Sign Up for Free Account", "Create an Account" or the like.

3. You'll be asked for much of the following:

   • Your first and last name.

   • To select a "user name". This will be the name for your e-mail account. See "Components of any e-mail address" (again, in an earlier section above) for more information.

   • You'll also be asked to select a password.

A word (or two) about passwords...

Don't make passwords too obvious. For example, avoid using your date of birth, spouse's name, social security number, pet's name, previous addresses or phone numbers, and so forth.

If someone finds your e-mail address – which is easier than you might think – they could just as easily "**hack**" your password by hunting down these obvious examples.

That said, here are some password tips:

• Look for a unique phrase. As an example, "worldsbestmom" or "ilovetheyankees".

• Add a number (either before or after or both). As example: "5worldsbestmom2"

• Capitalize some of the letters, but not in the way you'd normally expect. Here's a suggestion given our example: "5worldSbestmOm2

 As you look at it, it seems like a complex password, but if your age is 52 and you know where the capital letters are, it's actually a very simple password to remember (and next-to-impossible to "hack").

4. From here, you're usually asked to provide your gender, date of birth and, on occasion, your telephone number.

5. You might also be asked to provide answers to some basic security questions (for example, "what was the name of your high school?" or "in what city were you born?").

   All this information – while slightly intrusive – enables the e-mail company to verify who you are should you need to call them for help (or if you've forgotten both your user name and password).

6. At this point, you're done. You now have an e-mail name and account and you're ready to send messages, attachments and much more.

How to send an e-mail

Let's dive right in on how to compose an e-mail; attach a file; and much more.

1. First, sign into your e-mail account. (www.gmail,com, www.yahoomail.com and so forth),

2. You'll be asked to provide your user name and password. This is the information you registered when you signed up for the account (see our examples above).

3. Once you gain access to the e-mail account, you'll see **a button or link** marked "**Compose**" or "**New**" or "**Create a new message**". Click (left-mouse button) on that button or link.

> The **button or link** is usually located on the upper left hand corner of the screen.

4. You'll find a form that looks like our **graphic below**. (Depending on which e-mail account you sign up with, the design might differ slightly, but the basic form for all e-mails should remain the same.)

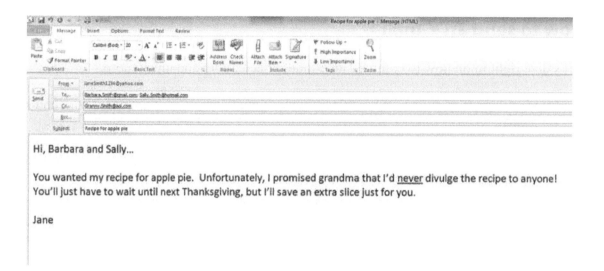

Hi, Barbara and Sally...

You wanted my recipe for apple pie. Unfortunately, I promised grandma that I'd <u>never</u> divulge the recipe to anyone! You'll just have to wait until next Thanksgiving, but I'll save an extra slice just for you.

Jane

5. In the first **field** – the "**From**" field to the right of the Send button – your e-mail address is automatically inserted.

> The "**field**" we're referring to are the blank rectangular boxes next to the "**From**", "**To**" and "**Subject**" headers.

6. Drop down to the second field – the "**To**" field – and insert the e-mail address of the person you're trying to reach,

   (Sometimes you'll need to contact that person the old fashioned way – usually by phone – in order to get their e-mail address).

7. If you want to copy the e-mail to someone – say, other family members – you'll insert their e-mail addresses into the third field – the "**cc**" field.

"**cc**" stands for carbon copy, a throw-back to the old typewriter days.

It means a copy of the e-mail is being sent to the people listed in this field.

When you put someone's name / e-mail address in the "cc" field, their name and e-mail address will appear on everyone's copy.

You can also send a "**bcc**" (which stands for "**blind carbon copy**"). In this instance, anyone's name you put in the "bcc" field will <u>not</u> be seen by anyone else in the e-mail chain.

A quick note re: "cc" and "bcc" fields. Some e-mail accounts – such as the Google gmail service provided below – don't automatically add these two additional fields.

Nonetheless, just under the "to" field, you will find links to add the "cc: or "bcc"

A word about the "Subject" line

All e-mail forms include a "Subject" line. In this line, you tell the receiver what the general content of the e-mail is about. (As in our earlier graphic example, we've created the Subject line as "Recipe for apple pie".)

Filling in the Subject line helps the receiver understand what's being sent. In these days of Spam and Junk Mail, it's extreme-ly important to know who is sending the e-mail (and what is being sent).

8. Type your letter or message into the large white space below the "Subject" line (designed for that purpose).

9. Once you've composed your e-mail letter and have added the appropriate e-mail addresses, you're good-to-go.

   Just click the "Send" button – common to all e-mail messages – and the e-mail is on its way.

Adding an attachment to your e-mail

You can also add an attachment to an e-mail.

Most attachments are **pictures or documents**.

> Theoretically, you could also **attach** a digital music or video file, but these files are usually very large (and most e-mail services have a cap on how large an attachment can be).

In order to add an attachment:

1. Compose your e-mail address (per the section above).

   In brief: Insert the e-mail address of the person "To" whom you're sending the letter; add a brief descriptive notation into the "Subject" line; then type your letter or message into the large white space (designed for that purpose).

2. At this point, click on the button or link that indicates "**Attach**" or "**Attach a File**".

3. Once you click on the "Attach" button, you'll be taken to a directory of your files.

   Fear not. Your computer – whether Microsoft Windows or Apple Mac – tries to organize all your files in a logical way. In Windows, for example, you'll find these folders – or Libraries as Windows calls them – arranged in self-explanatory groups: "Documents", "Music", "Pictures" and "Videos".

   Let's say you want to attach a **picture of your trip to Miami Beach**.

This is assuming you've **taken** the picture and **saved** it to your computer.

For more information, we suggest you take a look at Chapter 13 on Digital Cameras.

Go to the Library marked "Pictures"; scroll down until you find the right picture; select (click once) on the picture; then click the button marked "Insert" or "Attach".

That's it. A copy of your picture is attached to the e-mail. (The original picture will stay in its original folder on your computer.) Just hit "Send" and the picture is safely on its way.

A few things you should know about attachments

• As mentioned, when you attach a file – say, a picture – you're not sending the original.

Your e-mail attaches a <u>copy</u> of the picture and sends that along. Your original picture remains safely on your computer.

• Sometimes, an e-mail might not use the word "Attach". Instead, your e-mail account provides **a graphic representation of a paperclip**.

(This graphic is the same thing as "Attach" or "Attach File" – just click on the paperclip icon).

• If you can't easily find the document or picture you want to send – but know it's <u>somewhere</u> on your computer – we suggest this step:

Click on the Start button – the button with the Windows logo on the bottom left of your computer. (For Apple Macs, use "Finder").

You'll see a box marked "**Search Programs and Files**".

Enter the name of the file or picture. Even a partial name will do – for example, if you know "Miami Beach" is part of the label, just mark that down.

The computer will search for anything you've marked and will display both the file or picture (and its exact location).

• If you change your mind and want to delete an e-mail attachment, just highlight by clicking once on the attachment, then select the "**delete**" key from the keyboard. You can also use the "**cut**" key from the main menu or by right clicking on the attachment.

Replying to someone's e-mail letter

Quite often, you'll receive an e-mail from a friend or family member and will want to respond.

Nothing could be easier. (Okay, in theory anyway.)

1. First, open the e-mail to which you want to respond (by doing the following):

   a. Go into your e-mail account and click on your "**Inbox**" (where you should find all your e-mails messages).

   b. Double-click on the message. This opens the e-mail.

2. Most of the time, you'll find phrases and graphics like the one from Microsoft Outlook below:

As you can see, you can:

- **Delete**: Just click the "X" and you can delete the message.

- **Reply** – this replies <u>just</u> to the person who sent you the e-mail.

- **Reply All**: This replies not only to the person who sent you the e-mail, but to anyone else they may have been copied on the e-mail.

- **Forward**: You can forward the original e-mail – along with its contents – to another person. (We'll discuss this shortly).

- **Junk**: You'll also find a symbol marked "**Junk**" (or, occasionally, "**Spam**"). This marks the e-mail as content you no longer wish to receive.

  Unfortunately, there's no way around junk mail (or "**spam**" as it's also known). This button will help you sift through those annoying e-mails.

3. Once you click on reply, the e-mail will automatically enter the address of the person from the original e-mail message and will allow you to type your reply or comment.

4. Once you've finished composing the reply, just hit "**Send**" as you would on any other e-mail message.

5. There – you're done!

A word (or two) about forwarding an e-mail

Forwarding an e-mail can be quite handy – especially if you've received a document or picture and you want to send it to a friend or family member.

Ordinarily, you would have to save the attachment onto your computer, then attach it on a new e-mail.

Instead, by using "**Forward**", the e-mail can be sent along to anyone you choose including the original attachment.

When could you use this?

Suppose you receive a picture of several family members. Nice photo, you think.

If you "forward" the original e-mail, you can send the picture along to the other family members by just clicking the "Forward" button and typing in their e-mail addresses.

Useful? We think so!

Saving an attachment in your e-mail

Suppose you receive a document or picture that you'd like to save to your computer.

Again, the steps are simple enough:

1. Assuming you've received an e-mail with an attachment, first open the e-mail (by double-clicking on the e-mail itself).

2. Depending on the type of e-mail program you're using, you'll usually find a button that says "**Download**" or "**Save**".

   Occasionally – when no "download" button is easily apparent – you can click your right mouse button onto the attachment. This will give you the opportunity to save the attachment. (Sometimes, instead of a button marked "download" or "save", you'll see a graphic icon of a paperclip.)

   In all cases, we recommend you use the "**Save As**" button, which will allow you to name the picture or document any way you choose.

3. Save the attachment into the appropriate folder.

   As example, you would want to save your photos into the "Pictures" library; files into "Documents" and so forth.

File naming convention

- Try to be logical in the way you name your files.

  For example, if you name your pictures from California as "Disneyland.001", "Disneyland.002" and so forth, you probably won't remember which picture is which.

  Instead, if you name the pictures "John and Mary at Disneyland" or "Little Billy with Mickey Mouse", you have a better chance of remembering the contents.

- The same can be said about naming documents.

  Let's say you have written four draft letters to United Airlines.

  One way of naming these letters would be "United Airlines first draft", "United Airlines second draft" and so on.

  A *better* way might be to also date the files. For example, "United Airlines first draft (01-01-14)" and so forth.

- We suspect you get the idea. Any naming convention that will help you recall the picture or document is extremely helpful.

E-Mail: At a glance

The Pros

- A fast and easy way to keep in touch with friends, family and acquaintances. (In fact, <u>the</u> easiest way to stay in touch.)

- Inexpensive – most e-mail services are free – and learning everything you need to know about e-mails is surprisingly simple.

- Sending documents and pictures are easy and can simply be attached to any e-mail.

- There is no charge for sending any of these attachments. Compared with the cost of mailing these items via the post office or overnight services, e-mails are the bargain of the century.

- Any e-mail you send can be received in a matter of seconds – certainly, in only a matter of minutes.

The Cons

- Initially, tracking down the e-mail addresses for friends, family and associates can be frustrating at times.

- Once you begin to e-mail, you **lay yourself open** to receiving junk mail, spam, and even a barrage of advertisements and promotional material from places you shop.

If you're wondering '**how did they ever find me?**' understand that when you sign up for anything on the Internet, chances are the company you signed up with is likely to sell your e-mail address to direct marketers.

Annoying, not ethical perhaps; but technically legal.

Make sure you check a company's privacy notice before you sign up (and opt out if you have a choice).

Trust us…you'll get enough e-mails without having to sign up for additional promotions.

Certainly, you can "**unsubscribe**" from this barrage of advertisements and promotions; and you can mark them as "junk mail" or "spam" -- using the ever-handy right mouse button – so they'll be filtered out. Still, all this takes time and having your e-mail in-box cluttered with junk messages is irksome.

The Hidden Costs

- Although chances are very rare that this will happen, it is possible that your e-mail and password might get commandeered by a stranger.

  Again, these are rare occurrences, but occasionally a company's database might get 'hacked' and certain information (notably e-mail addresses) can be stolen.

  If this should happen, we recommend contacting your e-mail provider; cancelling your e-mail address; then setting up with an entirely new e-mail account.

  Not a financial strain, but annoying nonetheless.

Section 2: Entertainment

Chapter 7

Television

Who should read this section

If you're considering purchasing a new television set, this section will help you determine which one is right for you.

We'll guide you through the new types of television sets…most of which will cost you less than you imagine (and will certainly take up less space).

If you're interested in learning about the new features available in today's televisions, we'll show you what's on the market – and what's coming down the pike.

Who should skip this section

If you've already purchased your second, third or even fourth digital television, you're probably already an expert in this area.

(Even so, you might want to check out the latest "universal remotes" which we explore later in this chapter.)

Television 101

Ah, for the good old days when the word "**television**" was synonymous with a "**tubed television set**" and the only thing you had to worry about was the size.

Nowadays, it seems as though there are a myriad of choices.

Fortunately – although it seems overwhelming at first glance – there are really only three choices, (two of which are fast-becoming obsolete). We'll give you the rundown shortly, but first, we need to give you a brief history lesson:

Actually while the first television broadcasts began in the early 1950s, the changes which we're now seeing – and which now dominate our television lives and viewing habits – occurred as recently as the last 15-20 years.

Prior to the late 1990s, television was broadcast via over-the-air transmissions into what were termed **analog** signals.

> "**Analog**" is a process by which data is represented as physical quantities (say the picture on your television set) that change continuously.

These analog signals were captured by a **cathode-ray tube** (situated inside your clunky television) and, voila, moving images were displayed in the middle your living room.

You don't need to know the specifics of how a **cath-ode-ray tube** (**CRT**) operates – honestly, just image a vacuum tube with electrons flying around, all de-signed to create images.

For our current purposes, just know that these devices were referred to as "tubed television sets".

Since our culture loves to compartmentalize everything, the analog signals were standard-ized into a **525-line broadcast**.

In English, what that meant was that whether you were watching "Gunsmoke", "Masterpiece Theater", "Gilligan's Island" or some old movies on television, the **quality of the images all looked the same**.

So why do you need to know about 525 lines? Well, as inventors and developers began tin-kering around with broadcast images, they discovered they could improve the clarity of the image using terms we refer to in today television jargon as 720p and 1080p.

720p can be described as: "wow, that's clear".

1080p can be described as: "Double-wow, I can't begin to describe how clear those images are – I can even see the **lines and wrinkles on my favorite actor's face**".

> Obviously, a sore point for many actors; a boon to the television makeup industry; but hardly a subject to be explored in this book.

All this became known as **High Definition Television or HDTV**.

> **HDTV** simply stands for **High Definition TV**. The phrases "**High Definition**" or "**HDTV**" can be used interchangeably.

Well, you can imagine how happy all this digital tweaking and compression and inventions made the television manufacturers. With signals transmitted as digital rather than analog, they no longer needed our friendly cathode-ray tube. So, out went the clunky television set and in came the flat-screen television set.

And by "**flat-screen**" we mean <u>flat</u>!

Most of the new television sets –and we're including all the electronics stuffed inside – are only 2-4" thick. And there are apparently no limits: new televisions have now reached the marketplace that are no more than **1/4" thick**.

> That's not a typo, folks – that's **one-quarter of an inch thick** (and shrinking)!
>
> (If you're looking for the right imagery, try stacking four quarters together – that's about a quarter of an inch).

And while these televisions are not thick, they are certainly wide. Standard flat-screen television sets generally measure between **42" – 50" wide**. Newest flat-screen models can reach widths over 100" inches.

> The **dimensions** for flat-screen televisions are measured *diagonally* across the viewing surface. As a result, a 42" television set might actually be 44" or 45" wide (depending on the model).

So in 2006, with cathode-ray tubes practically a thing of the past, the **United States government** required that all over-the-air television stations cease analog broadcasting and, rather, broadcast in high-definition mode instead.

> Well, technically, the **Federal Communications Commission** (FCC)

Are we done with the history lesson?

Almost!

We have one more piece of the puzzle to describe to you – the four ways you can receive your television signal:

Over the air (free)

The first way – "**over the air**" broadcast – is the one most familiar to people. As the term implies, the signals are broadcast over the airwaves and you pick up the signal via a home **antenna**.

The **antenna** that takes up space on your roof or those famous-but-mainly-defunct "rabbit ear" antennas.

Unfortunately, you can only access those local stations close enough to allow you to pick up a signal. These usually include the major networks and, if you're lucky, a handful of privately-owned stations.

Consequently you cannot receive any of the cable networks – ESPN, Disney Channel and the like. As the name implies, they can only be received via cable (or satellite).

"Over the air" signals come to you free-of-charge. Of course, nothing is "free". Where the **networks** make their money is by selling commercials. They pocket the money from the advertisers and you, in turn, have to sit through the endless sales pitches for cars, aspirins, fast foods and so forth.

At the moment, there **are five major networks**: ABC, CBS, NBC, Fox and the CW network.

Cable television (pay)

The second way to receive a broadcast is via your **local cable company**.

> The **top cable companies** in the United States include Comcast, Time-Warner Cable, Cox Communications, Charter Communication and so forth.

In this process, the cable company comes to your door; hooks up some wires through your outlets; leave you with **a cable box**; and, presto, you're ready to go.

> You're usually responsible for the cost of the **cable box**, so make sure you return the box to the cable company in the event you move or relocate.

Unfortunately, you need to pay for cable television.

Here's the trade-off: You pay a certain monthly fee for your cable hook-up. The cable company, in turn, provides you with over 140 channels to choose from.

Some of these channels – such as ESPN, TBS, Discovery, USA Network, CNN and the Food Network – are included with your basic monthly fee. Others – such as HBO, Starz, Showtime, and special sports packages – are considered "premium" channels. You can still get them, but there's an **extra cost for these channels** which is added to your monthly bill.

The **cost** for these extra bells-and-whistles can add up, resulting in bills totaling well over $100 per month.

That said, cable television offers high-definition broadcast for most of their cable channels as well as the ability to hook up a digital recorder to record your favorite programs (see our next chapter, Chapter 8 on Digital Recorders).

Here's the bottom line…

Cable (or satellite) is an absolute must for people who live in areas where over-the-air broadcast signals are weak. Also, since you can't get cable network channels any other way, most people are willing to trade the monthly expense in exchange for the variety of programs.

Satellite television (pay)

The third way to receive a broadcast is via **satellite**.

At the moment, there are **only two satellite companies** in the United States: DIRECTV (888) 777-2454 and Dish Network (800) 823-4929.

In this process, you call the satellite company. They come to your door; place a small satellite dish on your roof or balcony; hook up some wires; and leave you with a satellite box. And again, presto, you're ready to go.

Sound familiar?

It should, since the process (and results) is exactly the same as cable television hook-up.

Everything else is pretty much the same. You pay a monthly fee and, in exchange, receive over 140 channels. Same channels as the cable companies provide; same premium packages; same offer of high-definition broadcast; even the same ability to hook up a digital recorder. Even the financial bottom line remains the same.

Cable versus Satellite: The final analysis

In the end, it comes down to research and personal preference.

1. Determine which local cable company services your neighborhood.

2. Check out how that company's record is received overall. (Ask your neighbors, friends and colleagues – most of whom will likely have an opinion.)

3. Compare the cable company's service with that of the satellite companies. (Again, ask neighbors and friends).

4. Make an informed decision.

5. If it comes down to a toss-up, just flip a coin. (Remember, both cable and satellite companies provide near-identical service.)

IPTV (in English, television via the Internet)

The last way to receive your television broadcast is rather revolutionary: access to your shows is accomplished through the Internet.

Unlike calling the cable or satellite company and letting them do the work, with **IPTV** ("Internet Protocol Television") you'll need to purchase a set-top box and hook up your Internet to your television. Most set-top boxes – such as Apple TV, Roku and Boxee – have wireless network built-in which allows for a (reasonably) easy set-up.

But many of you are already two questions ahead of us: You know that television doesn't broadcast over the Internet, so why bother?

Actually, while the Internet doesn't broadcast like regular television, many of the shows are available through websites. Hulu (and Hulu Plus) provide thousands of episodes while access to Netflix provides an equal-large number of movies and television series. Even the major broadcast and television networks have their own dedicated websites which allow viewing of recent episodes.

What's the catch with television over the Internet?

The cost!

Although the Internet professes to be free, in actuality, it's not.

First, there's the cost of the telephone (**broadband**) service that allows you to access the Internet. Then, add the cost of the set-top box to connect the Internet to your television. Finally, many of the websites – such as Hulu Plus and Netflix – charge a premium to access their shows.

In the end, IPTV is cheaper than cable or satellite, but not by much. You might want to think this over carefully before "disconnecting" from mainstream television.

So ends our history primer, although we think you'll agree that you've been given the foundation for our final segment, which explains the three types of television sets currently available to you:

Direct view (tubed) televisions

The first type of television set is the old work-horse: the **tubed television**.

> This **tubed television** is sometimes re-
> ferred to as **Direct View** or **Standard
> Definition** televisions.

If you've been following along, you know that these tubed television sets will soon be pass-ing the way of the dinosaur, the dodo bird, Polaroid cameras, eight-track tapes and the elec-tric typewriter.

Still, there are a few models around, but rather than elaborate further, let's just jump right to the basic "At a Glance…".

Direct view (tubed) televisions: At a glance

The Pros

- **Relatively inexpensive**.

> We use the term "**relatively inexpensive**" with a proverbial grain of salt.
>
> Prices for flat-screen televisions (see next section below) have been tumbling for years. If you shop around, you'll find these newer models available at comparable (or far less) cost.

(As you can see, we don't have much to commend these types of television sets. If you glance at the "Cons", the reasons will be very apparent.)

The Cons

- Bulky and heavy.

- Limited screen sizes. (Sizes for these televisions run no larger than 36" sets – not surprising since most televisions this size weigh over 200 pounds and are often 2-3 feet deep).

- Lower resolution which is often not compatible with high-end HDTV.

- **Hard to find**.

> As we mentioned earlier, this type of television is going the way of the dinosaur – few are being produced and they're extremely hard to find.

- Chances are this type of television – and its antiquated technology – will all-but-vanish over the next number of years.

The Hidden Costs

- Should something happen to the television – even a minor glitch – replacement parts are hard-to-impossible to find (and are often quite expensive).

Flat-screen televisions

Now we come to the bread-and-butter of the television manufacturing industry: **the flat-screen TVs**.

> Also known as **flat-panel televisions**.

Flat-screen televisions come in two distinct "flavors": **Plasma** and **LCD / LED**.

> **LCD** stands for **Liquid Crystal Display**.
>
> **LED** stands for **Light-Emitting Diodoe**s
>
> While manufactures and television purists will rant and rail over the notion that we're lumping these two kinds of televisions into one category…well, we are.
>
> See "LCD and LED Televisions: At a Glance" further below for nuances of these kind of television sets.

Essentially, both plasma and LCD-LED televisions provide the same excellent performance and durability, so choosing between the two models comes down to personal preference.

One major note of differentiation…

Plasma televisions are only available in large screen sizes (from 42" and above).

If you're looking for a television smaller than 42" (say, a 32" television for the kitchen counter top), the only choices you have available are LCD and LED televisions.

Meanwhile, here's our breakdown and analysis:

Plasma televisions: At a glance

The Pros

- All plasma televisions are flat-screen.

- Generally plasma televisions have a better **home-theater image quality** than LCD or LED televisions.

> In brief, **plasma televisions** more closely replicate the movie-going experience.
>
> Here's a quick way of assessing:
>
> If you tend to watch lots of movies on your television, you might consider purchasing a plasma television.
>
> If your viewing habits consist primarily of television shows rather than movies, then an LCD or LED television might be right for you.

- Thin, wide and (reasonably) lightweight.

- Larger plasma televisions (50" plus) are slightly less expensive than similar-sized LCD or LED televisions.

- Excellent viewing area from any angle in the room.

- Life span for plasma televisions is typically 60,000 hours or about 20 years if used 8 hours per day. (This is the same as for LCD-LED televisions).

- Superior **motion resolution**.

> **Negligible motion blur** caused by fast-action on the screen. This is advantageous if you (or someone in your family) play video games.

The Cons

- Only available in large screen sizes (from 42" and beyond). If you're looking for a television smaller than 42" (say, a 32" television for the kitchen counter), the only choice you have available are LCD or LED televisions.

- Screens usually reflect lots of light (perhaps an issue in very bright rooms).

- Possible "**burn-in**" image (faint after-image left on the screen), although new models are less susceptible.

> A "**burn in**" occurs when an image – such as a network logo or a stock ticker – gets etched permanently onto the screen.
>
> This usually occurs when the television is tuned to a single station for long hours with very bright settings. Very rare and, as we mentioned, the newer models are less susceptible.

- By in large, less energy-efficient than LCD or LED televisions.

The Hidden Costs

- Once you purchase your flat-screen television (and perhaps sign-up with a cable or satellite company), you'll probably find yourself purchasing ancillary devices – such as a **high-definition recorder or DVD player** – to enhance your viewing experience.

See our upcoming chapters on these devices.

- Television viewing is **addictive**, taking you away from hobbies, time outdoors, intimate conversations and so forth.

But you knew this already – didn't you?

LCD and LED televisions: At a glance

The Pros

- All LCD and LED televisions are flat-screen.

- More energy-efficient than plasma televisions.

- Generally LCD and LED televisions have a **sharper image quality** than plasma televisions.

In brief, **LCD and LED televisions** provide a crisp (some would say "too crisp") viewing experience.

Again, here's a quick way of assessing:

If your viewing habits consist primarily of television shows rather than movies, then an LCD or LED television might be right for you.

If you're a "purist" and tend to watch lots of movies on your television, you might consider purchasing a plasma television instead.

Here's a quick differentiation between LCD and LED televisions …

Picture Quality:

LED (generally) has better black levels and contrasts than their LCD counterparts.

Energy Efficiency:

LED uses less light to display the picture and is slightly more energy efficient than LCD televisions.

Price:

At the moment, LCD televisions are the best choice if price is your primary concern.

Size:

LED televisions are slimmer than LCD televisions – but not by much.

- Thin, wide and (reasonably) lightweight.

- Available in all sizes (from 5" models all the way up to 100" plus). If you're looking for a television smaller than **42"**, the only choices you have available are LCD or LED televisions.

Remember: The <u>smallest</u> plasma television size is 42".

- Life span for LCD-LED televisions is typically 60,000 hours or about 20 years if used 8 hours per day. (This is the same as for plasma televisions).

- Superior **motion resolution**.

> **Negligible motion blur** caused by fast-action on the screen. This is advantageous if you (or someone in your family) plays video games.

The Cons

- Larger LCD televisions (50" plus) are generally more expensive than similar-sized Plasma televisions.

- Narrow viewing area. Some viewing angles – especially from the sides and above – produce a (slightly) less-than-clear picture.

The Hidden Costs

- As with the plasma televisions, once you purchase your flat-screen television, you may find yourself purchasing ancillary devices – such as a **high-definition recorder or DVD player** – to enhance your viewing experience.

> See our upcoming chapters on these devices.

- Television viewing is **addictive**, taking you away from hobbies, time outdoors, intimate conversations and so forth.

> Worth repeating, since we can't stress this enough!

Before we leave our discussion of flat-screen televisions, we'd like to say a word about three-dimension (3D) television:

A word about 3D television

You're probably well aware of **3D** (**three-dimensional**) movies, whether from the old 1950s titles such as "House of Wax" and "Creature from the Black Lagoon" to the current slate of modern 3D movies.

Well, after the 3D box office bonanza for the movie "Avatar" (with box office receipts of over $2.7 <u>billion</u> dollars worldwide), it certainly didn't take long for television to jump on the 3D bandwagon.

Since costs to produce 3D programs are very expensive, the vote isn't in yet on whether 3D will be around for a while or will simply be considered a fad. (ESPN, for example, took a stab at launching a 3D sports channel, but has recently opted out, shutting down the channel and citing high production costs and low viewership.)

3D television sets, however, remain on the market. At the moment, many flat-screen models – both plasma and LCD – are available as 3D sets.

The cost for a 3D television set is only marginally higher than other comparable high-definition televisions, so if you're willing to gamble that 3D is here-to-stay, this might be a worthwhile purchase.

Remember: you'll need to purchase 3D glasses for every person who will be watching. Also, you'll have to pay an extra premium to your cable or satellite provider for the "pleasure" of watching any 3D channel or event.

Rear-Projection televisions

Much like tubed televisions, rear-projection televisions, which have been around for a number of years, are being phased out by the cheaper, thinner and more durable flat-screen televisions.

In case you're not familiar, rear-projection television uses lamps inside the set to project images onto the screen (again, all inside the set). Since describing rear-projection in more detail would probably take longer than these televisions will remain on the market, let's just cut to the pros and cons.

Rear-Projection televisions: At a glance

The Pros

- Reasonably inexpensive – although as the prices of flat-screen televisions continue to decline – this might not remain a "pro" comment for long.

  (As with our comments for tubed televisions, you can see we don't have much to commend these types of television sets.)

The Cons

- Bulky and heavy.

- Only available in larger sizes.

- You generally need a large stand to lift these televisions to eye level.

- Lamps inside these sets cost $200 or more and must be replaced every 3,000 to 6,000 hours, depending on your use.

- Lamps take up to 20-60 seconds to warm up and cool down. During the warm-up phase, the image is either dim or completely dark.

- Chances are this type of television will all-but-vanish over the next number of years.

The Hidden Costs

- Part are often expensive and aren't always easy to find.

Home Theater Projector

Technically, there is fourth type of television available on the market: the Home Theater Projector.

As the name implies, however, this is a front screen projector, not actually a television set. These front-projection televisions work pretty much the same way as rear-projection televisions, only the system is not contained in a television case.

Like any projector system, you need to center the television image on a separate fabric screen (although a white wall would also work).

While the main advantage to the Home Theater Projector is screen size, you're none-the-less limited to the size of the room. As a result, this project isn't for everyone – you need a **light-controlled environment** and a very large room with plenty of space.

> In other words, a very, very dark room.

While the technology is still evolving for the Home Theater Project, if you're looking for one with high-definition and a built-in television tuner, know that the price tag can be rather hefty.

Apps in televisions:

Okay, what's an "**app**" and what's it doing in my television?!

We actually cover variations of this same question throughout the book, but since "apps" are such a key component to this new "digital" conversation, we feel repetition is worthwhile.

So let's start off with: "what is an app?"

An "**app**" is slang: a shortened term for "**application**".

An "**application**" is a piece of computer software that has been designed to provide some unique service or services. These services can take the form of hobbies; special or personal interests; games; general information; and are even designed to enhance productivity at work or at home.

Some "apps" are available free of charge. Others, however, cost a nominal sum (usually between $0.99 - $9.99 each).

"Apps" are usually available via **computers; smartphones; iPads and tablets**; and, for the purpose of our current discussion: televisions.

> We discuss "**apps**" for these devices in various chapters throughout the book. Just check the table of content.

Here are a sampling of "apps" that come available on many new television models.

- Netflix. A monthly subscription that is available as an "app" and allows you to view thousands of movies and television shows anytime you want on your television screen.

- YouTube. A free "app" that allows you to view thousands of free videos – everything from old television clips to "how to" step-by-step videos on all manner of subjects.

- Pandora. A free "app" that allows you to listen to music from your favorite artists.

- Facebook. A free "app" that allows you to connect to your friends and family.

- Flickr. A free photo "app" that allows you to download and view your personal photos, as well as photo from friends and family.

- Fandango. A free "app" that gives you movie times, previews, reviews, and the ability to purchase movie tickets directly from home.

- Weather. Again, a free "app" giving you extended weather forecasts.

The list of "apps" just goes on and on. Some new television models have over 1,000 "apps" available for use.

"Apps": Good news / bad news

As we just mentioned, the good news is that "apps" (many for free) are available on your television set – and television manufacturers make the process of accessing these "apps" via your remote, very simple.

The bad news is that you need to hook up your television to the Internet. Some cable and satellite companies and Best Buy's "Geek Squad" will handle the set-up for you (obviously, for a fee). We suggest you check out our chapter on the Internet to get an overview on what's needed and wanted.

If you're planning to purchase a new television set, we recommend finding a model that allows you to access "apps" and go through the slight aggravation of hooking up the television to the Internet. In the end, you'll be pleased with the endless variety of services these "apps" will offer you.

Smart TV: Combining "apps" and the Internet

As we've just noted with new television sets, there is currently a trend towards integrating "apps" and the Internet, called "**Smart TV**".

> "**Smart TV**" is the phrase used to describe the integration of television and the Internet.

Several stand-along devices also serve this same purpose. The technology is still evolving, so we're only offering a qualified nod towards these products. Still, you'll probably hear about one or two of them by name, so we thought we'd just mention them here:

Apple TV

This small receiver – just under four inches square – is designed to play digital content notably from the iTunes Store, Netflix, Hulu Plus and others. The receiver has high resolution and contains a large hard drive (for storage of your favorite shows).

Apple TV is particularly handy if you have purchased or rented movies and television shows from iTunes and want to watch them on a big screen.

Google TV

The Google TV receiver integrates the Google Chrome web browser to create an interactive overlay on top of any television set with Internet capability. In addition to Google's YouTube and Google Play, the receiver allows you to connect directly with the Internet for searches and access to sites such as Netflix, Hulu Plus, Pandora and much more.

Roku, Boxee and NetGear's NeoTV

While they might not have the brand recognition of Apple and Google, Roku, Boxee and NetGear's NeoTV offer – to one degree or another – many of the same features, including wireless capability and services such as Netflix, Amazon Video-on-Demand, Pandora, YouTube and more. Interestingly, in several consumer analyses, Roku and NetGear's NeoTv edged to the front (with even higher ratings than Apple TV or Google TV).

Still, despite some appeal, **Smart TV** is an evolving concept. We're certain that television manufacturers are not about to step aside and let these receivers supplant their products. As a result, we'll wait and see what surfaces in the near future.

For now, you might consider these receivers a luxury rather than a necessity.

Your television remote

One of the most confusing elements about watching television isn't the television itself, but rather the remote.

Confusing with reason – every remote seems to have tons of features and buttons.

We won't begin to list all models of the remotes – instead, we suggest you take a look at the section which immediately follows on "The Universal Remote". We will, however, suggest the buttons you should look for and identify on any remote:

Power
This button turns the television on and off. Usually located at the very top or top-right portion of any remote.

Channels
Two options. You can simply input the channel number using the keypad. Another choice, most remotes have a channel up / channel down button (usually in the middle, often on the right).

Volume
There is always a volume up / volume down button. Same as the channel buttons, but on the opposite side (again, the middle, often on the left).

Mute
The mute button turns off the volume. You click it a second time to restore the volume. Very handy when you've had enough with those annoying commercials.

After these basic necessities, most manufacturers cram every option into the remote – with no logical or consumer consideration. Satellite and cable company remotes are often the biggest culprits with buttons marked "guide" or "lists" and so on.

The Universal Remote

We have one related topic that is worth discussing: the universal remote.

Since over 99% of homes in America have one or more television sets, we're going to assume you know what a remote is and how it functions.

However, like many households, you may have more than one remote lying around. One for each television; one for the cable or satellite box; one for a DVD player, one for a sound system. The number of remotes just grows and grows.

We just want you to be aware that there are universal remotes on the marketplace.

What a universal remote does is allow you to program all of your devices into one single remote.

- Television?   Check.

- Cable box?   Check.

- DVD Player   Check.

You get the idea. Very worthwhile, since you can tuck all those other remotes in a drawer and just access every one of your devices with a single click.

Several companies produce excellent universal remotes (the most well-reviewed is the company, Logitech, and their Harmony remotes). Their customer service personnel are very competent and they will take as much time as you need in order to guide you through the set-up.

Obviously, universal remotes are a luxury device and not for everyone. But if you're up-to-your-eyeballs in remotes, you might want to check this out.

Television: A glimpse into the future

We thought we'd offer you a quick glimpse into the near future.

A good deal of current research is being focused on voice-and-motion activation. In layman terms, this offers two potentially **important innovations**:

> Okay, perhaps "**important**" is too strong a word. Certainly, this current research will offer two potentially "interesting" innovations.

1. First, televisions which respond to voice commands.

    In this manner, anyone could walk into a room and simply address the television with any number of commands. "Turn on" and "Turn off" are the most obvious examples.

    In theory, you could also just ask your television to record your favorite show or, if your television is attached to the Internet, just ask what tomorrow's weather forecast might be. We trust you get the general idea.

2. Secondly, these new television innovations are being designed to recognize <u>who</u> is entering the room.

    Let's say you're a family of four. When you enter the room, motion sensors on the television will be able to recognize which family member is planning to access the television.

    In so doing, the television would automatically sort its menu to correspond to just the right television shows or recordings to match that family member's taste or pre-programmed choices.

3. Another new television innovation is the "**wire-free**" television. These have already hit the marketplace and you've probably seen the commercials. These "wire-free"

televisions have no cable cords; and allow you to actually take your television set from your living room and just bring it into your backyard or into any room of your choice.

Is this practical? Not really. Aside from the lack of clutter from cords, we don't care how lightweight your flat-screen television might be, the novelty of lugging your television set from room to room will undoubtedly grow old, fast.

4. Another important area that will influence our viewing habits in the years to come is what's called "**T-Commerce**", which is simply short for **Television Commerce**.

    What T-Commerce allows you do is interact with your favorite television shows (naturally with "commerce" as the prime directive).

    In short, if you're watching your favorite sports team, you'll be able to purchase a team hat or sweatshirt with just a click of a button on your remote. If you like what a character is wearing on your favorite television show? Again, just hit the remote and the product can be purchased and sent to you, literally overnight.

5. The very nature of your remote will undergo an enormous transformation. Devices such as your **iPad or Tablet** will serve as your television remote – this is being labeled as "**Second Screen**".

    In addition to being able to interface with your television to enhance T-Commerce, your iPad or Tablet will allow you to quick access your favorite actor's credits; your favorite team's sports statistics; latest news updates; and much more.

> See our chapter on **iPads and Tablets** (Chapter 14) for more details.

6. Finally, even the nature of high-definition is going through a complete overall.

4K television sets – also known as **Ultra High-Definition** or **Ultra HD** – have just been introduced onto the marketplace. As the name implies, the picture quality is four times as clear as the best high-definition television sets currently on the market.

At the moment, the prices of these 4K televisions are quite exorbitant. Still, prices are bound to drop to a more-affordable level in the near future.

Spark your fancy? Thinking of buying one?

Remember, there is currently little-to-no programming to support 4K televisions. Also, think about the cost to replace your movies or television shows into 4k quality discs.

(You should note that 8K televisions are currently in development and should reach the horizon of the consumer public within a few years.)

How well these new innovations will be **received in the marketplace** is a matter of much speculation. Also, whether these innovations will enhance our lives or simply be just "one more gadget" is also up-in-the-air.

> Or whether they'll even reach the marketplace at all.

At the very least, we thought you might want to get a glimpse at what innovators and manufacturers think you <u>might</u> need.

Chapter 8

Digital Recorders
(or you'll never watch live television again)

Who should read this section

If you watch a number of television shows during the week – many of which come on at odd days and times – digital recorders will keep track of them all and will record them every time they broadcast.

(What's even better: you no longer need those cumbersome video tapes, as these new digital recorders simply store all your programs inside one single device.)

If you want to record a television series (even for the entire year) with just one single entry, you'll love what digital recorders can do for you.

If your phone rings, you need to finish cooking or want a quick bathroom break, you can "pause" live television, and then resume watching when you're ready – all without missing a beat.

If you're annoyed by commercials and would love to fast-forward through them any time they appear, the digital recorder is the perfect device.

Who should skip this section

If you're generally a stay-at-home person; watch only a handful of shows during the week; and have no problem with commercials, well, maybe the digital recorder isn't your cup of tea.

Digital Video Recorders – or "**DVRs**" as they're often referred to – have replaced the old video cassette recorders ("**VCRs**").

Sometimes (but rarely) referred to as **Personal Video Recorder** or "**PVR**".

On occasion, you'll also hear people refer to their "**Tivo**". Tivo, however, is a brand name and, as one of the first, became quite popular on the marketplace.

Much like people use the word "Xerox" as synonymous with copier, people sometimes use "Tivo" as synonymous with DVR.

By in large, all digital video recorders operate the same way, so here are some of the basics along with key features:

- The **Digital Video Recorder** (DVR) is an interactive home-entertainment device that digitally records television content onto an internal **hard drive.**

The **hard drive** on a DVR is a way of storing digital information – in this case, television programming – and functions in much the same way as the hard drive on a computer. (See Chapter 1 as a refresher.)

Television programs are recorded onto the DVR hard drive. No tapes or any other media are needed. In short, a DVR programs, records and plays back, all from inside the device itself.

- The DVR hard drive comes in various sizes from **40 GB to 120 GB (or higher**).

> DVRs can hold 40 - 100 hours of recorded programs
> which, no matter how you slice it, is a lot of television.

- Since upgrading a DVR's hard drive storage capacity is hard-to-impossible, we suggestion you purchase the hard drive size that best meets your **potential viewing/recording habits**.

> Most DVRs will allow you to record your shows in high-definition – which, while offering crystal-clear pictures, regrettably takes up a lot more storage space.
>
> If you're planning to record shows in high-definition, we suggest purchasing a DVR with one of the larger storage capacities.

- While DVRs are generally inexpensive, there is usually some type of fee associated with the purchase of a DVR.

  Some DVRs offer electronic program guides for free, but to add certain features – which you'll generally need or might find worthwhile – you'll either need to pay a monthly subscription charge or an up-front cost for a lifetime subscription.

  Cable and satellite providers offer their own generic digital video recorders, albeit for a monthly rental fee. They also charge an extra fee to access high-definition (HDTV) content (which tends to mount up).

- Recording your favorite shows is quite simple and is all handled through the DVR remote:

To record a single show: You just navigate your way through the electronic program guide – which is displayed on your television screen. The guide is "populated" 2-4 weeks in advance. Just find the show you want and hit the "record" button on the remote. Simple!

To record a full-season of your favorite shows: Again, navigate through the electronic program guide until you find your show. Depending on the make and model of the DVR, you just select "Season Pass" or double click the "record" button to access the full season.

Nothing more needs to be done – the DVR will automatically record every single episode for an **entire season**.

> You also can "**instruct**" the DVR to either program only new episodes or, if you don't mind watching reruns, you can program for both first-runs and repeats.

When recording sports events, most DVRs automatically give you an option to add an additional 30 minutes (or more) in case the event goes into overtime. Very handy if you're fanatic about watching your favorite sports team; or if the start time to your favorite program runs late.

The electronic program guide usually allows you to narrow your search by categories. For example, you can narrow your search by movies, sports, news, family and kids, and more.

DVRs also provide a search feature which allows you to type in the name of your favorite show (or actor) and the search will bring up all future episodes involving that show (or actor). The search is done via an electronic "alphabet" viewed on the television screen and the remote allows you to input the name (letter by letter).

Since most DVRs work best in conjunction with cable and satellite providers, your guide is also populated with the ability to find and **view new movies** (often within 3-6 months from their original theatrical release). Naturally, there is a fee for the privilege (most ranging from $3.99 - $5.99).

> This feature is usually referred to as **"On Demand"** or **"Pay Per View"**.

Obvious (but maybe not)...

While you can record shows onto your DVR, don't forget that you can also "delete" shows from the DVR.

Once you're done watching something you've recorded, you can easily delete it from your "list" of recorded shows. Just use the remote and the DVR guide.

By deleting shows, the space is "restored" back onto your DVR so you never have to worry about running out of storage room.

- One of the key features on all DVRs is the ability to "pause" live television. The hard-drive provides an internal memory buffer that allows you to pause and fast forward any time you want.

- The ability to "fast-forward" on a DVR allows you to skip through commercials. Unfortunately, skipping through commercials only works on programs you've re-corded or paused. You can't skip through commercials while watching live television – at least, not yet.

Purchasing a DVR by brand name isn't important since most features are the same from one DVR to another. (Tivo is perhaps one of the most famous brand names by virtue of the fact that it was among the first of the DVRs to be released and just happened to catch the public's attention).

Since, as mentioned, the features of a DVR are consistent with any other, we recommend you shop around for the best deals.

Remember: if you're planning to connect your television and DVR via cable or satellite, make sure to contact your local provider before you make your purchase; and see whether they have DVRs available and whether they offer any special savings.

Finally, make sure you assess the right amount of hard drive storage space for your viewing / recording needs. And again, if you're planning to record your shows in high-definition, this will take up even more space, so plan accordingly.

Remember: televisions now broadcast (and record) in high-definition (HDTV). Make sure the DVR you purchase gives you the storage space needed for these high-definition standards.

Digital Video Recorder (DVR): At a glance

The Pros

- Inexpensive.

- Self-contained (no videos or other media needed to record).

- Even the most basic DVR can record 40+ hours of television viewing. If you watch 3 hours of television a night, that's over 13 days of programs you can record.

- All recordings are handled through the remote – usually with a single push of a button – making this a very simple process.

- Pause live television.

- Pause and fast forward through recorded shows – skipping over commercials.

The Cons

- Most DVRs – certainly all DVRs accessed through cable or satellite providers – are charged a **monthly fee**.

> This **monthly fee** is often in addition to the cost of purchasing the DVR itself.

- If you have purchased a DVR with the minimum amount of storage space, you might have to make choices on what to "save" and what to "delete" in order not to run out of space.

- Generally, most DVRs limit you to two recording choices at any one time. You can either record two shows at the same time; or watch live television while you're recording another show.

  (The good news is that you can record two shows and watch one of the shows you've already recorded; or you can purchase one of the new model DVRs which allows for more recording options.)

The Hidden Costs

- In addition to the monthly DVR fee, most cable and satellite providers will charge an extra monthly fee to view (and record) high-definition (HDTV) programs.

- Further costs can be incurred when watching first-run On Demand or Pay Per View movies, which are very easy to find and record onto your DVR -- expensive temptations if you're not careful.

Chapter 9

DVD Players

Who should read this section

If you'd like to watch your favorite movies and television shows in the highest clarity and resolution available.

If you enjoy watching (and collecting) your favorite movies and television series (in easy-to-use DVD disc formats).

If you are a movie or television buff and enjoy watching special features, behind-the-scenes, deleted scenes and more (which come readily available on most DVD discs).

Who should skip this section

If you're comfortable enough watching movies and television shows on your television set and don't need the extra expense of one more digital device (or the added costs of purchasing DVDs).

DVDs: An overview

Let's start with the term: DVD.

DVD stands for **Digital Video Disc**.

> Also: **Digital Versatile Disc** – although we've rarely met anyone who knows this.

As the name implies, Digital Video Discs hold digital video content. In English: these are lightweight **discs** that can store and play movies or television shows (along with a myriad of bonus features).

> Note that **Compact Discs** (or "CDs") are the audio equivalent of **DVDs**.
>
> **DVDs** are comparable to video cassette tapes that were used on the old Video Cassette Recorders (VCRs). Same principle, in that they show movies.
>
> The main difference: DVD discs are smaller, much more compact and far more durable than VCR tapes.
>
> The old VCR tapes also allowed you to record shows, although if you've ever had a VCR tape unwind inside your VCR machine, you might recall the enormous frustration to untangle the tape.
>
> If recording is your ultimate aim, you might want to look back at our chapter on Digital Video Recorders (Chapter 8).

Putting the pieces together:

A DVD Player is a device that plays movies and television shows.

You **connect** the DVD Player to your television set.

Here's how

Most new television sets have something called an **HDMI** (*High-Definition Multimedia Interface*) input. (See the section on "ports and plugs" in Chapter 1 for more details).

You simply purchase an HDMI cable, then insert one end into the television and the other end into the DVD player.

Honest, it's as simple as that!

Voila, you're done!

Here's how all DVD players work

1. Every DVD player has a tray into which the DVD is inserted.

2. You open the tray by using your remote or by pushing the button marked "Open" on the front panel of the DVD player (usually located on the far right).

3. Once you've opened the tray, you insert the DVD.

Obvious (but maybe not)

- DVDs need to be purchased or – through companies and kiosks like Netflix or Redbox – they can be rented.

  DVDs are readily available – you can even find them in grocery stores.

- Most-to-all DVD manufacturers affix a graphic image or title of the movie or show on the top surface of the DVD disc.

  When you insert the DVD into the tray on your DVD player, keep the graphic image or title on top.

- Try to avoid putting your fingerprints on the DVD (especially the bottom side, which is the side which contains the data). Fingerprints and smudges tend to distort the picture and need to be cleaned off.

  To avoid fingerprints or smudges, try holding (and loading) the DVD by grasping the disc by the edges.

- Keep DVDs away from extreme heat and direct sunlight.

---

4. After inserting the DVD disc – see above for some useful tips – make sure to **close the DVD tray**.

> In order to close the DVD tray, you press the "**Open**" button one more time.
>
> Yes: "**Open**" on a DVD player functions to both "open" and "shut" the DVD tray. (Hey, no one said technical inventors were particularly bright.)

5. Once the DVD is inserted and the tray closes, the movie or television show on the disc will automatically load and the display will appear on your television screen.

6. Most DVDs can be viewed with subtitles (including **English for the Hearing Impaired**); come with a variety of spoken languages to choose from (Spanish, French and so forth); and are usually filled to the brim with special features.

> Given the way contemporary actors "mumble", subtitles are a great boon for the majority of the adult population.

Options for these features are found on the DVD's Opening Menu (which appears when the DVD is first displayed). Your remote will allow you to navigate through the options and make the selections that are just right for you.

7. At this point, just select "**play**" or "**play movie**" and the movie or television show on the disc will automatically appear on your television screen.

8. Remote control buttons:

Since you'll be using the buttons on your remove quite a bit, we thought we'd provide a quick overview of what they look like and how they function:

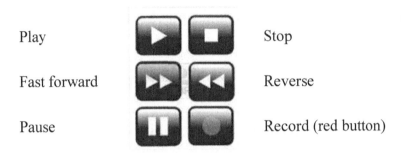

Play			Stop
Fast forward			Reverse
Pause			Record (red button)

Here's the great news: These buttons (and their functionality) are universal.

The button / image for "play" looks (and works) the same on <u>all</u> digital devices. In fact, we're willing to bet you'll find these exact same buttons / images on every one of your remotes.

Because DVDs are compact, they can store high-resolution digital content. Consequently, the image (movie / television show) that you see is crystal clear.

Even the sound from the DVD, because of its digital encoding, is ideal, especially when used with a home entertainment sound system.

Is there a catch?

Of course. If you've been reading along, you know that most of these digital devices come with some caveat or catch.

In the case of DVD players: the clarity displayed is only as good as your television set.

That's good news: if you have a brand-spanking-new television, the DVD movie or television show will play with optimum clarity.

If your television is a little antiquated, the results you'll see – while nonetheless impressive – aren't quite as sharp as they might be.

DVDs: Special features

Since digital DVDs can store a great deal of information, in addition to the main movie (or television show / series) you'll find a number of special features added to the discs themselves.

While each disc is unique in what it chooses to offer, here's a sampling of the kind of features you might find:

- **"Making of…"** or **"Behind the Scenes"**. This is the most common of the special features. They're short-length "documentaries" about the making of the movie or what transpired behind the scenes in the filming of the movie or television show.

- **Deleted scenes**. Often, especially with comedies, the studio might include **scenes that were deleted from the original production**.

> Although deleted, the scenes are generally interesting, occasionally even funny or poignant.
>
> In the end, however, you come to understand why they were deleted in the first place.

- **Running commentary**. Sometimes a DVD will also include a running commentary about the film or television show.

In these instances, usually the star and/or director engage in a **running commentary** about how the film was made; interesting anecdotes; or personal thoughts or observations.

> The **running commentary** overlaps the normal dialogue of the film, so you might not want to program the DVD to play this running commentary the first time you're watching a film (otherwise you'll miss most of the dialogue).

- **Preview**s. Since you're a captive audience planning to watch a movie or television show, most studios take the liberty of adding previews. Lots of previews.

These are some of the most common special features. Often, studios will try to "**recycle**" movies by adding more-and-more behind the scenes documentaries.

> This is why (say) the "Lord of the Rings" movies can be purchased as three individual movies; a 2-DVD set with the extra disc containing special features; all the way up to the "Extended Deluxe Edition" which includes 15 discs.
>
> Yes, you read that right – 15 discs!
>
> (That's the original 3 discs for the movies with an additional 12 discs reserved for Special Features).

DVD Players: At a glance

The Pros

- DVD players are inexpensive. Many models can be found for well-under $50.

- The DVDs themselves are also generally inexpensive, especially older titles than have been on the shelves for months (or even years)…so look for sales.

- Players are easy to operate and easy to hook-up to your television.

The Cons

- As digital technology advances in this area, the DVD and DVD player may soon find themselves obsolete.

- **Newer discs** have more clarity, higher resolution and are loaded with more bells-and-whistles.

> For these **newer discs**, continue to read about Blu-ray and 3D contained in this chapter (below).

The Hidden Costs

- If, as speculated, the original DVD technology becomes obsolete, you may find yourself having to replace many of your favorite movie or television titles – to say nothing of having to purchase the newest device capable of playing them.

Blu-ray DVDs: An overview

Pop quiz #1:

If you give a digital innovator a compact DVD with high storage, chances are he or she will:

- Squeeze more content onto the disc.

- Squeeze even higher resolution onto the disc.

- Call this new higher resolution DVD something else to confuse you…say, Blu-ray.

- All of the above.

We don't give hard quizzes – naturally, the answer is "all of the above".

So we reach the next incarnation: The Blu-ray disc and Blu-ray Player.

The name **Blu-ray** derives from blue-violet laser (Blue) and optical ray (ray). According to the Blu-ray Disc Association, the character "e" was intentionally left off so the term could be registered as a **trademark**.

Just wondering…

Was the term Blue-ray disc already taken? Is that why they had to drop the "e"?

No explanation on why the "r" in Blu-ray isn't capitalized.

Also, since DVDs use red or near-infrared lasers…why weren't they called Red-ray discs?

Blu-ray: What's the catch?

Although Blu-ray is (essentially) a bigger, better, faster version of the DVD, these discs (unfortunately) can't be played on the same player. Hence: you need a DVD player to play DVD discs; **but** you need a Blu-ray player to play Blu-ray discs.

> Digital commerce at its finest!

In comparing the Blu-ray with the DVD, experts will point to the even-higher resolution and the even-clearer images that are produced.

And, we must agree, all the claims of higher resolution and clarity are quite true.

Nevertheless…

- Blu-ray players operate much like a hard-drive. As such, they take an inordinate amount of time to load the movie or television shows onto the screen.

- Because of the sophistication of the Blu-ray player, you can connect them to the Internet (where they sometimes offer a feature called "**BD-Live**").

  BD-Live provides even more special features such as online games; downloadable featurettes and previews; even scheduled "chats" with the director – all accessed through **one disc**.

> We suppose this is more economical than the 15 set edition of "Lord of the Rings", but we wonder if this bell-and-whistle is worth the added cost of the Blu-ray disc itself.

Blu-ray Players: At a glance

The Pros

- Blu-ray players are **generally** inexpensive.

> While not as inexpensive as DVD players, you can find many Blu-ray players for under $100.

- The clarity and resolution of movies and television shows on Blu-ray is far superior to DVD.

- You can watch regular DVD discs on Blu-ray players

- While Blu-ray discs are more expensive than DVD discs, if you shop carefully, you can often find sales on older Blu-ray titles.

- Blu-ray players are easy to operate and easy to hook-up to your television.

The Cons

- Blu-ray discs are more expensive than DVD discs.

- Because of its hard drive technology, loading movies or television shows on Blu-ray discs can take several minutes (and is often frustrating while you sit and wait for something to happen).

The Hidden Costs

- While this technology will probably be around for a number of years, we recommend that you look at our section entitled "A Cloud on the Horizon" at the end of this chapter.

3D DVDs: An overview

Pop quiz #2:

Actually, we'll let you design this quiz yourself given the following:

- We started with the compact DVD with high storage.

- Digital innovators opted to squeeze even more content and resolution onto the disc.

- The new-and-improved discs were called Blu-ray discs.

- 3D movies became popular in the theaters.

- Ergo: digital innovators now plan to squeeze even more content and resolution to store the 3D image onto the disc.

- These even-newer-and-more-improved discs should be called **3D** (or 3D discs).

> Do we really need to mention that **3D** stands for **3-Dimension**, to connote the enhanced illusion of depth perception?

And yes, you guessed right – 3D discs cannot play on either a DVD player or Blu-ray player. You need a 3D Player in order to view 3D discs.

To make matters worse…

At least with a DVD player or Blu-ray player, you only needed a standard television set. (Of course, the newer the television set, the more clarity you're able to achieve.)

Unfortunately, with the 3D player, you need to purchase a 3D television set as well. 3D television needs to sync with the 3D player in order for the 3D discs to work.

And don't forget, when purchasing a player, you'll need to buy extra 3D glasses for each and every viewer…

You've probably already surmised the brand name of the player's manufacturer isn't important.

Here's our recommendation on how to purchase…

Simply determine which format you want to watch:

- **DVD**   Slowly become obsolete

- **Blu-ray**   High clarity and resolution but more expensive then DVDs

- **3D**   More expensive than Blu-ray and the vote isn't in on whether 3D is just a novelty or will be around for a while.

Once you've determined the format, just shop around for the best deal on the player.

3D Players: At a glance

The Pros

- The clarity of 3D movies continues to improve, making the viewing experience unique.

- You can watch Blu-ray and DVD discs on 3D players

- Players are easy to operate and easy to hook-up to your television.

The Cons

- You need to own a 3D television in order to watch 3D discs.

- You need to purchase a **set of 3D glasses** for every person watching.

- 3D discs are more expensive than DVD or Blu-ray discs.

Manufacturers differ. Many include one free pair of glasses with a 3D player; some include two.

3D glasses are expensive and if you have a large household or gathering, the cost for glasses can add up.

On the bright side, manufacturers are hard at work on new television models that will project the 3D image without the need for glasses.

The Hidden Costs

- Is 3D a new (lasting) trend or simply a fad?

  If 3D is a fad, the investment costs for the 3D player (plus the 3D television, plus 3D glasses, plus 3D discs) can be quite expensive. Again, we recommend that you look at the section entitled "A Cloud on the Horizon" at the end of this chapter.

Apps in DVD / Blu-ray and 3D players

First, we refer you to our section on "**Apps** in Television" (see Chapter 7) for a lengthier discussion of what is an "app" and what value it might have.

A quick refresher in case you don't want to jump around:

"**Apps**" is short for "**application**".

These "**application**s" are pieces of computer software that have been designed to provide some unique service.

These services may take the form of hobbies; special or personal interests; games; general information and so forth.

Among the most common and popular "apps" are Netflix, YouTube, Pandora and much more.

"Apps" have become a common feature on most new televisions.

But what if you have an older television; have no plans to upgrade; yet like what "apps" have to offer? In that case, you're in luck.

Most of the newer model players – whether for DVD, Blu-ray or 3D – now come with Internet access, as well as access to "apps".

Since the price for most of these players is far less expensive than purchasing a new television set, this might be the way to go if you want to keep up with the (technical) Joneses.

A "Cloud" on the Horizon

Have any of you spotted the "Emperor's New Clothes" issue?

That's where some bright person – like yourself – points out the obvious conundrum: if music CDs have all-but-vanished because of devices like the iPod, what's the life expectancy of the DVD – Blu-ray – 3D?

Welcome to **Cloud Computing** (or "**The Cloud**" as it's come to be known).

> We also cover "**The Cloud**" in our final chapter ("Beyond the Basics") in case you're interested in more.

The Cloud is one of the latest pieces of technological innovation. Essentially, your purchase is delivered as a "service" not as a "product".

Here's the way it's designed to work.

Let's say you purchase a movie. In the 'good-old-days', you would receive a disc – whether DVD, Blu-ray or 3D – which would be yours to keep.

Under the Cloud, the seller would simply provide you with "access" to your movie (no tangible product would ever be received).

Proponents of the Cloud gush how you can access your movie from any digital device: On your television; your iPad or Tablet; or your smartphone. You never have to worry about storage space – the seller will "store" it for you – nor would you ever have to be worried or concerned about **damaging or losing** the movie.

> Since the seller retains the original pristine copy, no damage or loss can occur.

We generally don't like to call ourselves naïve consumers, but here's what we're concerned about:

- We suspect that accessing our "Cloud purchases" might require the additional expense of a Cloud-compatible television or, at the very least, a Cloud-compatible device or player.

- As technology advances, the high-definition (HD) purchase of today will undoubtedly give way to new innovations in the **near-future**. Again, would this mean we'd have to purchase (newer) Cloud-compatible televisions or players?

- While the Cloud protects the copyright of movie and television producers, some of us enjoying **seeing and touching** what we've purchased.

> We're fans of much of the new technology in our lives, but we certainly would not enjoy a world without tangible books, movies, etc.

We're certainly not suggesting any "doom-and-gloom" prophecy. Quite the opposite.

If technology has taught us anything it's how resourceful manufacturers can be to protect their products and yet entice us with new ones.

Still, we wanted you to be aware of the implications: a world in which "digital products" might become obsolete and, rather, would be replaced by a single hub which distributes this content to all your digital devices.

To give you a preview of what will bridge this new "Cloud-based" technology into our lives, we suggest you continue on to our next chapter: Chapter 10: "Streaming" music and video.

Chapter 10

"Streaming" Music and Video

Who should read this section

If you're looking to understand (and access) music and video that can be "streamed" immediately onto your computer or television or any portable device, this section is worthwhile.

If you'd like a peek into the digital future, this section will show you how music and video will be viewed and delivered in the years to come.

Who should skip this section

If your music and video usage is limited, this section might not be right for you.

(Even so, we recommend checking out this section to gain a glimpse at the way most music and video will be accessed in the near-future.)

A brief look back (and forward)

In the early days of computers and digital technology, the only way you could access information from the Internet was to plug your telephone line into a **modem**, then dial up a connection. As anyone who went through this can attest, the process was lengthy and cumbersome.

> Simply, a "**modem**" is a device that modulates your telephone signal in order to transmit and receive encoded information from the Internet to your computer.

Back then, an Internet connection sometimes took hours to complete; and, quite frequently, the telephone would "drop" the call so that the process would have to be restarted from the very beginning.

Well you can only imagine how frustrated Internet users became. And, since many of the early digital technology innovators used the Internet to seek out and exchange ideas, fast and immediate access became a top priority for everyone involved.

Without a long lesson on those painstaking steps, let's just fast-forward to the present day.

Connecting onto the Internet now occurs via **high speeds**. Where an Internet exchange once took hours, now takes only seconds.

You may have heard telephone terms like **DSL** connections, **T1** lines or **cable** and **satellite** connections.

These terms are simply different designations for **high-speed Internet access**.

Whatever the high speed designation, know that some services are faster than others (and, naturally, you spend more money for the privilege of accessing those higher speeds).

What that high speed communication means is that chunks and chucks of digital data – like, for the purposes of our discussion, music and video – can be downloaded to your computer, television, cell phone or digital device at an astonishing rate of speed.

What is "streaming"?

Because of this ever-expanding high-speed connection, music and videos can now be delivered to you without any **lag or interruption**. This uninterrupted delivery is what is known as "**streaming**".

> Okay, all this is true in theory but not necessarily in practice.
>
> Whether or not you are delivered content without lags or interruptions often depends on the speed of your connection – the faster your connection, the less likely the interruption.
>
> That caveat aside, even the slowest of today's high-speed connections cause only a minimal amount of interruption.

As a result, new businesses sprang up – businesses which provided you with music and video content that you can listen to or watch the moment the urge overcomes you.

Before we continue, let's clear the air on an important distinction:

- Is "streaming music" the same as "radio"?

- Is "streaming video" the same as "television"?

The short answer is "yes".

But, since we're talking about new digital technology, nothing is quite so simple.

Yes, radio and television can be considered "streaming" since they come to you via the airwaves.

The new "streaming" music and video which we're talking about, takes that basic concept, but delivers them to you in unique ways.

Is there a cost?

Yes (and no).

Most of the "streaming" providers charge a monthly fee for their services. The fee is usually nominal, but it is a fee nonetheless.

Among these providers, some offer "free" access for scaled-down services. In exchange, however, you must put up with advertisements and you don't get many of the bells-and-whistles that are offered to monthly subscribers.

Still, the free service gives you the opportunity to test out the providers and see whether this type of "streaming" service appeals to you.

Let's take a look at some of the leading "streaming" providers, which should clarify matters.

Here are some of the more popular venues. We've broken them down by what they provide, rather than simply listing them by name:

Streaming music: Take your pick from a variety of formats

Sirius XM Satellite Radio

Sirius XM Radio bridges the old-fashioned radio notion with today's modern technology.

Their service provides over 140 unique stations (or "**channels**").

Sirius XM offers over 70 channels with commercial-free music. These include popular hits for every era from the 1940s to today. They also offer commercial-free music in most genres including rock-and-roll, Broadway, opera and country music. They even have designated channels that play songs of one particular artist or band (such as Elvis, Frank Sinatra, and much more).

In addition to music, Sirius XM offers 40 Sports channels featuring play-by-play broadcast of most professional sports as well as a variety of sports talk shows.

Sirius XM also features over 40 news, entertainment and talk shows (hosted by notable personalities such as Oprah Winfrey, Howard Stern, Martha Stewart and so forth). Even humor has its place as they provide 6 comedy channels to lighten up your day.

Good news / bad news...

Unfortunately, Sirius XM can't be picked up on your old radio. Instead, you need to purchase one of their special radios in order to listen to their music subscription.

On the plus side, many new cars manufacturers install Sirius XM radios and you can also listen to the music on your computer, smartphone and more.

Streaming music: Seek and ye shall find

Rhapsody

Rhapsody is one of a number of online music subscription services. You can search from over 14 million songs and can listen to the music on your computer or on a variety of **MP3 players and smartphones**.

> "**MP3 players**" are digital music players, such as the iPod.
>
> "**Smartphones**" are traditional cell phones with a myriad of features, including the ability to connect to the Internet.
>
> We cover both topics in more detail. Learn about MP3 players in Chapter 12 on Digital Music; and learn about smartphones in Chapter 15 on Cell Phones.

Online music subscription services charge a monthly fee and, unfortunately, you need a **computer** in order to access their service.

> By '**computer**' we also include digital devices such as cell phones, iPads and tablets and so forth. Anything, in fact, that is capable of connecting to the Internet.

That said, these types of services usually operate in a similar fashion:

1. First, you go **online** and sign up for their service.

> In this case, www.rhapsody.com.

2. As you sign-up, Rhapsody automatically downloads its site / service to your computer.

3. From within their site, you can search for the music you want from their music **catalog**. You can search by title, artist, genre, charts and much more.

> Again, over 14 million songs!

4. When you find what you're looking for, you can save the song or album to your Rhapsody library.

5. From there, you can play any song you want – there's no limit to the number of songs you can play (or, for that matter, the number of times you can play them).

One final note of interest: Rhapsody and others usually offer a 14-day free trial in order to try out their services. The free trial is certainly a good way to see whether this is something that appeals to your tastes (and needs).

Steaming music: Mix and match

Pandora, Spotify, iTunes Radio

Another type of online music service is represented by Pandora, Spotify and iTunes Radio.

These services offer music via the Internet. In part, they provide commercial-free music similar to the music steams offered by Sirius XM Satellite Radio.

Another more interesting distinction: these types of services allow you to select an artist, and then listen to additional music from that artist (as well as similar music from their contemporaries). In this way, you can create your own music "**channels**".

> Pandora, as an example, allows you to create up to 100 stations or channels of your own design.

As you listen to this Internet music, the service provides biographies about the artist, links to similar artists, lyrics to songs and more.

These types of music services have gone mainstream. Pandora, as an example, is now available via your television and, like Sirius XM, is offered by car manufacturers on many new model cars.

Streaming Music: At a glance

The Pros

- Access to millions of songs and a wide range of music

- "Streaming music" is available on a myriad of electronic devices.

- The ability to search and sort based on your music preferences

The Cons

- The monthly / yearly fees tend to add up.

- Generally, you need a computer to access and sign-up for these services.

- You need to be a music lover to full appreciate (and enjoy) "streaming music". For the casual music listener, the novelty can wear off rather quickly.

The Hidden Costs

- In the case of "streaming" music, it's the peripherals that add up. To access and listen, you definitely need to own a computer or some digital device that connects to the Internet; in the case of Sirius XM you need one of their designated radios; and, if you're planning to listen on your iPod or MP3 player, those costs must also be considered.

Taking a close look at "streaming" video

"Streaming" video operates in much the same manner as "streaming" music. The main distinction: the service streams video instead of music (obviously); and can be viewed on your computer, most digital devices, even your television.

Here are some of the more popular venues. Again, we've broken them down by <u>what</u> they provide, rather than simply list them by name:

Streaming Video: With a slant towards movies

Netflix

Initially, Netflix started out as a flat-rate DVD rental-by-mail service. The company was hugely successful, offering over 100,000 titles to a base of over 10 million subscribers.

In 2008, Netflix began to offer "streaming" video. Offering a wide assortment of titles, Netflix was able to "stream" these films directly to your computer (and, later, to your television).

Well, we don't have to tell you that "streaming" video took off. At the moment, Netflix has over 30 million subscribers and they are the biggest source of Internet traffic in North America.

The reason for the sizable jump in subscribers is that Netflix is no longer a computer-only platform to stream your videos. Television manufacturers have jumped on the Netflix bandwagon.

Most new television models offer **Internet access**, including the ability to sign up for "streaming" video services such as Netflix, Pandora (both discussed above in "streaming" music) and Hulu (which we'll discuss shortly).

Remember, **Internet access** on your television set means you have to "**hook up**" your television to the Internet – using an **Ethernet cord** or **wireless connection**.

We've covered this in Chapter 4 on the Internet.

The principles of connecting a computer or your television set are the same, so you might want to review that chapter.

Netflix offers a large number of movies and documentaries. Because of contract negotiations with the studios, many of the movies are classics and slightly-older titles. Still, the selections can suit most viewers' tastes and interests.

Netflix also provides a wide variety of television shows which you can stream on your television and other devices. Still, as you'll see from our discussion of Hulu (below), they have some catching up to do on more recent shows.

Finally, Netflix has also entered the original content arena by producing their own television series. Whether they're successful or not is still a work-in-progress, although recent Emmy Award nominations (and winners) point this trend in the right direction.

The way to sign into and access Netflix is the same as for most "streaming" sites:

1. First, you go **online** and sign up for their service.

> In this case, www.netflix.com.

2. As you sign-up, Netflix will offer you a variety of subscription **possibilities**. Once you make your decision, Netflix allows you full access to their site.

> "Streaming" video only. DVD rental only. A combination including "streaming" video and DVD rental. The choices go on and on.

> **Remember...**
>
> Netflix, like most of the "streaming" music and video services, charges a monthly fee.

3. Once you've signed up and accessed the site, the sky's the limit. You can link your Netflix account on your television; iPad or tablet; or smartphone. One fee for all devices!

4. Sign on; then search, using your mouse or remote to select the movie you want to watch. Use the video controls on your remote to maneuver through the movie.

   As a refresher, here are some of the basic controls:

Play	▶ ■	Stop
Fast forward	▶▶ ◀◀	Reverse
Pause	❚❚ ●	Record (red button)

Streaming Video: With a slant towards television

Hulu and Hulu Plus

If Netflix dominates the "streaming" movie arena, Hulu (and its sister company, Hulu Plus) dominate the "streaming" television marketplace.

Hulu began as a joint venture between NBC-Universal and Fox, with ABC-Disney soon coming into the fold. Needless to say, these powerhouses brought with them a ton of programming (new and old).

Hulu is a free "streaming" service; while Hulu Plus is a premium "streaming" service that charges a monthly fee. Here are some other distinctions that might clarify the difference:

Hulu	**Hulu Plus**
A free option but can only be watched on your computer.	Can be accessed on all digital devices, including your television.
Available as standard definition only.	Available in high definition (HD).
Offers only last 5 episodes that aired on TV.	All current-season episodes for many popular shows (and full seasons of many recent and old series).

Unfortunately, both services are scattered with ads...so there's no way around the dreaded commercial.

Streaming Video: With a slant towards the hodge-podge...

YouTube

And finally, but certainly not least, we have YouTube.

YouTube is a **video-sharing website**. What this means is that anyone with a video camera can record and post a video onto the YouTube website. (If you're interested in putting up your video on YouTube, see Chapter 23 for the step-by-steps.)

Your mind might boggle at that notion – as well it should. YouTube is available around the world, with, according to their statistics, several billion – yes, that's billions with a "B" – views seen every day (coupled with 60 hours of video content posted onto the site every minute).

At the moment, YouTube is free. Advertiser supported, naturally.

Back in 2006, the giant technology company, Google, acquired YouTube. Google is in the process of reshaping YouTube into a service much like Netflix, Hulu and Hulu Plus.

Already you can rent feature films on the site for a fee; and YouTube has begun to offer monthly subscriptions, although what will ultimately be offered is still in its evolutionary stage.

Why We Love YouTube…

YouTube seems to have video on almost every subject. When we went looking one day for information on Salvador Dali, we not only found documentary and interview footage on the painter / artist, but also a clip of his appearance on the old television show, "What's My Line".

YouTube also has a wide variety of "how to" instructional videos on a myriad of subjects.

Just two examples, but you should get the idea that the YouTube site is full of those nuggets.

Why We Hate YouTube…

Unfortunately, for every nugget you can find on YouTube, there are an endless number of nonsensical videos. We won't elaborate further, but if you get a chance to peruse YouTube, you'll quickly understand what we mean.

Streaming Video: At a glance

The Pros

- Access to a wide range of videos, movies and television shows.

- "Streaming" video is available on a myriad of electronic devices.

- Several "streaming" video sites are free.

The Cons

- While some sites are free, most are not. The monthly / yearly fees tend to add up.

- Generally, you need a computer to access and sign-up for these services.

The Hidden Costs

- As with "streaming" music, it's the peripherals that add up.

One more look at "The Cloud"

As mentioned in the last chapter, "**The Cloud**" is the latest piece of technological innovation. Both music and video stream from The Cloud. Essentially, you are delivered your purchase as a "service" not as a "product".

A quick review on the way it's designed to work:

Let's say you purchase a movie. In the 'good-old-days', you would be sent a disc – whether CD, DVD, Blu-ray or 3D – which would be yours to keep.

Under the Cloud, the seller would simply provide you with "access" to your movie (no tangible product would ever be received).

Proponents of the Cloud tout how you can access your movie from any device – on your television; your iPad or Tablet; your smartphone; and so forth. You never have to worry about storage space – the seller will "store" it for you – nor would you ever have to be worried or concerned about **damaging or losing** the movie.

> Since the seller retains the original pristine copy, **no damage or loss can occur.**

As you can see from our chapter on "streaming" music and video, the vehicle by which the Cloud can be set into place is already in motion.

Chapter 11

Digital Books / E-Readers

Who should read this section

If you enjoy reading, this piece of technology was invented just for you.

If you like to read and your eyesight isn't what it used to be, the expandable font sizes on these devices are just what the doctor (or optometrist) ordered.

If you tend to lug books around every time you travel, you'll love these light-weight, portable devices (which can hold and store hundreds-to-thousands of books).

Who should skip this section

If you only read a handful of books each year, this is 'just one more gadget' and might not be worth the cost.

If you savor the tactile experience of holding and reading a book.

If you read on occasion but equally enjoy watching movies or checking e-mail from your friends and family, you might want to check out the multi-purpose "tablets" that have hit the marketplace. (See Chapter 14 on "iPads and Tablets").

Digital Books / E-Readers: An overview

One of the most fiercely opinionated topics of conversation revolves around digital reading. Let's take a quick look at what's available (and how what's available might just get you to rethink the way you read).

You're already very familiar with the basic forms in which we read. Heading the list are hardcover and paperback books, newspapers and magazines.

As the computer developed, people found they were able to read documents directly upon their computer screen. This was particularly handy in the business community given the proliferation of e-mails; and it soon became commonplace to send memos, letters, documents back and forth.

Trying to read on the computer, however, was very cumbersome; and the flickering / headache-inspiring resolution of computer screens certainly wasn't conducive for the average reader.

So – in a recurring theme throughout this book – technology evolved to adapt to people's needs. In this case, they came up with the *mobile electronic device* – nicknamed "**E-Reader**" or "**E-Book**" for short.

Two elements were brought together to make the e-book practical for the average reader:

First and foremost, the device was mobile. You can take the device anywhere; much like you can carry a book, magazine or newspaper anywhere.

Secondly came the introduction of 'electronic paper' (also known as electronic ink or E-Ink). This revolutionary invention displayed reflected light onto a static page. More to the point, the result was an image of a page as bright and clear as any conventional book.

Typically, all e-reader have some form of Internet connection – either through a **wireless network** (also known as **Wi-Fi**) or through a wired connection (technically referred to as a **Universal Serial Bus** or "**USB connection**" for short) that links up the e-reader device directly to a computer.

> A **"wireless network"** is any type of computer connection that doesn't necessitate the use of cables.
>
> By this method, homes and businesses avoid the costly expense of running cables throughout the building (and from device to device).

Both types of connections allow you to access **"electronic books"** which you can store and read on your e-reader. Making life even simpler, most e-readers also have some direct relationship with a digital bookseller (such as Amazon, Apple or Barnes & Noble), which we'll elaborate on shortly.

You should know that you don't need any type of connection (wireless or otherwise) in order to order to read your book. In fact, we recommend you shut your wireless connection unless absolutely necessary – it drains your battery and (medically) probably doesn't help your brain cells.

That said: you do, unfortunately, need some type of connection to ***order*** your book.

> We're reminded of Joseph Heller's book *"Catch-22"*.
>
> Simply: Catch-22 is a situation in which an individual cannot solve a problem because of its contradictory rules or restraints.
>
> As you'll find with Amazon, Apple, Barnes and Noble and others, these companies take much delight in forcing you to access the Internet (and their site) whenever you want to order a book.
>
> Fortunately, once you purchase and download a book, you can read it without any further interference.

A look at the Kindle

The first e-reader that exploded onto the scene was the Amazon Kindle. We'll spend time examining the Kindle, especially since most of its features are common to all e-readers. Even the look of the Kindle – see graphic below – resembles the other popular e-readers.

The first thing you'll notice is that the Kindle is extremely small – about the size of a paperback book. This portable hand-held device has a 6" diagonal screen and is no thicker than a pencil.

Here are some of the key features for the Kindle. Again, remember that most of these features are common to all e-readers:

- The Kindle's screen reads like real paper with no glare and can be easily read both indoors or in bright sunlight.

- Amazon claims that the battery life can hold a single charge for up to 1-2 months, although most active readers will find their battery will realistically need to be recharged once a week.

- The Kindle can store between **1,400 - 3,500** books (depending on the model).

> The active reader reads about 50 books a year. Given this capacity, most e-readers can store over 70 years' worth of material – good enough for a lifetime of reading.

- The Kindle contains built-in wireless capability. The wireless connection is free and allows you to access and purchase books through the Amazon website.

- Like all e-readers, the Kindle has adjustable text sizes to allow for easy reading.

- A dictionary is pre-loaded for easy use.

- Because the Kindle allows you to purchase books directly from the Amazon website, you have access to over 1.5 million books.

- Additionally, many public libraries now offer the ability to "borrow" electronic books. (The book is downloaded directly onto your Kindle. Access to the digital book "expires" on the due date).

Currently, Amazon offers two basic forms of the Kindle.

The first type includes a keyboard at the bottom of the device. Pages are turned by click on "Next Page" or "Previous Page" tabs located on the sides of the device. There is a large button on the bottom right side of the keyboard which provides access to and helps navigate various menus.

The second type is the Kindle Touch. As its name indicates, everything is operated by **touching the screen**. Menus and the keyboard are accessed in this fashion and pages can be turned by 'tapping' or 'swiping' the screen either to the right or the left.

Although very much in vogue, touch screens aren't for everyone.

For one, the constant repetitive motion could lead to carpel tunnel syndrome. For another, you tend to spend more time swiping and tapping and less time reading.

Remember...

You don't need any type of connection (wireless or otherwise) to actually read your books. You do, however, need some type of connection to <u>order</u> your books.

Kindle begat Kindle Fire: Amazon's variations of the Kindle

Kindle (basic)

The basic, and least expensive, model (but essentially with many of the Kindle bells-and-whistles).

This version comes with **advertising**. As a scaled-down version, this Kindle is not touch-screen, so you have to navigate via a 5-way controller which is rather cumbersome.

> **Ads? Ads???!!**
>
> Yes. You pay less for a device with ads, but, over time, the annoyance factor just isn't worth the savings.

In addition to being able to link the device via your computer, this Kindle has a built-in wireless connection.

Kindle Touch

A low-priced model that features a **touch screen**. Simply put, you turn the pages by either 'swiping' or 'tapping' on the screen. As with the prior variation, this Kindle can connect via your computer and has a built-in wireless connection.

> While we voiced some reservations about touch screens earlier, they are nonetheless the wave of the future.
>
> Still, we strongly recommend you try one out before you decide.

Both the Kindle Touch and Kindle Touch 3G (below) include a feature called **Paperwhite**, which has a built-in light to allow you to read under any-and-all conditions.

Kindle Touch 3G

Identical to the Kindle Touch, with one exception. In addition to the built-in wireless connection, this version has a **3G wireless access**.

> Sounds complicated? Not really. Here's a simple way to understand it:
>
> **"Wireless or Wi-Fi"** means you must access a wireless network.
>
> Public libraries usually offer wireless networks as do popular venues such as coffee houses, bookstores, hotels, even supermarkets.
>
> Still, while plentiful, only having a wireless connection means you have to hunt down an available wireless network before you can connect.
>
> **"3G network"** means you can don't need a designated wireless network. Instead, you can connect like you would via any cell phone. In the case of the Kindle, no dialing is required.

The 3G wireless access is free – Amazon absorbs the costs, calculating that they'll more-than make up for the freebie by the number of books you purchase through their website.

The main advantage to the Kindle Touch 3G is that you can access their Amazon website – in other words, 'purchase your books' – from just about anywhere.

(Don't expect to be able to order books from remote / rural locations where neither wireless networks nor cell phone coverage are available. Make sure you stock up on digital books before you head off to some far-off locale).

Kindle Keyboard

A solid Kindle workhorse. This version has a keyboard as opposed to a touch screen. Obviously, the keyboard is small – barely suited for the hand of even the tiniest Munchkin – but it gets the job done. This particular Kindle has built-in wireless connection and a 3G network.

Kindle Fire

Currently, Amazon is offering its latest device called the **Kindle Fire**. In many ways, this device is remarkably similar to the Nook Tablet that Barnes & Noble is offering (see further below).

The Kindle Fire is attempting to compete with the various surge of tablet devices, such as the iPad.

In addition to reading books, this reasonably low-cost device offers access to the Internet; the ability to download applications ("**apps**"); view movies; and so forth.

(We only mention the device here briefly as we provide a more in-depth look in our Chapter 14 on "iPads and Tablets").

Kindle: At a glance

The Pros

- Inexpensive.

- Lightweight and portable.

- Font sizes are adjustable, so you can find just the right size for comfortable reading (without eye strain).

- Access to over 1.5 million books, including most of the popular best-sellers.

- Digital books usually cost much less than hardcover and paperback editions.

- Easy connection (to the Amazon website) which makes purchasing books a breeze.

- Easy reading whether indoors or in bright sunlight.

- Storage capacity for thousands of books. One of the joys of owning an e-reader is that you can stock up on plenty of books when you travel.

- Kindle applications ("**apps**") allow you to read books on other devices, such as phones, iPads and so forth.

The Cons

- Somewhat fragile – they don't like to be dropped and need to be protected from the elements.

- Kindle books are proprietary to Amazon. This means you can't read these books on any other device (except through Amazon **applications**).

These Amazon **applications** are (thankfully) free, but are still a minor inconvenience to find and download.

- Menus are cumbersome and controllers (on the keyboard models) are awkward to use.

- Constantly leaving the "wireless" mode turned on can drain the Kindle's battery.

- No easy "filing" system for your books. You can search for a book and sort by title and author, but, as your digital library increases, it's easy to lose sight of which books you own.

- There is no easy way to "skim" a digital book.

The Hidden Costs

- While many of the books on Amazon cost $9.99 or less, publishers have started to raise their price of popular "digital" bestsellers. At times, the price of a digital book might even cost more than a reduced hardcover or paperback.

Kindle Competitors

Since the Kindle was the first e-reader device out of the gate, they quickly dominated the e-book marketplace, fueled by clout of Amazon's website. Other e-readers soon appeared, vying for their share of the market. Among the most notable:

A look at the Nook

The Nook is an e-reader from Barnes & Noble. Much like the Kindle, the Nook is a hand-held device with a 6" diagonal screen. Again, like the Kindle, the Nook provides clear, crisp text; a long battery life; backlighting; scalable text sizes; free wireless connection and access to millions of books through the Barnes & Noble website.

The Nook (called the "Nook Simple Touch") is a touch-only device; its keyboard and menus can only be accessed via the screen itself.

Unlike the Kindle, the Nook has a color **e-reader** (called, appropriately enough, the "Nook Color") which allows for the display of color graphics. One should note, however, that in most digital books, the only portion of the book in color is usually just the jacket cover.

Calling this device an e-reader is perhaps a misnomer since the **Nook Color** allows you to download applications, view movies and more.

If these features intrigue you, you might want to purchase the Nook Tablet instead. The price is practically the same as the Nook Color yet the Nook Tablet has more 'horsepower' and additional bells and whistles.

In keeping with the iPad craze, Barnes & Noble also offer a **tablet** (called the "**Nook Tablet**") which, like the Kindle Fire, we cover in more depth in Chapter 14 on "iPads and Tablets".

A "**tablet**" is a mobile computing device – larger than a mobile phone / smaller than a laptop – with a flat screen that is operated by touching the screen rather than using a physical keyboard.

The Nook: At a glance

The Pros

- Inexpensive.

- Lightweight and portable.

- Competitive with the Amazon Kindle.

- Font sizes are adjustable, so you can find just the right size for comfortable reading.

- Access to slightly more titles than the Kindle, including most of the popular best-sellers.

- E-Ink allows for easy reading whether indoors or in bright sunlight.

- Storage capacity for thousands of books.

- The Nook Color has shading which allows for reading in dark or low-lit spaces.

- Magazines look great on the Nook Color.

- The Nook Color provides **several features** found in the iPad and tablets.

> If you're interested in these features, you might want to consider the Nook Tablet instead (see our earlier caveat).

The Cons

- Fragile. Like the Kindle, they don't appreciate being dropped and need to be protected from the elements.

- Menus are cumbersome.

- The Barnes & Noble website is often counter-intuitive, especially when compared with the Amazon site.

- There is no physical keyboard (touch-screen only) so navigation can be awkward.

- Constantly leaving on the "wireless" capability drains the battery.

- There is no easy way to "skim" a digital book.

The Hidden Costs

- Generally, books are priced higher than on Amazon. At times, the price of a digital book might even cost more than a reduced hardcover or paperback.

- There are some unexpected hidden costs for the Nook Color and Nook Tablet that are unique to iPads and Tablets, so we recommend you check out our chapter covering those devices.

A look at the Sony Reader Wi-Fi

The Sony Reader Wi-Fi looks very similar to the Kindle and the Nook and shares many of the same features. Like the Kindle and Nook, the Sony Reader Wi-Fi is a hand-held device with a 6" diagonal screen. This device provides clear text; a long battery life; scalable text sizes; wireless connection and access to books via the Sony website.

The Sony Reader Wi-Fi is a touch-only device; therefore its keyboard and menus can only be accessed in this fashion. One added feature: the device also includes a stylus by which you can touch (and even write on) the screen.

> While the notion of a **stylus** sounds appealing, there's nowhere on the current version of the Sony Reader Wi-Fi to store or even hold the stylus.
>
> If you're like our household, the stylus will probably be lost or misplaced in less than a week.

The Sony Reader Wi-Fi: At a glance

The Pros

- Inexpensive. Lightweight and portable. Competitive with the Kindle and Nook.

- Font sizes are adjustable.

- Access to slightly fewer electronic books than Amazon and Barnes & Noble

- E-Ink allows for easy reading whether indoors or in bright sunlight.

- Storage capacity for thousands of books.

- Only one basic model, so you don't have to compare against other variations.

The Cons

- Fragile. Made of plastic.

- Menus are cumbersome.

- Navigation on this device is very awkward.

- The refresh rate of the screen is slower than the Kindle and Nook, so the spaces (as you turn pages) are more noticeable.

- Many of the features are counter-intuitive. For example, you can only turn pages by swiping the page, not tapping the screen.

The Hidden Costs

- Much like the Nook, books purchased via the Sony site are generally priced higher than Amazon.

Understanding iPad / iBooks

The iPad is a tablet <u>not technically</u> an e-reader; and **iBooks** is simply an application within the iPad that enables you to read books (purchased through the Apple store).

Here's a quick overview of what an **iPad / tablet** is (and how it differentiates from the traditional e-reader):

> Technically, the iPad <u>is</u> a tablet – much like Xerox for a while became synonymous for all brands of copiers.

Like the e-reader, the iPad is a portable device. The iPad comes in two sizes: the regular iPad (9.7") and the iPad Mini (7.9").

Here's the easiest way to think of it: the iPad is a form of wireless computer. As such, you can do a variety of tasks, such as write notes; check e-mails; store your calendar and contacts; watch movies…the list goes on and on.

While some of these functions are built-into the iPad, most require downloading an application (or "**app**" for short). Some of the apps are free – in fact, some very good apps are available for free – but the majority requires a nominal **payment**.

> Most **apps** cost between $0.99 - $9.99.
>
> Apple makes their website store very user-friendly and there are often reviews by users to help decide whether the app is actually worth purchasing.

The inherent different between a tablet and an e-reader: the iPad and other tablets allow you to engage in a variety of activities. The sole purpose of most e-readers, however, is simply **to read**.

> The exceptions – as we've pointed out in this chapter – include the Kindle Fire and Nook Tablet. (And, to a large degree, the Nook Color.)

So, our usual caveat: If you want to find out more about the iPad and other tablets, check out Chapter 14 on "iPads and Tablets".

The iPad / iBooks: At a glance

The Pros

- Lightweight and portable.

- A bright screen with dazzling color.

- Font sizes are adjustable, so you can find just the right size for comfortable reading.

- Storage capacity for thousands of books.

- Magazines and newspapers look great on the iPad.

- The menu / design of the iPad is well-thought out, making navigation easy.

The Cons

- **Expensive.**

> Remember, you're buying a computer-like device, not a designated e-reader.

- Since the iPad and tablets can't avail themselves with E-Ink, reading outdoors is difficult-to-impossible.

- The number of books available to purchase at the Apple store are **somewhat limited**.

> Most bestselling books are available, but when you try to dig deeper for a favorite book, chances are it might not be there.

- But the biggest negative is in the nature of the beast – the iPad was never designed solely as an e-reader. You might start reading a book, but you'll soon find yourself distracted by the dozens of other applications that are vying for your attention.

The Hidden Costs

- Books are generally higher priced.

- The iPad / tablets come in a variety of assorted configurations – each one higher priced than the next.

- While the initial cost for an application ("app") might seem minimal, the costs tend to mount up.

- Unlike most e-readers which provide free 3G connection, you actually must subscribe to one of your local telephone carriers in order to access this feature.

One final caveat about E-Readers...

We're big fans of reading in general and E-Readers in particular.

That said, whether these devices – singular to 'reading only' – will remain around for much longer is highly doubtful.

With the coming-of-age of the iPad / Tablets, consumers now have a device that provides their entertainment and basic computer needs <u>and</u> allows them to read their books as well.

As Amazon and Barnes and Noble spend more and more time innovating and promoting their Kindle Fire and Nook Tablet, we doubt whether the basic E-Reader models will be around for much longer.

Chapter 12

Digital Music

Who should read this section

If you love music – any kind of music – this piece of technology should be #1 on your personal Top 10.

If you have albums or CDs taking up space deep inside your closet, we'll suggest some easy-to-use devices that will help you convert those long-lost memories onto your digital music player.

If you're intrigued by the notion of bringing your entire music library with you every time you travel, these devices are just the ticket.

Who should skip this section

If you're surrounded by a music turntable, a cassette player, a CD player – and you haven't noticed (or care) that these music players have become obsolete – then, digital music might not be anywhere on your radar.

If you're an audiophile who swears by every pop and hiss on your vinyl records, you're probably already offended by the term 'digital music'.

So what is "digital" music?

We won't get too technical on you – we promise! – just a few basic pieces of information.

Most early music – whether on the traditional 33-1/3 rpm record albums, 45 rpm 'singles', the 78 rpm gramophone discs and even cassette tapes – were the result of **analog recordings**. These analog recordings were susceptible to noises and distortions that some audio 'purists' find endearing.

> "**Analog recording**" is a technique by which signals are stored into or on a media.
>
> As a simple example, the sounds produced by an orchestra (the signals) are stored onto a record or tape (the media).

With the introduction in the early 1980s of the **compact disc** (also known as "**CDs**"), these analog signals were converted into **digital form**.

> The **digital form** is a series of binary numbers or "bits" – the specific process by which music is turned into numbers is a discussion better left to obsessive people on long, lonely nights.

Okay, but what does any of this have to do with you, right?

Well, in simple terms, once you've created a digital file, you can do all sorts of things with it. You can copy it; you can move it; and you can even shrink it. And, from that shrinking (or compression) the MP3 file came into existence.

The **MP3** file is an '**audio-specific format**' or, in English, it's **a music file**. Because the file is compressed, it doesn't take up much space; and, because the file is digital, the clarity remains exceptionally high.

Technically: **MP3** is a patented digital audio encoding format that compresses voice and music files for transfer from one electronic device to another while always retaining its original CD-like audio quality.

Whew!

A look at the iPod

So let's start right in with the music player that currently dominates the marketplace: the **iPod**.

> The name **iPod** was the brainchild of Vinnie Chieco, a freelance copywriter. After seeing a prototype, Chieco thought of the movie "2001: A Space Odyssey" and the phrase "Open the pod bay door, Hal!"
>
> From that little anecdote, history was made.

While by no means the first music player to come on the scene, the **iPod** quickly surpassed all other music players and now controls between 70-80% of the market. Why? As you'll see, the iPod is portable, easy-to-use and has a unique relationship with the Apple store that is as simple as can be.

> While it seems to have been around forever, in actuality the **iPod** didn't appear on the scene until October 2001.

Here are some key features and information regarding the iPod:

- Like most Apple products, the device start-up is instantaneous.

- As with all music players, you'll need earphones to listen to your music. The iPod contains a free set of **earphones** in the box that's shipped to you.

The **earphones** shipped with the iPod are called "**ear buds**". These earphones sit loosely in your outer ear (and, yes, they're too big to slip into the ear canal).

Surprisingly, these earphones are compact, inexpensive and produce decent sound. Still, these earphones are not for everyone.

Fortunately, all brands of earphones will work with the iPod, so you have a wide variety of styles and quality to choose from.

- The battery life ranges from 15 – 40 hours of music depending on the model you choose. Seems like a lot of time, but, as most iPod users will probably agree, you should probably charge the device every few days.

- All iPods are controlled by a digital media center (called iTunes) that lets you purchase, organize and play your music, movies and TV shows on your computer <u>and</u> on your iPod.

We'll discuss iTunes in a moment. Meanwhile, you're probably already seeing the main caveat: Yes, you'll need a computer to format, stock and organize your iPod.

iTunes (why do you need it and how to use it)

Remember…

First, you have to download the iTunes program before you're able to access any music, movies or video (and synchronize everything to your iPod).

You can go online (to www.YouTube.com) and look for iTunes tutorials on how to download and set-up iTunes.

If talking to a real-live human is more your style, you can call Apple directly (800) 275-2273 and one of their representatives will be more-than-willing to help you with any questions or concerns.

"iTunes" is the digital center that acts as the hub for all your music, movies and videos – and which, quite frankly, is the only way to access and store them onto your iPod.

Just as you can't drive a car without an engine, you can't operate an iPod without iTunes.

Here are the simple steps to download and access iTunes:

1. Turn on your computer.

2. Go to the following website: www.apple.com/itunes

3. Prominently displayed on the page is the latest iTunes version with a button which reads: "Free Download".

4. Click on that button.

5. On the next screen, you'll also be asked to decide whether you want iTunes to send you **news and special offers**. Either click (or unclick) the boxes to your preference.

> If you have no interest or want to remain anonymous, simply unclick the boxes.

6. Once you've indicated these preferences, click on the button marked "Download Now".

7. Depending on your computer, you may be given some additional choices. Suffice it to say, iTunes is a legitimate download, so click "ok" or "run" accordingly.

8. Your computer will then download iTunes automatically.

Once you've downloaded iTunes, you'll find an iTunes icon located on your computer desktop.

1. Double-click on the icon.

2. iTunes will begin to configure itself on your computer. This process will take a few minutes, so be patient.

3. Soon, a set-up screen will appear. You'll be given a **variety of choices**. Make each selection based on your personal preferences, and then click your way through the series of "Next" buttons.

---

iTunes will ask these following choices:

- First, you'll need to agree to iTunes Terms and Conditions. (Hardly a 'choice' because if you don't agree, iTunes won't let you continue.)

- Do you want iTunes to automatically search your computer for existing music?

- Should iTunes maintain your music folders (as opposed to doing it yourself)?

- Automatically download album artwork?

- Do you want to be directed to the Apple store?

---

4. Depending on your selections, you'll eventually find yourself inside the iTunes home page.

Here's a brief description of what you'll find on your own version of iTunes:

- A menu near at the very top of the page (containing File, Edit, View, Control, Store, Help). Feel free to explore each one, as they'll give you more options to fine-tune your music collection.

- Above the menu are music controls (Play, Next Track and so forth) that will actually allow you to play your music on your computer.

- The main body of the screen is the **iTunes Store** which allows you to scan, search and ultimately purchase music tracks, movies and so forth.

> If you are planning any purchases, you'll need to sign up for an account on Apple's iTunes store and give them your credit card number to keep on file.
>
> Security is quite good. Once you've put your credit card number on file, you simply click on a music or video selection to purchase and download your choice.

- On the far right, you'll find a section marked "Library" and underneath that, labels with headings such as Music, Movies, and TV Shows.

  Initially, your Library will be empty except for these headings. Once you've purchased some music or a film or transferred your music from your own CDs to iTunes **(we'll explain how-to shortly)**, they'll all be stored in this Library area. We'll get back to these labels in a moment.

> We'll not only explain how to transfer your CDs to iTunes, but we've also dedicated a separate section – see Chapter 17 – on how to transfer your record albums and cassette tapes to iTunes.

- You'll also find a link to the iTunes Store. Other options include ways to access your particular iPod, **Playlists** and more.

Playlists are fun. You simply create a title for your playlist – for example, Favorite Country Songs – then drag the songs you'd like to hear from your Library / Music folder into the playlist.

ITunes neatly transfers a <u>copy</u> of the songs into the playlist which you can listen to on your iPod anytime you're in the mood.

Remember...

If all this seems overwhelming or confusing, there are a myriad of help opportunities to guide you through the process.

You can go online (to www.YouTube.com) and look for iTunes tutorials on how to download and set-up iTunes.

If talking to a real-live human is more your style, you can call Apple directly at (800) 275-2273. One of their representatives will be more-than-willing to help you with any questions or concerns.

Once you get your iTunes up-and-running, you can begin to explore the labels under your Library.

In the graphic below, you can see one of the many **views** that iTunes provides. In this instance, we've chosen the Songs label within the Library (circled in the center area).

You can configure these **views** to meet your personal tastes or needs, including views that show the album covers (which is always a fun way of viewing your music collection).

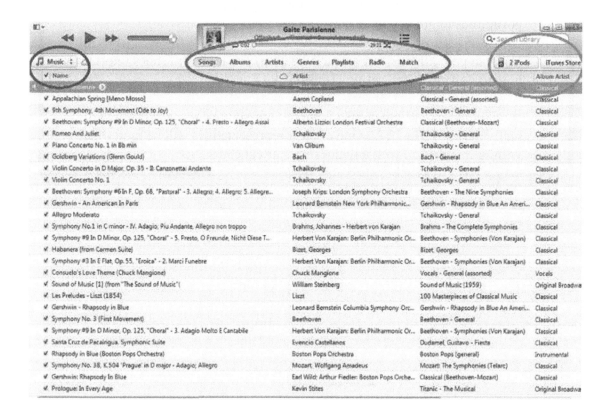

In this particular view, songs in the library are divided by **Name**, **Artist, Album** and so forth (see the menu headings at the top of the list of songs). A few tips:

- If you click on a label (say, on the Name label), iTunes will automatically sort your listing alphabetically…from A-Z or, if you click a second time, in reverse from Z-A. This is true for all the headings.

- If you use your computer mouse and Right Click on any empty space within that line of headings, you'll be given a seemingly-endless list of ways you can **view or sort your music**.

> To make life simple, we suggest limiting your choices to only a handful – perhaps just Name, Artist, Album, and Genre to start.
>
> iTunes also gives you the opportunity to "rate" your songs on a 1-5 star basis and even allows you to make comments about the song.
>
> You're also given a setting to "shuffle" your songs, allowing you to play some or all of your music in random order.

- When you begin playing a song, iTunes automatically shows you the album cover.

- If you're importing a song of your own and the album cover artwork is missing, it's actually an easy process to find, copy and paste the cover art into your iTunes. (We explain these steps in detail shortly in the section on "Downloading Music from your CD to your iPod").

As you can also see from the above graphic, iTunes also lets you configure your music library by Albums, Artists, Genres, etc.

In the area circled on the right, iTunes lets you know what devices are connected and allows you to go directly to the iTunes Store.

Clicking the down arrow in the area circled on the left, iTunes lets you select and configure your Music, Movies, TV Shows, Podcasts, Books, Apps and so forth.

Before we turn to the specific iPods, let us leave you with a brief overview of iTunes using our usual Pros, Cons and Hidden Costs.

iTunes: At a glance

The Pros

- An excellent storage / digital center to house all your music and/or videos.

- The iTunes Store is relatively easy to navigate.

- Purchasing a product on the iTunes Store is simple and effortless.

- iTunes help desk is extremely friendly and accommodating (especially if you're within their complimentary **90-day technical support period**).

> You can always get additional technical support beyond the 90 day period, but, unfortunately, you're charged for each incident.

The Cons

- Unfortunately, you need a computer in order to download, set-up and configure iTunes.

  While the process is straightforward, if you're doing this for the first time, you might want to bring along a friend or relative for support. If not, remember an iTunes representative is only a quick phone call away.

- In signing up for an Apple / iTunes account, you'll need to provide them your e-mail address, a password, and, ultimately, your credit card information. By-and-large, the Apple / iTunes information is secure and your information is well-protected.

- While iTunes is relatively easy to use, there is a slight 'learning curve' as you try to navigate your way around. Be kind to yourself for the first 1-3 days as you learn its ins-and-outs.

The Hidden Costs

- Although music in the iTunes store is inexpensive (between $0.99 - $1.29 per song), the costs can quickly mount up, especially as you try to build your music library. iTunes adds to the temptation by offering up similar songs to the ones that you have purchased.

Back to the iPod

Okay, enough about iTunes – let's turn our attention to the iPod itself.

The illustration below shows four different iPod models. First, we'll give you some general information, followed by a brief rundown on each:

- Three of the four iPods models have screens. The iPod Shuffle does not.

- Two of the models – the iPod Nano and iPod Touch – can be navigated by touching the screen. The remaining two – the iPod Shuffle and iPod Classic – navigate using a **wheel**.

> We're fans of the iPod, but using the **wheel** to navigate through songs is rather laborious and cumbersome.

- All four models can play music, audio books and **podcasts**. Two of the models – the iPod Classic and iPod Touch – can also play video.

A **podcast** is a type of digital media consisting of episodic series of files which are downloaded or subscribed to. Usually for free.

In English, these can be lectures or discussions that you can download directly to your iPod – with topics ranging from art, history, wine, sports, even a wide variety of classroom studies.

The iTunes store makes downloading podcasts simple. They've even devoted two sections to podcasts: one to general topics (which also include broadcasts of radio shows) and one specifically designed for the classroom (iTunes U, which is short for iTunes University).

- Two models – the iPod Shuffle and iPod Nano – are no larger than a book of matches. The iPod Classic is the size of a deck of cards while the iPod Touch is the size of a cell phone.

- Each model can also be purchased with different storage capacities. Storage is measured in gigabytes (abbreviated as "GB"). We won't bother with a definition, but rather will give you an approximation of the amount of music (or videos) they can store.

Storage	Number of songs	Number or albums or films	Name of device
2 GB	500 – 600 songs	50 albums	iPod Shuffle
8 GB	2,000 – 2,500 songs	200 albums or 5 films	iPod Nano / iPod Touch
16 GB	4,000 – 5,000 songs	400 albums	iPod Nano
32 GB	8,000 – 10,000 songs	800 albums or 20 films	iPod Touch
64 GB	16,000 – 20,000 songs	1,400 albums or 40 films	iPod Touch
160 GB	40,000 – 50,000 songs	4,000 albums or 100 films	iPod Classic

A snapshot of Apple's iPod variations

iPod Shuffle:

Extremely small (the size of a book of matches). The simplest and least expensive of the iPods (although that's not necessarily meant as a compliment):

The Shuffle is the one iPod with no screen. As a result, you can't see what's playing (although an annoying VoiceOver feature tells you what you're listening to).

On the other hand, the Shuffle is perfect for people who love to walk or exercise. Just load the right kind of music and you're on your way.

iPod Nano:

The Nano is as small as the Shuffle (again, the size of a book of matches) but features a touch screen. Its small size makes the Nano ideal for exercise or just to carry around in your pocket or purse.

In addition, the Nano features an FM radio and an accelerometer (a device which allows you to keep track of how many steps you take during your walks or exercise).

While the Nano cannot display video, it allows you to store and view photos. Although small, the Nano comes with enough capacity to store an ample number of songs and photo (as many as 4,000 songs and over 10,000 pictures).

iPod Classic

This is the granddaddy of iPods. With ample storage, the device has more than enough horsepower for most music collections.

The iPod Classic is approximately the size of a deck of cards. While the screen is small, the clarity is surprisingly good for **videos**.

While we wouldn't recommend watching an entire movie or television show on such a small screen, it is certainly more-than serviceable if you have a few minutes while waiting in line; or are at a doctor's office.

Because the iPod synchronizes through iTunes, you'll be able to continue watching from the spot you last left off using on any Apple device.

iPod Touch

The Touch has enough features to satisfy most people's needs. The size of a standard cell phone, the Touch has a large viewing screen for crystal-clear images and video.

The Touch also contains a wireless connection that allows you to easily download songs or movies on the go. If that weren't enough, the Touch has a built-in camera that allows you to take pictures or even high-definition video recordings.

That said, we have one major caveat on the device:

The iPod Touch costs about the same price as an iPhone – and the iPhone does all of the above; functions as a cell phone; and has additional bells-and-whistles to boot.

Once you picked the right model for you, here's a quick **step-by-step on how to synchronize your iPod**:

These steps remain the same, no matter which iPod you purchase.

When you **synchronize** (or "**Sync**" as the term is often called) your iPod, iTunes automatically matches the content from your Library against the content on your iPod. Any additions, deletions or changes are automatically copied, deleted or transferred.

1. Download iTunes (see section on iTunes above).

2. Purchase music from iTunes Store (or see our section below on how to transfer music from your albums or CDs and place that music into iTunes).

3. Connect the USB Cable that each iPod includes in its packaging – one end goes into your computer, the other end connects directly into your iPod.

4. Once the USB Cable is properly connected, your iPod will automatically synchronize with your iTunes.

5. After the iPod is synchronized – which usually takes no more than a few minutes, depending on the size of your music library – you can disconnect your iPod and you're ready to go.

Remember...

- Creating Playlists (see our earlier remarks) is a fun way to group your favorite songs into easily-recognizable and easily-playable lists.

- You need to keep your iPod charged after use. You can reconnect the iPod back to the USB Cable and onto your computer (but that means you need to keep your computer on while the iPod charges).

  We suggest using an iPod Power Adaptor instead. One end plugs into the iPod while the other end plugs directly into an electrical outlet. Most (but not all) iPods are pre-packaged with a power adaptor. If not, you can easily purchase an adaptor directly from the Apple / iTunes store.

---

iPod: At a glance

The Pros

- Lightweight and portable.

- Easily synchronizes with iTunes to make transferring and listening to music effortless.

- iTunes has a more-than-ample selection of music, no matter what your listening preference.

- Cost per each individual song is reasonably inexpensive.

The Cons

- Using the "wheel' on the iPod Classic and iPod Shuffle can be cumbersome to navigate.

- While the touch screen on the iPod Nano and iPod Touch are easier use than the 'wheel', the content on the screens are not easily visible in bright sunlight.

- The small sizes of the IPod Shuffle and iPod Nano make them easy to lose or misplace.

- You must have a computer to access iTunes (and, therefore, to synchronize your iPod).

- You are dependent upon your own iTunes to synchronize your own music library. If you have a second computer or want to access a friend's computer, the process gets a little more complex.

The Hidden Costs

- The cost of purchasing music from the iTunes store tends to mount up and becomes expensive.

Downloading music from your CDs to your iPod

Before we leave the topic of iPod and iTunes, we want to make sure you know how to convert your CDs into digital music that can be played and stored on the iPod.

We're making two assumptions:

First, that you have a **collection of compact discs (also known as "CDs").**

For the purpose of this conversation, we hope you have at least one or more CDs.

We'll get to those vinyl albums and 45 singles in a little bit.

Second, that your computer has a disc player. Since 99% of all computers have a disc player, we're fairly confident you have one on your computer.

The disc player is the tray-like device on the computer by which you insert discs. You've probably already used this disc tray to load programs – hopefully, you're aware that this disc player will actually play your CDs as well.

Here is the step-by-step to **convert** your CDs to your iTunes / iPod.

Converting your CDs is also known as **"ripping"**.

Contrary to popular belief, the word does not derive from the phrase "rip off" or "stealing", but is rather an acronym RIP or Raster Image Processing (which concerns the speed of copying a file).

That was probably more information than you actually needed.

---

1. Turn on your computer.

2. Double-click on the iTunes icon – which should be located on the computer desktop. This will open the iTunes program / library.

3. Insert your CD into your computer disc player.

4. iTunes will **automatically** display the tracks on your **CD**.

If the tracks are unnamed and simply display "Track 1", "Track 2":

1. Go to the top menu bar on iTunes. Select "Edit", then click on "Preferences".

2. Look for the section near the bottom that says "Automatically retrieve CD track names from Internet" and make sure that box is checked.

As long as your CD is found on the iTunes online database (and most are), iTunes will find the information for you and will retrieve the track names.

If you're still running into a problem, try reloading the CD. Otherwise, select Advanced on the top menu and click on "Get Track Names".

You don't have to "rip" every song from every CD.

If you hate a song and don't want it as part of your library, just uncheck the box in front of the song name and iTunes won't convert it.

5. When you're all set, click the "**Import CD**" button on the lower right side of the display.

6. A status display will now show the progress of the conversion. If you choose to cancel, you can just click the small "x" next to the progress bar.

7. iTunes will chime when it's completed transferring the songs – the transfer is surprisingly fast.

That's it – your songs from the CD are automatically loaded into your iTunes library. From there:

- You can double-click on any of the songs to listen directly on your computer.

- You can create a new playlist and drag these new songs into that playlist (or any other playlist for that matter).

- You can plug your iPod into the computer and iTunes will automatically synchronize your songs and playlists so you can listen to your new music on the go.

Converting your albums and tapes to your iPod

Sometimes technology invents devices that are simple and smart.

If you have old records that you want to digitally convert into your iTunes library / iPod, there are a number of turntables on the market that are inexpensive and can easily convert your music.

Generally, these turntables should have the following features, but make sure to double-check before you purchase any:

- A **USB cable** that runs from the turntable to your computer. These turntables are usually compact and lightweight, so they can easily rest on a chair or small table which you can set near your computer.

- Look for turntables that have **3-speeds**, so you can play your 33-1/3 albums, your 45 rpm 'singles' and those priceless 78 rpm gramophone discs.

In addition to converting your albums, most of these turntables can also play your records – an added bonus.

- The turntable should also have supplied software that will make the interface between your albums and your iTunes library easy to use. You just install the software and follow the prompts. It's usually straight-forward and simple to understand.

To be on the safe side and save any frustration, ask the store or call the manufacturer to make sure the enclosed software is compatible with iTunes.

In addition to turntables, there are similar devices for cassette tapes. We've seen devices that have both a turntable and a cassette player built into one. If you have a large number of albums and cassette tapes in your personal library that you want to convert, that all-in-one device might be for you.

So where can you buy these turntables / cassette players?

We'd recommend starting with your local retailers, especially those that have a large selection of computers and electronic equipment. If that doesn't work, you might want to try **Brookstone**. They have stores around the country, especially at airports, and you can always try their customer service number (800) 846-3000 for additional information.

> We hate to be a shill for any particular company, but **Brookstone** has a selection of these turntables and cassette players which are easy to use. If all else fails, give them a try.

Moving on: iPod Competitors

Since the Apple iPod controls over 70 - 80% of the music player marketplace, there are slim pickings for other music players – especially ones that can compete with the iTunes interface and the enormous selection on the iTunes Store. As a case in point:

What happened to Microsoft Zune?

For a few years, Microsoft tried to compete with Apple in the music player marketplace. They came out with a music player called **Zune**.

In case you're wondering about the name "**Zune**", there's no specific derivation.

Microsoft was just looking for a name to compete with iPod and Zune sounded like a fun name to them.

The Zune music player had the look and feel of an iPod. Unfortunately, customers didn't agree. Sales of the Zune were less than stellar, so Microsoft quickly removed the music player from the market.

You'll still find Zune available as a digital center on the Microsoft gaming console **X-Box** as well as on computers and cell phones that feature Microsoft software, but as a music player, just cross it off your list.

See Chapter 16 on "Gaming" for more details on the **Microsoft X-Box** and other gaming consoles.

A look at Sony Walkman

Yes, the Sony Walkman – which had its heyday as a cassette and CD player in years past – is still around, now as an MP3 music player.

You get a sense of the music player's priority in the company by visiting the Sony website (www.sony.com). The Walkman is buried deep in the menu under Electronics, then Personal Audio and Phones. Not the easiest way to track it down.

Still, the Sony Walkman is certainly competitive and, in many ways, resembles iPods. The main difference is that Sony doesn't have a seamless digital center interface like iTunes. As a result, you generally have to keep your music in individual folders and **drag** the music files into the Walkman.

The **Sony Walkman** also has wireless models, but as we discussed earlier with the iPod Touch, the devices so closely resemble high-end cell phones, that you'd almost be better off purchasing one of these smartphones instead.

Most new smartphones can play music and videos and have an astonishing array of bells-and-whistles to make them an alluring alternative.

The Sony Walkman also has a variety of models – the A Series; E Series (their traditional and low-cost model); the S Series and the Z Series (their top of the line).

Like the iPods, the Sony Walkman comes in array of colors and storage capacities. The E Series uses wheels and buttons to navigate; while the A, S and Z series are all touch screen.

Here are some features for the Sony Walkman that are worth noting:

- The basic Walkman E Series has a built-in FM radio and up to 50 hours of battery life without recharging. The E Series also has a Karaoke Mode, which lowers the vocals on the track in case you want to sing along.

- The Walkman A Series is a touch-screen; has wireless capability including the ability to listen to your music via wireless headsets; and includes a premium set of ear bud headsets.

- The Walkman S Series is also a touch-screen music player and includes a set of Bluetooth headphones for wireless listening.

- The latest Walkman Z Series with built-in wireless connection also connects with the Android market for applications. The Walkman Z Series functions much like the iPod Touch. As we've mentioned in both cases, make sure you compare with the equivalent smartphones – which give you more features and also provide cell phone capabilities.

Sony Walkman: At a glance

The Pros

- Comparable to other music players.

- Synchronizes well, especially if you have other Sony products, such as their television and stereo equipment.

The Cons

- Not at the top of Sony's product line and runs the risks of vanishing much like Microsoft Zune. Probably unlikely, but worth thinking about.

- Sony's interface to obtain music and video is not as seamless or as plentiful as the iTunes store.

The Hidden Costs

- As with the iPod, purchasing music tends to mount up as you build or fill in your music library. This can tend to become expensive.

And finally...other music players

We would be remiss if we didn't at least mention some additional music players that are on the market. Creative Labs offers its Zen series music players. These MP3 players are less expensive than the iPods and Walkman, but the features in the Zen players are not quite up to par, especially when compared with the others.

SanDisc has the Sansa MP3 player; Philips has the GoGear Spark player and Archos also has a variety of music players. All these music players function pretty much alike, so you can experiment with any of these in case the more popular iPods or Walkman don't measure up to your taste.

Chapter 13

Digital Cameras

Who should read this section

If you enjoy taking pictures.

If you want an overview of the world of digital cameras and digital photography.

If you'd like to take (and send!) pictures to your family and friends.

Who should skip this section

If you're not a picture-taker and have no interest in cameras (digital or otherwise).

Digital Cameras: An Overview

Typewriters. VHS tapes. Vinyl albums. Film for your camera.

What do those four have in common? Well, while they are not quite **obsolete**, they've become increasingly difficult to find.

> At least, not yet. Whether they become **obsolete** in another generation or two is, unfortunately, highly likely.

In fact, over **80%** of people who take pictures do so on a digital camera.

> And that **percentage** continues to grow, especially since digital camera have become incorporated into cell phones, iPads and tablets, and so forth.

Which is as good a lead-in as any into our discussion of digital cameras...

The major breakthroughs in technology over the last twenty years have revolved around the same principle: converting analog information into digital information.

This is true for many of the topics we've covered: **CDs** (music), **DVDs** (movies), **HDTV** (television), **MP3** (music) and **DVRs** (digital recordings / television).

In the same way, today's cameras have replaced film (**analog**) with digital content (**digital photographs**).

Digital cameras / photography have many distinct advantages over film photography:

- Digital cameras – especially the point-and-shoot variety – are relatively inexpensive.

- With digital photos, you can see the results instantaneously.

- Digital photos don't require the costs of film and developing.

- Digital photos are suitable for software editing on your computer.

- Digital photos can be uploaded to the Internet or sent to family or friends via an e-mail or even via the cell phone.

- Almost every digital camera has a video mode, allowing you to record video images.

We would be remiss in pointing out that devotees of old-school film photography are often quite **passionate** about their cameras. This isn't the forum, however, to discuss "shutter release time", "low light focus" and other terms that film photographers banter around.

> This is similar to the notion that some music lovers are **passionate** about vinyl records (and ridge up against digital / MP3 music).

One claim is certainly relevant: film cameras have manual backups while digital cameras are entirely dependent on an electronic supply (most-usually, batteries).

Basic tips…

Since digital camera depend on batteries in order to operate, make sure you carry an extra battery or two tucked in your camera case.

If your camera allows for chargeable batteries – certainly, the most economical way to go – make sure you keep the battery charged, especially if you're going on a trip or plan to take pictures at an event or family gathering.

So how do digital cameras work?

Going under the assumption that most of you are familiar with the basic make-up of a camera, we'll try to focus on some of the unique components within a digital camera.

Memory card

First, you need to understand that digital cameras function and operate much like a mini-computer. As a result – instead of film – most digital cameras stores data (images / pictures) on what is called a **memory card**.

> Also referred to as **memory chip**, **memory stic**k, **flash card** or **multimedia card**.

While the memory card (see graphic above) has no scale to give you an accurate representation, know that they are always small – usually little more than an inch – and are re-recordable.

The memory card fits into a slot, usually along the side of the camera.

- Think of the memory card like a piece of toast that gets inserted into the slot of a toaster.

- Notice the strip along the bottom of the right image (above). That's where the data is retained.

  Much like a CD or DVD, there's only one correct way to insert the card. Don't try to force the card into the slot. If it doesn't insert easily, try flipping the card around. If in doubt, check the camera manual.

All digital cameras come equipped with a memory card.

There are several types of memory cards formats:

- Among the most popular formats are SD ("Secure Digital") and CompactFlash.

- Not all cameras use the same type of **memory card**.

> If you already have one digital camera and are thinking of purchasing another (or giving one as a gift to a close family member), **make sure the memory cards are compatible**.
>
> That way, you can swap or exchange memory cards easily, if you so desire.

In addition to format types, memory cards vary in the amount of storage space available on each card. Memory cards range from 1 GB (gigabyte) of storage to 128 GB.

What this means in English: Assuming you're using one of the newer digital cameras, 1GB of storage means you can take about **200 pictures**; 4 GB of storage means over 800 pictures; and so forth.

> **Obviously, we're giving you estimations, especially since each camera model is different.**
>
> Remember: memory cards are re-recordable, so you can always move / save your photos onto your computer, then start all over again with a clean slate.

Megapixels

The basic term used to assess a digital camera – determined by the quality of a picture – is called its **megapixel** rating.

> Let's start with "**pixel**" which, in digital imaging, is the smallest, controllable element of a picture.
>
> "**Megapixel**" is one million pixels, which is the way a camera calculates the number of elements (rows times columns) in a digital display.

In simplistic terms: "**Megapixels**" are the total number of "**dots**" in a picture. So, for example, 3 megapixels would contain 3 million "dots" (which would define the totality of the picture).

That's it on the science lesson.

Just know: cameras are defined (more accurately, labeled) by the largest number of megapixels in a single picture.

Cameras range in size from 2 megapixels to 10 or more megapixels. The average digital camera usually comes in around 5 megapixels (with newer models ranging from **10-14 megapixels** or higher).

> Cameras with these **higher-end megapixels** are more-than-enough if you're planning to take serious artistic photos; sell your photos as prints; or post high-resolution photos on the Internet.

Most manufacturers will agree that a camera assessed with 6-9 megapixels is the equivalent to most 35mm film cameras.

Why do I need to know about a high megapixel count?

- Most new cameras are already available (pre-packaged, if you will) with a high megapixel count.

- You can find basic point-and-shoot cameras available with a high megapixel count – and many are inexpensive to boot.

- By in large, the higher the megapixel count, the greater the resolution.

- Finally, a high megapixel count will allow you to edit (or "tweak") your picture with greater accuracy on your computer.

The Viewfinder

Another element that is slightly different on the digital camera is its **viewfinder**.

Everyone who's used any kind of camera is aware of the viewfinder – the opening in the camera, which is usually located at the top center; and which allows you to find, view and focus a picture.

Like conventional film cameras, most digital cameras also have a viewfinder. Unlike conventional film camera, all digital cameras also have an **LCD screen**.

> **LCD** stands for **Liquid Crystal Display**. As you'll see from the graphic, this allows you to view the entire picture that's being framed on a clear display.

As you can see from the **two graphics above**, the LCD screen is a way of viewing the picture you're about to take (without squinting through the viewfinder).

Most digital cameras offer LCD screens that resemble the above image on the left, in that the screen dominates a large portion of the rear of the camera.

Some digital cameras offer LCD screens such as the above image on the right, wherein the LCD screen can be tucked to the side and can often rotate for your best viewing angle.

Both types of LCD screen positions function well and are only a matter of personal preference.

How does the camera's LCD screen work?

Quite simply, instead of peering through the viewfinder, you hold the digital camera a foot or so away from your eye so you can find and frame the picture on the LCD screen.

Once the picture is framed properly on the LCD screen, you just push the button and, presto, the picture is taken.

If the light outside is too bright to properly see the LCD screen…don't worry. You can always revert back to the viewfinder any time you want.

Camera in your cell phone

One item worth mentioning is that most cell phones – even your basic models – contain a built-in digital camera.

Many of you might be thinking: A camera inside a cell phone – how good can that camera be?

Actually, the opposite is true. Innovative strides have been made regarding cameras in cell phones. The average cell phone cameras are now 2-5 megapixels which is more-than-enough for most photographs.

Quite a few of the newer cell phone cameras, in fact, range from 8 megapixels or higher which can provide high-quality photographs.

Why even bother mentioning cameras in cell phones?

Two important reasons:

1. First, most people own a cell phone. If so, you might already be sitting on a better-than-average camera without even realizing it.

   To highlight once more: great strides have been made regarding the quality of cameras within cell phones. Many of these cameras are an excellent choice for the average user / photographer.

2. Secondly, if you'd like to consolidate this seemingly-endless array of technology, perhaps investing in a cell phone – <u>with</u> a powerful camera already built-in – might be just the ticket.

How to send / download / print pictures

There are a variety of software programs available to help you with your pictures. Many will help you organize your photos; and all – to one degree or another – will help you edit your pictures as well.

Many of these programs – for example, the software programs put out by **Adobe** – contain more bells-and-whistles than the average consumer will ever use.

> Look for programs such as Adobe Photoshop or Adobe Photoshop Elements.

What's more, they're often expensive and, surprisingly, aren't always easy to use for the simple tasks.

Fortunately, today's computers recognize people's zest for cameras and their need to send, save and print pictures. As a result, they've made the process extremely simple.

Here are some sample scenarios which should guide you through the basics:

Scenario #1: You've received a photo by e-mail and want to view it

Easy as pie:

1. The photo will be received as an attachment to your e-mail.

2. Every Internet provider – that's the company you signed up with to receive your e-mails – stores their attachments as a link or file in an area marked (appropriately enough) "**Attachments**".

> In certain providers, "**attachments**" might also be found alongside the graphic icon of **a paper clip.**

3. Using the left button on your computer mouse, just double-click on the link or file.

4. Presto, the photo will **automatically open**.

> In Windows, for example, the photo will open automatically in a built-in program called **Windows Photo Viewer**.

An alternate way to opening the photo:

1. Instead of using the *left* button on your computer mouse, use the *right* button and just click (once) on the link or attachment.

2. You'll be presented with a series of possible actions.

3. Pick (click) the one that says "Open" or "View".

4. Again – presto, the photo opens automatically.

Why we love the right button on the computer mouse

We can't say this enough: using the right button on your computer mouse always unveils an array of possibilities.

For the purpose of our current scenarios, you'll find options that will allow you to Open, View, Save, Print and more.

If you ever find yourself "lost" on how to perform some computer activity, we always suggest trying (clicking) the right button on your mouse. A majority of the time, you'll find the perfect activity you're looking for right there.

Scenario #2: You've received a photo by e-mail and want to save it

1. We assume your photo is received as an **attachment** to your e-mail.

> See "**Scenario #1**" for specifics on where to find the photo attachment.

2. Using the left button on your computer mouse, click once on that link, file or attachment.

3. While each Internet provider is different, you should receive a choice that allows you to "Save", "Save As" or "Download".

4. Where possible, we recommend you select (click) the choice that allows you to "Save As".

5. Once you've clicked on "Save As", you'll be given the opportunity to save and re-name the photo.

6. We recommend you rename the file to appropriately **identify the photo**.

> As example: "Cousin Billy in front of the Eiffel Tower"; or "Aunt Helen, Spokane, Washington". You get the idea…

An alternate way to save your photo:

1. Instead of using the left button on your computer mouse, use the right button and just click (once) on the link or attachment.

2. You'll be presented with a series of possible actions.

3. Pick (click) the one that says "Save As".

4. Again, we recommend you rename the file to appropriately identify the photo.

Why should you rename photos?

Digital cameras are machines; and, as such, when they assign a series of sequential letters and numbers to each picture. For example: 100-001_IMG, 100-002_IMG. (Remember, this is just an example, and the coding for each digital camera is different.)

Image you've just gone to Disneyland and have taken 200 pictures. Certainly the best way to find that special photo of your spouse standing alongside Mickey Mouse is by renaming the photo.

(Some of you are groaning at the thought of renaming 200 individual pictures.)

Now you can understand why there's a thriving business in computer software that will help you organize your photos – for example, Adobe Photoshop Elements.

The process remains somewhat laborious, but these types of software programs are often handy, especially as the number of pictures you take (and begin to save) increases.

Scenario #3: You've received a photo in your e-mail and want to print it

Again, an easy process…

1. First, locate your photo in the **attachment** to your e-mail.

> See "**Scenario #1**" for specifics on where to find the photo attachment.

2. Using the left button on your computer mouse, click once on that link, file or attachment.

3. While each Internet provider is different, you should receive a choice that allows you to "Print" or "Quick Print".

4. Just click on either of these options and your picture will print.

An alternate way to print your photo (you've probably already figure this out):

1. Instead of using the left button on your computer mouse, use the right button and just click (once) on the link or attachment.

2. You'll be presented with a series of possible actions.

3. Pick (click) the one that says "Print" or "Quick Print".

4. Then, voila, just head to your printer to retrieve your printed picture.

An important reminder...

Make sure your printer is turned "<u>on</u>" before you start to print.

Scenario #4: You've returned from vacation and want to download and save your pictures

In this case, digital camera manufacturers make the process (relatively) easy...

1. When you purchase your digital camera, most cameras come pre-packaged with two items:

   - A USB plug (in which one end of the plug attaches to the camera and the other end attaches to the computer).

   - Digital camera manufacturers also provide a computer disc, complete with a program to help you download and edit your pictures.

2. **Install** the software program from the computer disc onto your computer.

As a refresher: Just insert the disc into your computer tray.

All computer discs are self-loading, so the disc will automatically begin to install.

Often, you will need to answer some basic-but-dumb questions (like, "do you want to install the program?")

---

3. Attach one end of the USB plug to your camera; the other end to the USB port on your computer.

4. The program you've just installed will automatically recognize the camera and will navigate you through a series of choices to help you download and save your pictures onto your computer.

Depending on the number of pictures you've taken (and the speed of your computer), this process should take a few minutes, so have a soothing cup of tea or coffee ready just in case.

5. Once the picture has been downloaded – and you've verified that they now are located / saved onto your computer – feel free to delete the pictures from the memory card.

    (Again, make sure to verify the pictures have been saved onto your computer – there's nothing more aggravating than deleting pictures from your memory card that have not been saved.)

Scenario #5: You want to send one of your photos to a family member

> We're assuming that both you and your family members have computers and access to e-mail.
>
> If not, you might just have to print out a picture (Scenario #3) and send it by regular mail (via the post office).
>
> If the latter is the case, we might also suggest you buy them a copy of this book to help them understand this digital world we now live in.

We'll assume one of two mini-scenarios:

You've received a picture as an e-mail attachment and want to send it to a family member:

1. While each Internet provider is different, you will be offered a choice that allows you to "Forward" your e-mail.

2. Select (click) the icon or tab marked "Forward".

3. Selecting "Forward" will automatically include the photograph attachment.

4. Just type in your family member's e-mail address, then click "Send".

One cautionary word...

While selecting "Forward" automatically includes the photograph attachment, it also includes the text of the original e-mail message.

If you don't want the family member to see that original e-mail message, just delete the text in the message box. (You also have the ability to write a message of your own, if you so choose).

You've come back from vacation and want to send one of the pictures you've just taken to a family member

1. First, download / save the pictures to your computer (see Scenario #4).

2. Open your Internet provider / e-mail program and create /compose an e-mail message.

3. Type in the family member's e-mail address; **add some description in the Subject line**; and write a short note (if you so choose).

For example: "A picture from our trip to Disneyland".

Putting text in the Subject line is important because it helps the person at the other end (in this case, your family member) know what's being sent.

4. Click on the button or icon that says "Attach" or "Attach a File".

5. You've be given a navigation menu – often, on the left side of the screen – to find the correct file.

6. Pictures are generally stored in the Library marked "Pictures", so either click directly on "Pictures" or navigate by double-clicking on "Libraries", then double-click on "Pictures".

7. Depending on the number of pictures in your "Pictures" library, you might have to scroll down to find the right photo.

8. Select (click) on the picture you want to send and then click **"Open" or "Insert"**.

> The terms **"open"** or **"insert"** vary depending on our Internet provider, but they mean the same thing – they attach the photo to your e-mail.

9. Once you've inserted the picture; have inputted the family member's e-mail address; and added any message, just click "Send" and your picture will soon be received at the other end.

A look at video cameras

The **video camera** – also referred to as **camcorder** – is a way of taking "moving" pictures.

The technology for digital video cameras has improved to such a degree that some high-end models camcorders can actually rival the quality of professional film and television production.

Here are some points worth noting:

- Most regular digital cameras – especially within the middle-to-high end models – contain a "video" mode which allows you to shoot moving pictures. The quality of these moving pictures is quite good – especially if you purchase a camera that allows you to take high-definition (HD) moving pictures.

> ### Remember...
>
> Taking moving pictures from a regular camera uses up a lot of storage space. If you're planning to take moving pictures, you might want to purchase a memory card with a lot of storage space.
>
> (See our earlier section on Memory Cards. Remember, you can purchase and insert memory cards with as much as 128 GB of storage, which should be more-than-enough for even the most prolific user).

- If you're planning to take moving pictures with an eye to posting them on the Internet – for example, posting a video onto YouTube – you might want to consider pocket video cameras.

Sony and Kodak are among the manufacturers of these pocket video cameras. They are lightweight; come available in high-definition (HD) capability; and often include a UBS plug which allows you to plug the video camera directly into your computer (and upload the video instantly to the Internet).

- Finally, you can take moving pictures from a variety of camcorders. Surprisingly, these cameras aren't very expensive and many are available with high-definition (HD) capacity.

If you think you'll have a strong need to take moving pictures / videos – for example, a newborn child or a budding filmmaker in the family – than we suggest a designated video camera.

If taking videos isn't your biggest need, most people can probably make do with the "video" mode feature on standard digital cameras.

A quick lesson on picture (and computer) files

All computer files (including digital pictures) have a three or four letter extension at the end. These letter extensions are preceded by a dot or period – in other words ".doc", ".jpg", ".tiff" and so forth – and are known as a file "extension".

These extensions help the computer identify (and categorize) the types of program associated with each file.

Consider them like a telephone area code. When calling someone, you enter the area code (i.e. 212) before the actual number. With a computer file, you have (say) ".doc" at the end of the file name to identify the type of program associated with that file.

Chances are you will never see those three letters on your file name, since Windows and Mac keep those extensions "hidden" (as they don't want you changing these extensions as it confuses the computer).

Among the more common file extensions:

".doc"	Refers to Microsoft word processing files.
".wav" or ".mp3"	Refers to music files.
".bak"	Refers to backup files.
".txt"	Refers to text files.
".pdf"	Refers to portable document files (also called Adobe files).
".zip"	Refers to compressed files.

Pictures and photos also have unique file extensions. Among the most common:

".jpg"	Short for JPEG or Joint Photographic Expert Group.
".tiff"	Short for Tagged Image File Format.
".png"	Short for Portable Network Graphic.
".gif"	Short for Graphic Interchange Format.
".mpg" or ".wmv"	Short for...well, equally obtuse extensions for video files.

We could go on, but as you can see the names and initials were compiled by computer geeks (with no logic and far too much time on their hands).

You're probably asking: "So if we don't see the file extensions, why should we bother reading this?"

Unfortunately, the same computer geeks – remember them, the ones with no logic and far too much time on their hands? – are also the same geeks who write the manuals for your digital cameras.

So…if you pick up a digital camera manual, you'll undoubtedly see the terms "JPEG" files and so forth.

We just wanted to give you a little background so you can be better prepared.

Digital Cameras: At a glance

The Pros

- Most digital cameras are slim, portable and inexpensive.

- Since photos are stored on a re-recordable memory card, there is no longer the expense of buying (and developing) film.

- Digital cameras are available in a wide assortment of choices – the majority for the inexperienced-to-average user, but then ranging upwards to even the most avid professional.

- Point-and-shoot cameras are easy to use and produce excellent photos.

- The cameras that come pre-loaded onto your cell phone often produce good-to-excellent pictures; and are a wonderful way to combine two devices for the price of one.

The Cons

- While digital cameras allow you to take excellent pictures in a wide range of **settings**, these settings are sometimes "buried" in a series of menus (usually located as a button or wheel on the camera).

> Portrait photographs; pictures in low-light; wide panoramas – the list of these **settings** just goes on and on.

As a result, the learning curve to **fully understand and operate your camera** may take a while to master.

> Don't groan – this was also true with the old conventional film camera.

- In cost-cutting measures, many digital camera manufacturers only provide a basic 2-3 page "how to get started" printed brochure. The full manual – while available – is usually found in the **pre-packed computer disc**. Accessing the manual, therefore, can become awkward (and, sometimes, frustrating).

- The tiny menu settings and dials can sometimes be difficult to read (because of the small print and small screens). Make sure you get a camera whose screen size makes it easy for you to see.

The Hidden Costs

- The more pictures you take, the more cumbersome the process of organizing your photos. This often necessitates the need to purchase third-party software to help you organize and edit your photos.

Chapter 14

iPad and Tablets

Who should read this section

If you enjoy being on the leading edge of new technology.

If you would like to purchase one single easy-to-carry device that performs a myriad of functions (such as the ability to send e-mails; watch videos; read books; and much more).

Who should skip this section

If you tend to compartmentalize your entertainment needs – for example: watch movies in the movie theater; read books at home; send e-mails on your computer – and don't feel the need for yet-another device (no matter how all-in-one handy it might be).

iPad and Tablets: An overview

First, let's clarify something right off the bat: An iPad <u>is</u> a **Tablet**.

By "**tablet**" we mean tablet computer.

Tablets are mobile computers, larger than a cell phone, with a flat touch screen and primarily operated by touching the screen (and by use of a virtual onscreen keyboard).

iPad is simply the brand name that Apple uses to describe its tablet.

(This is similar to the early days of copiers when Xerox <u>meant</u> copier. In actuality, Xerox was the company brand name and was just one of many copiers. Because it was the first – and had the most high-profile visibility – people just associated the name with the function. In actuality, Xerox <u>is</u> a copier and the iPad, in actuality, <u>is</u> a tablet).

That said, we'll continue to refer to them as iPad and tablets – just to distinguish between the brands.

A closer look at the iPad

So let's start right in with the device that currently **dominates** the marketplace: the iPad.

Okay, that's no longer true...

The iPad no longer **dominates** the marketplace. Android tablets (see further below) have recently surpassed the iPad in sales.

Still, the iPad has name-recognition and, like a fading-but-still-popular movie or TV star, we've decided to give the iPad top billing.

(At least for the moment.)

Computer manufacturers – including Apple with its early-tablet incarnation called Newton MessagePad 100 – made numerous (unsuccessful) attempts to launch a computer tablet.

It wasn't until 2010, when Apple repackaged and launched the device now known as the iPad, that these devices caught on. Capitalizing on the touch-screen success of Apple's **iPhone**; and the existing seamless integration of iTunes and the iPod, the iPad became an instant success.

> See Chapter 15 for specifics on the iPhone.

So, although no longer as dominant as in years past, we'll focus on the iPad – with the understanding that many of its features are also found in other tablet computers.

Here are some key features and information:

- The device start-up is instantaneous.

- The iPad (and most tablets) contains a large 9.7" touch-screen; is 0.37 inches thick; and only weighs 1.4 pounds. In English: the iPad and tablets have a large screen – are thinner than your finger – and weigh about as much as a can of soda.

- The newest iPad has an enhanced Retina display, with a resolution that is 1 million pixels more than is found in most high-definition televisions.

- The battery is rechargeable and has a battery life of approximately **10 hours**.

> However – as most iPad users will probably agree – you should probably charge the device frequently (at least overnight) for uninterrupted flow.

- The iPad features a 5 megapixel camera (called **iSight**). Cameras and megapixels are covered in depth in our chapter on Digital Cameras (Chapter 13).

  We'll save you having to look: A 5 megapixel camera is quite respectable and can take good-to-excellent pictures. In addition, the digital camera on the iPad is also capable of taking high-definition (HD) video recordings.

- You can connect your iPad through a built-in wireless network.

- You don't need to buy a keyboard or mouse as the iPad has a built-in virtual keyboard and the movement of your finger on the glass replaces the mouse.

- The latest iPad has a Dictation feature which allows you to write an e-mail, search the Internet or create a note – all with your voice.

- You can download over **400,000** "apps" uniquely designed for the iPad. (We'll discuss this in more depth shortly).

> At the moment, there are approximately 1 million "apps" (and climbing) available on the iTunes Store. Most are for the iPhone – which can also be viewed on the iPad. The 400,000 we referenced are "apps" specifically designed to maximize the size, shape and features of the iPad.

- All iPads are controlled by a digital media center (called iTunes) that lets you purchase, organize and play your music, movies and TV shows on your computer and on your iPad.

We've discussed iTunes in depth in our discussion of the iPod in Digital Music (Chapter 12). You might take a moment to look over that section for a fuller understanding of how iTunes operates.

Meanwhile, most of you are probably already aware of a basic caveat: Yes, you'll need a computer to format, stock and organize your iPad.

Three choices fits all (for now)…

Like many other Apple products, the latest iPad has added, refined or en-hanced features from their earlier models (including a gorgeous high-reso-lution Retina screen display).

Three "choices" within the iPad:

1. All iPads contain a built-in wireless network. You can, however, purchase an iPad that contains the wireless network <u>and</u> a 4G network.

    The latter – which must be activated through your telephone provider and which requires an addition cellular monthly charge – allows you to access the iPad through a cellular network. (Not as powerful as the wireless net-work, but sometimes handy when no other connection is available).

2. While there is only one basic model of the iPad, it can, nonetheless, be purchased with various levels of storage space: 16 GB – 32 GB or 64 GB.

    For the specifics of what can be stored in these respective storage spaces, we refer you to our chart in the chapter on Digital Music (Chapter 12).

3. Finally, Apple has launched a smaller 7" version of its iPad – known as the iPad Mini – to compete with Kindle Fire and Nook Tablet (which we'll discuss towards the end of this chapter).

Apps for your iPad

We've discussed "apps" or "applications" in other sections. Since "apps" are central to the iPad, let's review some of that basic information. (Forgive us for some repetition).

So let's start off with: "what is an app?"

An "**app**" is slang: a shortened term for "**application**".

An "application" is a piece of computer software that has been designed to provide some unique service or services. These services can take the form of hobbies; special or personal interests; games; general information; and are even designed to enhance productivity at work or at home.

Some "apps" are available free of charge. Most, however, cost a nominal sum (usually between $0.99 - $9.99 each).

"Apps" are usually available for use in **computers; smartphones; televisions and digital recorders**; and, for the purpose of our current discussion: the iPad.

> We discuss "**apps**" unique to these devices in various sections throughout the book. Just check the Table of Contents.

There are over 1 million "apps" available through the iTunes store. 400,000 are unique to the iPad. Most of the remainder, while designed for the iPhone, can nonetheless be **played and viewed** on the iPad.

> Because they're designed for the smaller iPhone, they don't take advantage of the iPad's large screen and brilliant colors and resolution.
>
> In every other way, however, they still work fine on the iPad.

Most of the "apps" are designed by third-party developers (under Apple's strict guidelines).

Apple has designed certain "apps" internally – a relatively small number in comparison with the total number of "apps". Nevertheless, we'll focus on their "apps"; and, as we discuss some of these applications, they should offer you an overview of what "apps" can do (in general) and how they can be used on the iPad.

Certain "apps" come pre-installed with the iPad. Among them:

- **Safari**   This is Apple's web browser and the primary way to access the Internet on the iPad.

- **Mail**   The ability to send and receive e-mails.

- **iBooks**   An "app" to read and purchase books on the iPad.

- **Photos**   With this "app" you can view, edit and organize your photos.

- **FaceTime**   Using the iPad's built-in camera, you can place video telephone calls to your friends and family.

- **Messages**   Let's you send text messages to anyone with an iPhone or an iPad.

That's just a sampling. Other pre-installed "apps" include ways to access video, music, magazines, your calendar and contacts, YouTube and much more.

All the above "apps" are free and most come pre-installed.

Additional "apps"

Apple also offers a series of "apps" for work productivity, call iWorks. Among the applications are Pages (a word processor to write letters, flyers, reports and more); Keynote (a program that allows you to create, deliver and share presentations) and Numbers (a program designed to create and edit your spreadsheets). These programs are obtained via the Apple Apps Store and run $9.99 each.

Other "apps" available from Apple – which also must be purchased, but which cost far less than the iWorks programs – allow photo editing (iPhoto); movie editing (iMovie); the ability to play and record music (Garage Band); view movie trailers (iTunes Movie Trailer); and access to the world's largest catalog of free educational content (iTunes U).

These are just some highlights, but we think you can see the wide range of possibilities that can be accessed via the iPad.

How to setup and synchronize your iPad

Here's a quick step-by-step on how to setup and synchronize your iPad:

1. Download iTunes onto your computer first (refer to our section on iTunes in Chapter 12).

2. Connect the USB Cable that each iPad includes in its packaging – one end goes into your computer, the other end connects directly into your iPod.

3. Once the USB Cable is properly connected, your iPad will automatically synchronize with your iTunes.

4. Once synchronized, you'll see the entry for your iPad under "Devices" on the far-right button (right next to the "iTunes Store" button).

5. Select (click) on the iPad under "Devices".

6. You'll find the **iPad Summary** dominating the center of your screen.

> Within the **iPad Summary**, you'll find basic information about your iPad (including the serial number) and a series of options on how to connect and manage your iPad.

7. In addition, on the menu bar at the upper center of the screen, you'll find a series of tabs:

    *   Summary   Includes the ability to backup (save) contents on the iPad.

    *   Info   Helps you sync your calendar and contacts

    *   Apps   Helps you organize and move your "apps".

- Music   Allows you to sync your music and playlists.

- Movies   Allows you to select movies to view on your iPad.

- TV Shows   Allows you to select TV Shows to view on your iPad.

- Podcasts   Allows you to select and sync podcasts for your iPad.

- Books   Allows you to select and sync books for your iPad.

- Photos   Allows you to organize photos and videos for your iPad.

- On This iPad   Shows the entire content on this particular iPad.

(While there are sections for "apps", music and movies, you will need to purchase the actual items themselves from the iTunes store in order for them to show up).

We recommend you review these various tabs and adjust / tweak your iPad to what works best for you.

8. Finally, once the iPad is adjusted (synchronized) with your ideal settings, just unplug the device from the computer and away you go.

iPad: At a glance

The Pros

- Thin, lightweight and portable.

- A self-contained "entertainment" center with the ability to read books, watch movies, check your e-mail and much more.

- Availability of hundreds of thousands of "apps" to enhance entertainment and productivity.

- The ability to check e-mail and search the Internet, all while on-the-go.

The Cons

- Despite the "wow" factor, the iPad remains a portable middle-of-the-road device. If your emphasis is on work productivity, you'd probably be better off with a laptop. If your emphasis is on taking pictures, a digital camera would be better. If your emphasis is on entertainment, most television sets would fit the bill. You get the general idea.

  Still, if you're looking for something that does a little of everything, the iPad could be tailor-made for you.

- The virtual keyboard for the iPad takes some getting used to (and leaves much to be desired).

- Although there are hundreds of thousands of "apps" available, finding the best ones – to say nothing of the "apps" that are just right for you – is a daunting (and mysterious) task.

The Hidden Costs

- Feeding your iPad habit can become costly. What we mean is that purchasing movies, television episodes, music, books and "apps" for your iPad can add up – and, as we've discovered, those purchases can become addictive.

A look at other tablets

Although Apple's iPad was the first on the marketplace, competitors abound and Apple's once-insurmountable lead has eroded (with Android tablets now taking the lead in sales).

Every major digital manufacturer – Sony, Samsung, Hewlett-Packard, Dell, Asus, even Microsoft…the list goes on and on – are all developing tablets to compete with the iPad.

Naturally, the question becomes: how can I choose from all these other tablets?

Distinguishing between these various types of tablets lies within their underlying *operating systems*.

At the moment, three types of operating systems dominate the landscape. Here's a look at the three systems along with some of their advantages and disadvantages.

Apple's operating system (called iOS)

Apple's operating system runs the iPad, the iPhone and iPod Touch and, as such, is one of the most popular mobile operating systems on the market (and has been proven reliable by millions of satisfied users).

Among the advantages: this system has a very large "apps" store selection and is ideal for **games and media playback**. There is also a seamless integration with other Apple products, such as Apple TV, the Mac computer and so forth.

> We've covered most of this in our iPad section, so just refer to the information provided in the previous pages.

Among the disadvantages: the operating system only functions on Apple hardware. Also, the operating system lacks **Adobe Flash** compatibility. As such, you can see many of the videos posted on the web (but, unfortunately, not all).

> **Adobe Flash** is a widespread multimedia application that delivers animation, video and interactivity to web pages.
>
> Flash is gradually being replaced by a new format HTML5, supported by most operating systems – notably for our conversation, Apple's operating system for the iPad.
>
> While HTML5 and its future incarnations may ultimately dominate the market, Adobe Flash can still be found and, as such, is not compatible with Apple's iPad, iPhone and iTouch.

Google's Android operating system (called Android)

You may be familiar with Google's Android operating system (often referred to as Android OS) from its advertisements. Smartphones running Android OS have become among the biggest competitors to Apple's iPhone.

The Android OS has spread to the tablet marketplace and has gained the same popularity it mustered with the smartphone (supplanting Apple's iOS for the lead in sales). Android OS can be found on tablets manufactured by Sony, Samsung, Toshiba and more.

Advantages: There is a large variety of "apps" and the start-up boot time is very quick. Android OS supports a broad range of hardware and has a seamless integration with Google services (Google Search, Maps, E-mail and so forth).

Disadvantages: At the moment, many Android features are more suited for smartphones than tablets; there are compatibility issues from manufacturer to manufacturer; and its entertainment (media and gaming) content isn't yet on pace with Apple.

Microsoft Windows' operating system (called Windows)

Currently, Microsoft Windows' operating system dominates the computer marketplace. The same, however, cannot be said for the tablet marketplace.

The current operating system, Windows 8, allows for touch screen for tablets and phones. In fact, Microsoft has released its own tablet, known as "Surface". Windows operating systems can also be found on tablets manufactured by Lenovo, Archos, Asus and others.

Advantages: Most people who use computers are familiar with the Windows landscape and interface. Windows is ideal for multitasking and is compatible with a wide range of software and hardware.

Disadvantages: Currently, Windows 8 on the tablet's touch screen takes some getting used to. In addition, Windows has a (slightly) longer **boot time**, especially when compared with Apples iOS and the Android operating system (see above).

> "**Boot time**" is the amount of time it takes to start up your device – which, for the iPad and Android tablets is near-instantaneous.

Two other tablets of note

Finally, we'll point out two other devices that started out as digital e-readers, but which are fast becoming inexpensive, user-friendly tablets: **Amazon's Kindle Fire** and **Barnes & Noble's Nook Tablet**.

> We've already mentioned these devices in our chapter on digital books / e-readers (see Chapter 11 for details).

Since both devices are hybrids – straddling the line between digital e-reader and tablet – we'll lump their pros and cons together.

Advantages: The price. Both the Kindle Fire and Nook Tablet are less expensive than most tablets on the marketplace.

The Kindle Fire has the clout of the Amazon store which certainly rivals – and in many areas exceeds – the Apple online storefront.

With its recent business venture with Microsoft, the Barnes & Noble Nook Tablet is now poised to join the other tablets in the competitive race with the iPad. (Although, if you've been keeping up with the business news, their competitive climb has been extremely laborious.)

Disadvantages: The major disadvantage that both devices face is that they were originally designed as e-readers and, despite great strides to function as a tablet; they still find themselves slightly behind the Android-based tablets and well-behind the Apple iPad.

Still, as we've tried to stress throughout the chapter, changes and innovations in this arena are occurring at a furious pace and the ability to predict the leader in another year or two is still up-in-the-air.

One final look

If you're looking to purchase an iPad or tablet, here's a **quick assessment**:

> **A disclaimer**: Our assessment is highly subjective and, given the rapid changes in technology for these devices, this assessment might change (say) tomorrow.

- You probably can't go wrong with the Apple iPad – especially if you have compatible devices for phone (iPhone) or music (iPod / iPod Touch) and are therefore familiar with iTunes and Apple's synching. It's been proven (and vetted) by millions of users.

- Tablets run on the Android operating system are closer in look and feel to the iPad. Since tablets vary from manufacturer to manufacturer, you might want to check them out (personally) or get a recommendation from a (reliable) friend or family member.

- Microsoft Windows will always be a factor (and, for some, a favorite), but they're current running a distant third in the tablet arena. If Windows 8 can be revamped to compete with the Apple iOS and Android OS, Microsoft may carve out a higher share of the market. At the moment, however, that's not the case.

- Don't discount the Amazon Kindle Fire or Barnes & Noble Nook Tablet. While a hybrid between a digital e-reader and digital tablet, they are nonetheless quite inexpensive and can certainly satisfy the average, less-demanding consumer. Remember, too, Apple has its 7" iPad "Mini" to compete with these devices.

Ultrabook – Touch screen - Tablet

A new variation of the traditional laptop has recently hit the marketplace and will only increase in functionality and gain further popularity over the next few years:

Currently known as the **Ultrabook** – although we suspect this generic name will change as manufacturers create new names to carve out their own brand identity – this laptop has the following key features:

- Super thin

- Extremely lightweight

- Has a touch screen

- Most have (or will soon have) a swivel hinge that rotates the touch screen to form into a tablet.

This laptop is a three-in-one hybrid with the full power of a traditional laptop; the flexibility of a touch screen device; and the portability of an iPad / Tablet.

We wouldn't be surprised if these Ultrabook - Tablet devices become the wave of the future.

Chapter 15

Cell Phones

Who should read this section

If you already have a cell phone, but are confused or intimidated by the new features on the next generation of cell phones, we'll guide your way through them.

If the only phone you have is the one in your home (your "landline"), it might be time to see what's available and how the new generations of cell phones can add to the quality of your life.

If you're unsure of the meaning of the term "smartphone", we'll give you the latest "411".

Who should skip this section

If you've already gone through a number of smartphones and understand the nuances between cell phone carrier services, you're ready for the master class (and can probably skip this section).

The Cell Phone: An overview

> We've seen it spelled "**cell phone**" and "**cellphone**".
>
> At the moment – according to most American dictionaries – cell phone (with a space) is the accepted and preferred spelling.
>
> Still, if you use the other spelling "cellphone", people will certainly know what you mean.
>
> (As an aside, Australian dictionaries have both spellings listed.)

Of all the devices that are covered in this book, the cell phone is probably the single device that is at once the most understood / most confusing; the most appreciated / most defiled of them all.

If you still tend to think of your cell phone as, well, just a phone, you might want to reconsider. Here are some features your cell phone can do for you:

- Alarm clock

- Calendar

- E-mail and Internet access

- Texting and instant messaging capability

- Tip calculator

- Measure your walking steps

We love statistics – that's actually a sarcastic statement since statistics can be manipulated in so many ways. For our purposes:

- Over 90% of Americans use (or at least own) a cell phone.

- 19% of people drop their cell phone down the **toilet**.

> Whether accidentally or on purpose is probably up for debate.

- Nearly 50% of people who use mobile phones have "smartphones" (which we'll discuss shortly).

- Over 25% of American households have a cell phone only (no landline phone).

The gist of the statistics: just about everyone in America has a cell phone.

Given that most of you know something about telephones, here are some words we'll be bantering back and forth throughout the chapter:

Landline telephone (also known as a fixed line, dedicated line)

A **landline telephone** refers to a phone which uses a solid telephone line – such as a wire or fiber optic cable – for **transmission** (to send or receive calls).

This is distinguished from a mobile phone (discussed in the next paragraph) which uses radio waves for transmission.

Mobile phone (also known as cellular phone or cell phone)

This is the device that can make (and receive) telephone calls over a **radio link** while moving around a wide geographic area.

> We won't get technical. Telephone use a **radio link protocol** (RLP) to send and receive calls.
>
> In English: we usually just call these wireless or cellular networks.

In addition to sending and receiving calls, modern mobile phones also support a wide variety of other services such as text messaging; e-mail; Internet access, short-range wireless communication (infrared, Bluetooth), business applications; gaming and photography. All of which we'll cover in this chapter.

> ### Are cordless telephones "mobile" phones?
>
> The short answer is "no".
>
> Cordless telephones rely on a fixed base station (the landline) and can only operate within a short range (feet or yards as compared with the cell phone's ability to span the globe).
>
> Technically, the cordless telephone uses a "wireless" connection from the handset to the base, but don't misconstrue the language on the box – this isn't a mobile cell phone.

There are two types of mobile / cell phones:

Feature phone

Since feature phones account for approximately 60% of the cell phone market share, if you have a cell phone and aren't sure what kind – chances are, you're using a feature phone.

Feature phones, while not considered as smartphones (see below), nevertheless have features and functions over and above standard mobile services. Generally, they are intended for customers who want a lower-price phone with some – but not all – of the features of a smartphone.

Much as we'd like to refer to these as "dumb" phones – to distinguish from smartphones (below) – that's hardly the case.

For example, today's feature phones typically can connect to the Internet and has capabilities such as a camera, touchscreen, GPS navigation, music player and much more.

(What might have been considered a smartphone ten years ago is now considered standard on most feature phones today).

Smartphone

The main distinction between smartphones and feature phones is in the range of options and "apps" available.

Since "apps" are central to smartphones, here's a quick review:

We'll start off with (again): "what is an app?"

An "**app**" is slang: a shortened term for "**application**".

An "application" is a piece of computer software that has been designed to provide some unique service or services. These services can take the form of hobbies; special or personal interests; games; general information; and are even designed to enhance productivity at work or at home.

Some "apps" are available free of charge. Most, however, cost a nominal sum (usually between $0.99 - $9.99 each).

"Apps" are usually available via **computers; iPads and tablets; televisions and digital recorders**; and, for the purpose of our current discussion: the smartphone.

> We discuss "**apps**" unique to these devices in various sections throughout the book. Just check the table of content.

Over a million "apps" are available – most accessed through your smartphone manufacturer or providers such as Apple, Amazon and more.

(We suggest taking a look at Chapter 14 on "iPad and Tablets" which will give you sense of what some of those applications can do.)

Most smartphone "apps" are designed by third-party developers (under smartphone manufacturer's strict guidelines).

We'll give you a more in-depth depth look at the features that are available on most smartphones and feature phones. For the moment, let's just cover one more important area: your cell phone *provider*.

A few words about your cell phone provider

No matter what type of cell phone you might have – whether a feature phone or smartphone – there's one inescapable fact: you can only get **service** through the telephone company.

> This service is referred by a slew of names: often called **"cell phone service"** or **"service provider"** or **"cell phone carrier"** or **"phone company"** or some similar combination. They all stand for your local telephone company.

Before we continue, we have one personal disclaimer: we hate the phone company.

Okay, "hate" is perhaps too strong a word, but we're not enamored with any company that keeps its rates hidden from the consumer. Phone companies have an endless variety of "plans" involving minutes used; minutes used to other cell phones; minutes used to family members; minutes used after 5:00 pm (except for calls occurring within the state of Wyoming).

We're joking, but you get the idea. Yet until phone companies explain their plans and policies to their customers in ways that are easy to understand, we'll stay true to our personal opinion.

Among the major cell phone companies (known as **"carriers"**):

- ATT

- Verizon

- T-Mobile

- Sprint

There are a number of other carriers and local services, but we've just highlighted the largest ones.

Cell phone providers usually package their plans in three ways:

- **Voice**: This is for the phone calls made and received.

- **Data**: This is for the amount / volume of access to the Internet; sending and receiving of data or document; and downloads (music, movies, "apps")

- **Messaging**: Usually designated for text messages.

Okay, what's the difference between "text message" and "e-mail"?

In theory, there's very little difference:

Text messages originate from a cell phone (and are usually sent to another cell phone).

E-mails originate from an Internet provider / e-mail account – for example, Yahoo, Outlook, Gmail, AOL, MSN and the like – and are generally sent to another Internet provider / e-mail account.

Very simplistically: think of "text messages" as a message going from one cell phone to another; think of "e-mails" as a message going from one e-mail account to another.

On provider data plans which include Internet access, you would be able to send and receive both e-mails and texts on your phone.

We've already expressed our personal opinions about cell phone companies, so we won't go through another tirade. Here's our suggestion on how to get the best deals possible:

- We're a big fan of ***Consumer Reports*** magazine which tends to offer periodic issues with thorough-and-unbiased assessments of cell phone providers and their various plans. They generally assess the phone companies' service on a regional or state-by-state basis.

> Chances are many of you are not regular subscribers to ***Consumer Reports***. Fear not. Most local libraries carry back issues of the magazine.

- We also suggest you place multiple calls to the phone company – making sure you get a different representative each time you call. (Ask each representative about their "best" plans. You'll be surprised at the number of choices you're given. Just keep calling until you get a 'general consensus'.)

One large caveat…

When it comes to cell phones and cell phone carriers, one size does <u>not</u> fit all.

For example, if you had purchased an early iPhone, the only carrier available was ATT. (Newer models of the iPhone can now access the other carriers). To be on the safe side, check the cell phone model to determine which provider it can access.

Chicken or the egg?

You can either shop for a phone first (and then you're stuck with whichever carrier they can accommodate); or you can search for the best carrier in your city / state (and then seek out the best cell phone that the particular carrier supports).

We actually recommend the latter.

There's nothing worse than purchasing a new cell phone only to discover the service you're stuck with is horrid.

Better to research the best carrier for those areas where you live, work and play and purchase a cell phone accordingly.

What are the essential differences between cell phones?

You've seen the ads and probably have loads of questions. Among them: are you better off getting an Apple iPhone or are Android phones better?

Come to think of it: what's the difference?

The essential difference between cell phones lies within their underlying operating systems.

We've discussed operating systems in our last chapter on iPads and Tablets (Chapter 14), but we feel that a review at this juncture would be worthwhile.

At the moment, three types of operating systems dominate the landscape. Here's a look at these three systems along with some of their advantages and disadvantages.

Apple's operating system (called iOS)

Apple's operating system runs the iPhone (as well as the iPad and iPod Touch) and is one of the most popular mobile operating systems on the market (with proven reliability by millions of satisfied users).

Among the advantages, this system has a very large "apps" store selection. In fact, hundreds of thousands of "apps" have been created specifically for the iPhone. There is also a seamless integration with other Apple products, such as iPad, Apple TV and so forth so you can use most of your apps on each of the devices without any extra charge.

Among the disadvantages: the operating system only functions on Apple hardware. Also, the operating system lacks **Adobe Flash** compatibility. As such, you can see many of the videos posted on the web (but not all of them).

> **Adobe Flash** is a multimedia application that delivers animation, video and interactivity to web pages.
>
> Flash is gradually being replaced by a new format HTML5, supported by most operating systems – notably for our conversation, Apple's operating system for the iPad.
>
> While HTML5 and its future incarnations may ultimately dominate the market, Adobe Flash can still be found and, as such, are not compatible with Apple's iPad, iPhone and iTouch.

Google's Android operating system

Smartphones running on Google's Android operating system (often referred to as **Android OS**) have become among the biggest competitors to Apple's iPhone. In fact – depending on which statistics you opt for – Android smartphones have surpassed the iPhones in sales and Internet traffic.

Advantages: There is a large variety of "apps" available for Android smartphones and the start-up / boot time is very quick. Android OS supports a broad range of models and has a seamless integration with Google services (Google Search, Maps, E-mail and so forth).

Disadvantages: Certainly, its entertainment (media and gaming) content isn't yet on par with Apple.

Microsoft Windows' operating system (also known as Windows Mobile or Windows Phone)

While Microsoft Windows' operating system dominates the computer marketplace, the same cannot be said within the smartphone marketplace.

Advantages: Most people who use computers are familiar with the Windows landscape and interface. Windows is ideal for multitasking and is compatible with a wide range of software and hardware.

Disadvantages: While Microsoft's latest operating system works well with the smartphone's touch screen, the new Windows 8 takes a little getting used to – especially for the Windows user used to earlier releases. In addition, Windows has a longer **boot time**, especially when compared with Apples iOS and the Android operating systems.

> "**Boot time**" refers to the amount of time it takes to start up your device – which, for the iPad and Android tablets is near-instantaneous.

Features you can find in your cell phones

Whether you own (or plan on owning) a smartphone or feature phone – and the line of distinction between them is blurring with every new cell phone model and upgrade – they all have features and capabilities that are worth noting.

We'll give you an overview of some of these features. Remember, these features aren't found on all cell phones, so compare the individual models to make sure they have what you want:

Keyboard

All phones have some type of keyboard. There are three types of keyboards:

1. **The basic keyboard is the phone pad itself**. Although we use the word "basic", this is perhaps the most difficult keyboard to use, since typing often means you hit a key anywhere from 1-6 times to reach the right letter or symbol.

2. **The phone incorporates an actual physical keyboard**. These are a little handier – at least if you type an "a", you get an "a" – but to use these physical keyboards you need fingers as small as Munchkins. Accurate but cumbersome.

3. **The phone has a "virtual keyboard"**. Virtual keyboards are becoming the most prevalent type of keyboard available on smartphones.

> **"Virtual keyboard"**. A picture of a keyboard is displayed onto the screen – in this case, the screen of a smartphone – and you then touch the key / the letter in order to type and enter text.

Virtual keyboards come built-in with touch-screen smartphones. A virtual keyboard appears on your phone's screen every time you prepare to type. Like the physical keyboards (in example #2), they're handy, but because of the small keys, somewhat cumbersome.

Also, because the keys are virtual and can't be accessed by "touch" like with a physical keyboard, **you need to stop whatever you're doing to look at the keyboard in order to type**. A minor-to-major annoyance.

> This, in case you're wondering, is one of the primary reasons why so many automobile accidents occur when people are driving and "texting".

Camera

All smartphones come equipped with a camera. As we've discussed in our chapter on digital cameras (Chapter 13), built-in cell phone cameras shouldn't be scoffed at as they produce high quality pictures and videos that rival many digital stand-alone cameras.

Internet access

All smartphones allow you to access the Internet.

> **Why would I need to access the Internet?**
>
> First things first: you don't "need" to access the Internet.
>
> That out of the way, sometimes the ability to access the Internet is quite handy. For example, if you're looking for the specific address of a restaurant; or are in the middle of argument about which actor starred in a particular film.
>
> Cell phones give us the ability to call people while on the road. Smartphones increase our functionality with access to the Internet.

E-mail and text messaging (also known as "texting")

Another handy feature for all smartphones is the ability to access your e-mails (via your e-mail account) as well as to send and receive messages directly from phone to phone ("**texting**").

Much like whether you need to access the Internet or not, the ability to send messages or access your e-mails is a personal decision. Still, this capability is one more useful tool for the smartphone and untethers you from computer-based tasks.

"Apps"

The bread-and-butter of the smartphone is the ability to access "apps". We've already discussed this earlier in the chapter, as well in Chapter 7 on Television and Chapter 14 on iPads and Tablets, so we won't go into as much detail here.

We'll cite just one handy free "app": Yelp. Available at yelp.com or by searching an apps store, Yelp gives people's reviews of restaurants, businesses even medical providers. If you're looking for something in your neighborhood, chances are Yelp can provide you with some insight into the goods or services being offered. A handy "app" indeed.

Other "apps" include GPS navigation, the ability to watch movies, television shows and even read books. Some are conducive to the small smartphone screen. Many are not. Eventually, often (unfortunately) through trial-and-error, you'll find just the right "apps" that suit your needs.

Voice activation

Several of the new smartphones – notably new releases of Apple's iPhone and Samsung's Galaxy – allow the user to ask the smartphone questions.

At the moment, accurate responses are more a function of the simplicity of the question (for example, "what is the weather in London?") and the vote is still out whether they are more a novelty than useful tool. As the technology improves, however, voice activation might become a handy feature and one worth considering.

An apology to my wife (and, by extension, to many of our readers)

My wife was very excited about our chapter on cell phones. At last, she thought, someone will give her step-by-step instructions on how to add a Contact to the Address Book; or we would show her how to quickly retrieve Recently Used phone numbers.

Alas, these instructions won't be forthcoming.

As we discovered in researching a myriad of different cell phones, each manufacturer has its own unique way of accessing contacts, the address book, recent calls, and so forth.

So, unfortunately, there's no way around it: you'll have to read the cell phone manual (a nightmare, we admit). Some sellers of cell phones provide free in-person classes to help you get acquainted with your smartphone. Also remember that a wide variety of YouTube videos exist on smartphone topics.

We can only make one suggestion: When you purchase a new phone – and statistics indicate that people obtain a new cell phone every two years – you might want to stick with the same brand (especially if you're already happy with the phone and the service).

In this way, by selecting the same brand, accessing most of the common features should remain the same.

A few tips and techniques you might be interested in

While each smartphone is different, we'll try to give you some general guidelines:

How to send someone a text message (from your phone to their phone)

1. Get the person's cell phone number. (We suggest you store the number in your smartphone, rather than trying to remember the number each time.)

2. Go to your phone's "Menu". Look for "Messages" or "SMS". Depending on your phone, that choice might be prominent on your main menu.

"**SMS**" stands for **Short Messaging Service**".

Remember, you might want to identify yourself by including your name at the end of any text message (since the person receiving your text might not recognize you from your phone number alone).

---

3. Select "Create Message" (or some variation in order to create a new message).

4. In the "To" box, enter the person's telephone number.

   Some phones will take you to the "Text" box first (see #5 below for instructions) and will ask for the person's telephone number when you're ready to send the text.

5. In the "Text" box, type the message you want to send.

   Typing can be easy or frustrating depending on your phone. As we've pointed out, phones will either have a keypad or keyboard (physical or virtual).

   Most smartphones contain a built-in virtual keyboard, while a handful of phones have an actual physical keyboard. If you have one of those two options, typing should be easy – just start tapping the appropriate alpha-numerical keys.

6. Once you've typed in the message, just select "Send". (On some phones, you might have to choose "Options" first and then choose "Send".)

How to receive your e-mails on your smartphone

We're just going to give you general guidelines here, not a step-by-step – although we'll tell you where to get those step-by-step instructions:

1. Refresh your memory about the name of your **Internet Provider**. You could have a Google Gmail account; a Yahoo account; a Microsoft Hotmail or Outlook account; or some account based on your telephone or cable provider.

> Take a look back at the chapter on e-mails (Chapter 6) for a refresher.

2. Go the Internet Provider's website. For our example, we'll use Google Gmail – which would be www.gmail.com.

3. Enter your user name and password.

4. Go to "Settings".

5. You'll find a tab marked "Forwarding and **POP / IMAP**".

> **"POP"** stands for Post Office Protocol while **IMAP** stands for Internet Message Access Protocol.
>
> In English: These are formats by which you can download messages from your Internet Provider's services onto your computer or mobile devices.

(If you can't find this easily on other Internet Providers, try using the "Help" feature. Search for "Email forwarding", "Forwarding", "POP" or "IMAP". One of these should get you to the same place.)

6. Select the tab. You're looking for a section marked "Configuration" or "Configuration Instructions". In our example, it is located half-way down the center of the page.

   If you're uncertain, there are links for "help" or "learn more" which will give you more detail.

7. Select the appropriate configuration instructions. You might have (say) an Apple phone or Android smartphone, There are specific-yet-separate configurations for each device.

8. Each configuration has step-by-step instructions.

   Once you've located the configuration for your device, we suggest you print out these instructions.

9. Now go back to your smartphone and follow the step-by-step instructions.

10. Once you're done, you'll be able to receive (and send) your e-mails directly from your smartphone.

How to access a QR Code

Okay, first things first – what's a QR Code?

QR Code stands for **Quick Response Code**. Those are barcode-like images that have been popping up for the last few years in magazine ads, product shelves, billboards and so forth. (If you've seen them in magazines, they're usually about one inch square and look like a mass of squiggles).

These QR Codes provide information, coupons, images, videos and so forth and can be accessed through your smartphone or tablet.

QR Codes are usually connected with a product and are advertising or marketing specific. On occasion, a QR Code might be found on a business card and would give you additional information about the person (and company).

You'll need an application to be able to "read" your QR Code, but here's the easy step-by-step:

1. Start up your smartphone.

2. Go to your smartphone's "App" store.

3. Search for – and download – a QR Reader "app". The "app" is free and should be easy to locate.

4. Once you've downloaded the app, start it up.

5. Just point your smartphone's camera lens at the QR Code and, presto, you'll be taken to the endless world of advertising and promotions.

Deposit a check to your bank (using your smartphone)

Many banking institutions now allow you to deposit your check into your bank account using your smartphone.

The process is easy (and secure). Again, you'll need an application for your smartphone, but here's the easy step-by-step:

1. Identify your banking institution and double-check to make sure your bank (and account) can handle **mobile check deposits**.

> Also referred to as "**RDS**" or **Remote Deposit Service**.

You'll need to sign up for your bank's online service first. Specifically, you'll need a name and password to log into your account (see #7 below).

2. Start up your smartphone.

3. Go to your smartphone's "App" store.

4. Search for – and download – your **bank's** mobile "app". The "app" is free and should be easy to locate.

> At the moment, Chase is the leader, followed by Bank of America and others. You'd look to download your bank's specific mobile "app".
>
> For Steps #5 – 12, we'll use the Chase "app" as our model.

5. Once you've downloaded the app, start it up.

6. Once the app opens, you'll be asked to log into your bank account.

   On your first log-in to your bank's app, you will also need to verify your smartphone. The bank, in turn, will send you a code – usually eight digits or so sent via text or voicemail – which you will then need to enter into the Identification Code box in your log-in sequence.

7. Once you've logged into your account, select "Deposit". (Again, you'll need to sign-up and click the terms and conditions).

8. Select your account and enter the amount of the check.

9. You'll be asked to take a picture of the front and back of the check.

10. When you select the front of the check, make sure that the entire check is framed by your smartphone's camera.

    (You are recommended to place the check on a flat surface and take the picture from above. The image must be clear, not blurry.)

11. Once the check is framed properly, tap the "Camera" icon in the application. You'll be shown an image of the check. If complete and you can "Use" the image, the app will take a picture of the check.

12. Repeat the process (#11 and #12) for the rear of the check – which must be endorsed.

13. You'll then be taken to a verification page. If everything meets your specifications, you can "Submit" the deposit to the bank. (Banks usually recommends that you hang onto your check for approximate 15 days.)

As you can see, somewhat cumbersome at the moment; but we suspect the process will simplify as more people utilize this service.

Smartphones: At a glance

The Pros

- With over 90% of Americans already owning a cell phone, upgrading to a smartphone – with its wider array of features – makes sense.

- The ability to access the Internet and check your e-mail – anywhere, anytime – makes your life more portable and time-efficient.

- Although the size of its small screen is a factor, a smartphone's self-contained "entertainment" center – with the ability to read books, watch movies, check your e-mail and much more – is a plus.

- Hundreds of thousands of "apps" available to enhance entertainment and productivity. The smartphone untethers you from functions you might previously have needed a computer or laptop for.

- Easy to operate camera; photo access; and the ability increase the size of photos by **touch-screen**.

> You actually "**pinch**" your fingers directly on the photo.
>
> You **pinch** your fingers together to **shrink** the photo; and **separate (widen)** your fingers to increase the size of the picture.

The Cons

- Unfortunately, owning a smartphone – or any cell phone for that matter – puts you always within reach. We suggest turning off your phone during part of the day or, dare we suggest, leave your phone at home. "Disconnecting" from the world for a few hours at a time can reduce stress.

- Given smartphones' wide array of features, the "learning curve" to fully understanding and operate your phone can take a while.

- Smartphones are more expensive than many feature phones.

- Because of its array of features, smartphones also utilize data and messaging plans that increases the basic monthly cost.

The Hidden Costs

- Feeding your smartphone habit can become expensive. Purchasing movies, television episodes, music, books and "apps" can add up. Still, the **all-in-one** features of the smartphone can help you save money by not purchasing an array of other digital devices.

> Accessing the Internet; obtaining your e-mail; utilizing "apps"; ability to watch movies and read books; these are all part of the all-in-one features a smartphone can provide.

Chapter 16

Games

Who should read this section

Anyone who wants to understand why games dominate computers, cell phones, iPads and tablets, even social media sites such as Facebook.

Also, if you want to understand why video games often financially out-perform many motion pictures box office receipts, then you might want to read this chapter.

Surprisingly, while the statistics are close, there are more people over 50-years old playing video games (or **"gamers"** as they're referred to) than gamers under 18.

Who should skip this section

If you have no interest in video games – of any sort – then just skip this chapter. (We'll keep this chapter short, however, just in case you want a quick look.)

Basic information about "gaming" and the gaming industry

A video game is an electronic game that involved human interaction – yes, that means "you" – through a **user interface**, all to generate movement and action on a **video screen**.

> "**User Interface**". This could be as simple as a computer, mouse and keyboard to more sophisticated devices with an array of buttons and even a joystick (which looks remarkably like the control lever in an airplane cockpit).

> "**Video Screen**". Sometimes, it is your computer monitor. More often, it can be on hand-held devices like your phone, iPad or tablet; or, for full visual effects, your television screen.

Games have come a long way since shuffling a deck of cards and playing solitaire.

- The animation within video games is sharp, clear and surprisingly life-like. In many ways, it rivals motion picture quality.

- The sound (voices, sound effects and so forth) for most games will even give the most discerning audiophile pause.

- You can move your character – usually the game's hero or anti-hero – quite effortlessly.

- Movement and action within the game flows seamlessly. You feel like you're in the middle of a movie.

- You can even play games online…competing with other players around the world.

Let's go back to statistics for a moment – with our usual warning that statistics can often be manipulated. Much of this information was gleaned from reports a year ago, so you should adjust (upwards) accordingly:

- Over 67% of households in the United States play video games.

- 40% of all gamers are female.

- Video game revenue for consoles (which we'll discuss shortly) declined slightly, while gaming for **mobile devices** – cell phones, smartphones, iPads and tablets – and at **social network sites** – Facebook being the most notable – increased significantly.

Console games versus hand-held games

In simple terms, you can play video games on a computer or a **gaming console**; or while on-the-go using hand-held devices such as your phone, iPad or tablet; or even portable gaming devices, which are miniature on-the-go versions of their larger console counterparts (see below).

> A "**gaming console**" is a stand-along device – devoted primarily (but not exclusively) to games – that you plug into your television or monitor.
>
> Newer gaming consoles can also play movies, including Blu-ray discs, and can connect to the Internet for online gaming.

Here's a quick overview:

Computers

This one's easy:

1. You can purchase a video game in a store (boxed) or download it directly from the dealer's website.

2. Assuming you purchase in a box, you'll be given a DVD (and, thankfully, instructions).

3. Just insert the DVD into the computer tray and the **installation will automatically initiate**.

> This installation is called "**the setup**".

4. This process will probably take a few minutes – and you'll probably have to click "Next" and "Yes" a bunch of times – but in the end, the program is loaded onto your computer. Most-often, the game will open upon completion.

5. In the future, just double-click on the game icon –usually the program automatically sets an icon with the name and picture of the video game on your computer desktop – and away you go.

6. If you download the video game directly from the Internet to your computer, you'll be asked to "run" the program. Click "yes" or "okay" and the program will automatically download and install. From here, go to step #4 above and continue in the same manner.

Consoles

There are three major / best-selling game consoles:

Sony PlayStation

> They continually come out with new models. As the moment, the latest **PlayStation** is referred to as PS3 (with PS4 due out shortly)..
>
> The portable hand-held PlayStations are called PSP Go or PSP 3000.

Nintendo Wii

Pronounced "**whee**"…

The current model is simply **Nintendo Wii**, recently upgraded to Wii U (as in "whee you").

The portable hand-held models are Nintendo 3DS, DSi. DS Lite, and DSi XL. (As you can see, Nintendo has a variety of hand-held models).

Microsoft X-Box 360

Referred currently as **Xbox 360** (soon to be upgraded as **Xbox One**).

Microsoft has no hand-held models.

Each player device manufacturer sells video games configured expressly for their consoles. Unfortunately, they are not compatible with one another, so you can't use the game from Sony PlayStation on either Nintendo or Microsoft's consoles.

Some games are packaged in a variety of forms such as DVD discs or cartridges. The console manufacturers place their company brand name and logo prominently on each game, so there's no chance you can mistake which game goes with which console.

How to set up the console and play games

1. First, connect the console to either your computer or television.

2. Each console's plug-in is slightly different, but most new consoles allow you to hook up their device to the computer or television using an **HDMI cable**, the best plug for high definition.

> If you're drawing a blank, review the section on **HDMI ports and plugs** (Chapter 1).

This is a fairly common cable for all new televisions and computers, so you should have no difficulty accessing one.

3. Once you've hooked up your console, you're ready to install the video game.

4. Insert the DVD or disc or cartridge into the console. The game will automatically load and away you go.

A few console / video game features worth noting

- Most of the best-selling games are available in high-definition or Blu-ray formats, providing state-of-the-art clarity and movement – especially when seen in conjunction with a wide-screen television.

- Many consoles allow you to both play DVDs and Blu-Ray discs, enabling the console to be used for dual purposes (instead of purchasing a separate DVD or Blu-ray player).

  Further, many of these consoles allow you to connect to the Internet and, by extension, to play online games with video gamers around the world.

- Most of the consoles also allow you to connect to social network communities (Facebook and the like).

- All of the newer consoles – with varying degrees of effectiveness – allow for motion sensing games. The console's controller picks up your movement or the motion of a hand-held instrument and then moves the action on the screen accordingly.

  If you delve deeper into the gaming world, you'll hear terms like "Wii Motion Plus" or "Xbox Kinect" which refer to the game's motion sensors.

> Even more exciting to gamers, newer models have added voice commands to compliment these motion sensors.

A (subjective) word of caution

Playing video games can become highly addictive.

The realism and surround-sound motion and activity makes one lose focus on the time or, for that matter, where they are. (This, of course, is the intention of every game manufacturer – the "purpose" of the game if you will.)

You might start to play a game and – suddenly, it seems – hours have gone by.

You might want to consider setting an alarm clock or timer to keep track of where you are and how much time you've spent.

Video Games: At a glance

The Pros

- Video games allow you to immerse yourself into an interactive movie-like experience (where you are at the controls.).

- You should be able to find just the right video game for your tastes. There is a wide variety of video games, ranging from the educational and informative to the first-person shoot-'em-up.

- Most new model consoles offer a multitude of functions (and can serve as a DVD or Blu-ray player as well as the ability to connect with your television to the Internet).

The Cons

- Purchasing video games is far more expensive than purchasing most movies / television shows on DVD or Blu-ray.

- Learning to master video games takes time.

The Hidden Costs

- Playing video games can become very time consuming and, as such, the hidden cost involves your "quality of life".

The Old Made New

Sometimes technology invents devices that can help bridge the gap between the old and the new.

In this chapter, we'll take a look at ways in which you can convert your old media to use in the new digital devices; and we'll show you old standbys that have been reconverted to adapt to new technology.

Turntables: Converting your albums into digital music

Do you have old records that you want to digitally convert into your music library?

There are a number of turntables on the market that are inexpensive and can easily convert your music **from albums into digital files**.

> No, you're not wrong – we've covered some of this material in earlier chapters, for example our chapter on Digital Music (Chapter 12).
>
> We apologize for any duplication, but thought all this material deserved a chapter all to itself.

Generally, these turntable converters should have the following features, but make sure to double-check before you purchase any:

- A USB cable that runs from the turntable to your computer. These turntables are usually compact and lightweight, so they can easily rest on a small table or chair which you can set near your computer.

- Look for turntables that have **3-speeds**, so you can play your 33-1/3 albums, your 45 rpm 'singles' and those priceless 78 rpm gramophone discs.

> In addition to converting your albums, most of these turntables can also <u>play</u> your records – an added bonus.

- The turntable should also include software that will make the interface between your albums and your music library **easy to use**. You just install the software and follow the prompts. It's straight-forward and simple to understand.

> To be on the safe side and save any frustration, ask the store (or call the manufacturer) to make sure the enclosed software is compatible with iTunes or your specific music library venue.

So where can you buy these turntables?

We'd recommend starting with your local retailers, especially those that have a large selection of computers and electronic equipment. If that doesn't work, you might want to try **Brookstone** – they have stores around the country, especially at airports, and you can always try their customer service number (800) 846-3000 for additional information.

> We hate to be a shill for any particular company, but **Brookstone** has a selection of these turntables and cassette players which are easy to use. If all else fails, give them a try.

Cassette Players: Converting your cassette tapes into digital music

There are also a number of cassette player converters that are available on the market. Like their sister-turntable-devices, these cassette players are inexpensive and can easily convert your music from cassettes into digital files.

Much like turntables, these cassette players should have the following features. Make sure to double-check before you purchase:

- A USB cable that runs from the cassette player to your computer. Like the turntables, these cassette players are usually compact and lightweight; and can easily rest on a small table or chair which you can set near your computer.

- Unlike the turntable models, you don't have to worry about the three speeds for your albums. With cassette players, one device is **suited for all cassettes**.

> The obvious exception: these cassette player devices cannot record from those clunky-but-lovable eight-track tape cartridges.

- In addition to converting your cassette tapes, these cassette players have the added ability to play all your cassette tapes.

- Like the turntable models, these cassette players also have supplied software that will make the interface between your albums and your music library **easy**. You just install the software and follow the prompts. It's straight-forward and simple to understand.

To be on the safe side and save any frustration, ask the store (or call the manufacturer) to make sure the enclosed software is compatible with iTunes or your specific music library venue.

You can buy these cassette players at local retailers, especially those that have a large selection of computers and electronic equipment. Look at our recommendations in the Turntable section (above) for additional suggestions.

All-in-one Players: Converting both your cassettes and albums into digital music

Just a quick note: we've seen devices that have both a turntable <u>and</u> a cassette play built into one.

If you have an unusually large number of both albums and cassette tapes in your personal library that you want to convert, the all-in-one device might be just right for you.

Again, to purchase, take a look at our recommendations in the Turntable section (above) for suggestions.

Converting your 35mm slides and photos into digital images

A number of slide and photo converters (**Digital Image Converters**) exist on the market-place which allows you to convert your 35mm slides and photographs into digital images.

You can purchase a well-reviewed digital converter around the $100 range. These converters usually come in two forms:

- Flatbed scanners (similar to the scanners discussed among the accessories in Chapter 2).

- Stand-alone converters.

The flatbed scanners are ideal for photographs; while many of the stand-alone converters come highly rated, especially those which utilize an internal high-resolution fixed camera to capture slides.

Among the features you should look for in deciding which converter to purchase:

1. **Image resolution**. The resolution of an image – see our discussion on "**megapixels**" in our chapter on Digital Cameras (Chapter 13) – is extremely important when choosing a digital converter. The best slide converters create images with a resolution of 14 megapixels. Remember: the higher the megapixel count, the clearer the image.

    Most converters also include features to enhance the quality of the digital image, such as brightness controls and color correction.

    You might also think of investing in software designed expressly to enhance your digital images (Adobe Photoshop or Adobe Photoshop Elements being among the most popular as they offer a wide range of photo enhancing features).

2. **Conversion time**. You should expect an average conversion time of less than 15 seconds per slide; but the best digital converters time in around 3 seconds per slide.

    (Most of these devices convert slide and film, but not all of them convert printed photos. If photos are important to you, look for a device that converts all three forms of media – slides, film and photos).

3. **Help and support**. If you're planning to invest time and energy converting your slides, you want to make sure that the converter you're purchasing contains at least a one-year warranty; and that support for the converter is available by phone and e-mail.

We wish it weren't so: A word about digital converters

Something to keep in mind if you're planning to purchase a digital converter:

Unfortunately, you're not going to turn your old slides and photos into digital images that rival pictures taken with today's digital cameras.

Digital converters will record scratches, dust and color imperfections on the slide. While some converters and photo software will help minimize these imperfections, don't expect a pristine duplication.

---

iPod-playing digital clock radios

Digital clock radios are available at just about every major retail center and online stores, including Costco, Amazon, Target, Walmart, K-Mart and others (even large drug stores).

You're familiar with versions which have a large digital time display and can play AM / FM radio stations.

The newer digital clock radios also include a port (also called a "**docking station**") to hold your iPod.

If you have an iPod, there are several distinct advantages to these digital clock radios:

- Instead of waking up to a harsh alarm or the jarring sounds of AM or FM radio stations, these digital clock radios will allow you to wake up to the iPod music of your choice.

- The clock radio will allow you to play your iPod **inside your bedroom**, without the need for earphones.

We're assuming your clock radio is located in your bedroom.

- Most clock radio ports will also let you charge your iPod at the same time.

Digital picture frames

One "old-fashioned" item that has received a digital make-over is the picture frame.

Digital picture frames allow you pop in a memory card or USB thumb drive and instantly create a slideshow with your family photos, vacation pictures and more. (These digital picture frames display digital photos without the need to print them or attach them to the computer.)

These digital picture frames are reasonably priced. Here are some suggestions on what to look for:

- Look for picture frames with the highest available resolution. The higher the resolution – certainly 640 x 480 pixels or higher – will provide clarity to your pictures.

- Digital pictures frames come in an assortment of sizes, generally between 6-9 inches. Make sure you pick the right size for your needs. (We recommend looking at **Consumer Reports** for the best rating and value.)

- You might want to look for a digital picture frame with built-in wireless capability (in order to "grab" photos from your cell phone or computer).

- Extra space in the digital picture frame's memory card or USB thumb drive is a plus, allowing you to store more pictures for your slideshow.

Section 3: Connecting with Family and Friends

Chapter 18

Social Networking

Who should read this section

If you're looking for a simple way to connect with family and friends, social networking may be tailor-made for your needs.

If your family and friends are scattered around the country (or around the world), using social networking – and its video counterparts, YouTube, Skype and Facetime – may be just the right gathering place.

If you would like to post pictures and personal comments to wide groups of people.

With social media sites like Facebook soaring over 1 <u>billion</u> users (nearly one-seventh of humanity), even if you have no personal interest in choosing this communication vehicle, it makes sense to see what the hubbub is about.

Who should skip this section

If you have a small circle of family and friends, or are a private person, you may not feel a need to reach out in this way.

If you feel social interactions should be in person – and not via online 'gatherings' – this chapter might not be right for you. (Still, we do offer new ways for you to think about exchanging ideas, recipes, etc. that you may not have considered.)

Social Networking: An overview

There are a host of social networking sites. For our purposes, we'll focus on Facebook, LinkedIn, Twitter, Google +; video networking sites such as YouTube, Skype and Facetime; as well as social sites such as Pinterest, Instagram and Vine (sites or "apps" that have gotten lost under the shadow of the giants).

One thing you should know before we begin: social networking sites are **"free"**.

Well, nothing is entirely **"free"**. For starters, you're providing these sites with your e-mail address and, quite often, with your personal preferences.

To the advertising industry, all this information is a dream come true.

Meanwhile, here's an easy way to distinguish between these social networking sites.

Facebook

The behemoth social networking site is **Facebook**. Even if you're not familiar with how to use the site, you're undoubtedly familiar with the name, since Facebook has been in the news for years.

Facebook is the world's most popular social networking site and is generally used to connect friends and family. You can **post** your thoughts, pictures, areas of interest and much more; and you can allow your friends and family to view everything you post.

> For our purposes, "**post**" is the term used when you display something online.
>
> What you choose to display (or "**post**") can include a wide variety of information: random thoughts, pictures, music, video, links to useful information and so forth.

As such, Facebook is considered a personal social networking website.

LinkedIn

In contrast to Facebook, **LinkedIn** is a social networking site that focuses on business and the business professional.

LinkedIn presents your business profile to your friends and associates. On this site, you'll be asked to provide employment history, education, and skills, all designed to display your business prowess and background to anyone who might be interested (including former colleagues and prospective employers).

If Facebook is considered the premier <u>personal</u> social networking website, LinkedIn is considered the top <u>business</u> social networking site.

Twitter

Twitter is a social networking site that allows you to broadcast your random thoughts to the world in general.

Although you're limited to **140 characters**, your composition – known in the Twitter world as a "**Tweet**" – can address any topic or emotion that suits your fancy. Whether you want to 'stand on your soapbox' or 'shout from the rooftops', all can be accomplished via Twitter.

In case you're curious how long **140 characters** might be, they are <u>exactly</u> the total number of characters found in this sentence.

Although you're limited to 140 characters per Tweet, you can sneak around that limitation by adding a link as part of your comment.

The link can then direct anyone to a particular website or blog or article (where you're <u>not</u> limited by the number of characters).

YouTube

Although not as structured as Facebook, LinkedIn or Twitter, **YouTube** is a loosely-configured social networking site in which video content rules the day.

As we've pointed out in **other chapters**, access to video cameras is quite prevalent and common – chances are, even your cell phone already has a built-in video camera inside. All that's needed to post your video on YouTube is to set up an account, then launch your video for everyone to see. We'll give you specific step-by-steps shortly in our YouTube section.

For example, see our chapters on Digital Cameras (Chapter 13) and Cell Phones (Chapter 15) for specifics.

Skype and Facetime

Theoretically, neither **Skype** nor **Facetime** are officially social networking sites. Still, we're including them here, because they allow you to interact – via a webcam and microphone – with friends, family and associates.

Think of Skype and Facetime as **video phone calls**. Again, we'll provide more details shortly.

Additional Social Networking Sites

Under the shadow of the giant threesome – Facebook, LinkedIn and Twitter – loom a host of additional social networking sites. Some are for fun; some are focused on specialized interests; and some aim to compete with the giants head-to-head.

Among the other sites and services we'll cover:

Google +

Google + (pronounced "**Google Plus**") is using the clout of search engine giant Google to offer itself up as a social networking site in direct competition to Facebook.

Google + isn't quite in the same league as Facebook, but with over 400,000 members, Google + is certainly is no slouch as a social network.

Pinterest

For those with a visual eye, **Pinterest** is a site worth looking into.

Instagram & Vine

With cameras everywhere – especially on your cell phone – **Instagram** and **Vine** are (today's) hottest new activities which allows you to take photos and videos from your mobile phone and post them seamlessly and effortlessly on a variety of social networking sites.

Same Day Delivery

We'll also give you the rundown on sites that allow you to purchase a product with **same day delivery**!

Does one size fits all? A word of caution

It's becoming increasingly common for non-related websites to allow you to sign in to their sites by just logging onto your Facebook, LinkedIn or Twitter account. On the surface, this seems an easy and seamless integration of information.

Make sure, however, that the website doesn't ask for "access to your personal information" from these social networking sites. It's already annoying that social networking sites play 'loose' with your personal information. Do you really want non-related websites to have access to all this information? Give much thought before agreeing!

Now that you have a brief overview, let's plunge right in:

Chapter 19

Facebook

Who should read this section

As the world's largest social networking site, Facebook is the perfect place to sign up for if you're considering connecting online with family and friends.

If you have a urge to post your thoughts, pictures, areas of interest and much more for your friends and family to view and comment upon, Facebook could be the ideal site for you.

Who should skip this section

As we pointed out earlier, if you have a small circle of family and friends, there may not be a need to reach out beyond e-mails, letters and phone calls.

Facebook: What you need to begin

Here's what you need before you can sign up for a Facebook account:

1. A computer (see Chapter 1 for specifics)

> By the way, you can also access **Facebook** via an "**app**" on your smartphone, iPad or tablet. In fact, you can access it using any digital device that allows you an Internet connection.
>
> (Handy, if you become addicted to Facebook!)

2. Internet access (see Chapter 4 for specifics).

3. A valid e-mail account (see Chapter 6 for specifics).

How to sign up for Facebook

Just follow these simple steps:

1. Go to the Facebook website: www.facebook.com

2. You'll be taken to the Facebook sign-up page (see below):

   Remember: Popular sites such as Facebook tend to change the look and feel of their websites – often, and without much notice. If you see something a tad different than the image below, don't fret. The basic sign-up process, nevertheless, should be the same.

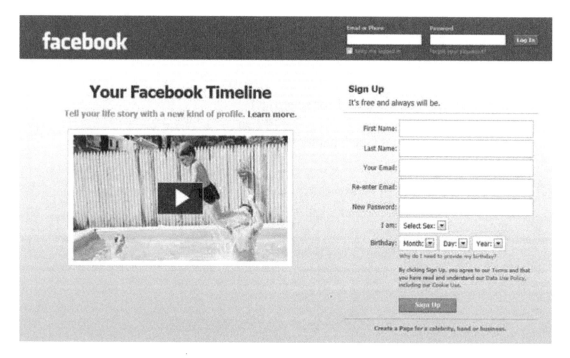

3. Fill in the content under Sign Up: Your first name, last name, e-mail address, gender and birthdate.

   We suggest you enter the information accurately. Remember, you <u>want</u> people to find you – that's the whole purpose behind Facebook. So don't be cute and shave 10 years off your age by juggling your date of birth…otherwise, your old childhood or high school friends might never find you.

4. Click "Sign Up".

   Depending on your browser, you might be asked to type in a series of letters and symbols as part of the security check. (This is to make sure you're actually a person, not an automated device that is trying to access Facebook illegally).

5. Facebook then takes you through **a series of steps** to help you get started and find friends.

As we mentioned before, Facebook and other popular websites have the annoying habit of changing the look of its website.

What this means is you might not see these exact images, but the information required should nevertheless remain the same.

In Step 1, you can search for friends using one of your existing e-mail accounts. Facebook attempts to match people you might know – as it scans your address book – with people you already know (and asks them to "friend" you).

Yes, accessing your address book is a rather large **violation of your privacy**, but it does save time in matching you with friends and family who have existing Facebook accounts.

Facebook tends to violate your privacy a great deal, but, no worries, in a little while we'll show you where you can tweak your privacy settings to suit your personal comfort level.

If you want, you can click "Skip this step". Facebook will ask a variation of 'are you sure?', but if you keep clicking "Skip this step" you can move on.

6. You'll next be asked in Step 2 to provide some basic profile information: High school, college / university, and employer.

The purpose of this step is to help identify and locate friends and associates from school or work.

Again, you can "Skip" this step is you so choose. You also do not need to fill in all the information.

A basic piece of Internet advice

Just because a website asks for information, doesn't mean you <u>have</u> to provide it.

Sometimes certain information is required in order to help the website or sign-up process identify who you are (usually, a name, e-mail address and password).

But providing other information is often at your discretion. Websites are notorious for wanting as much information as possible. (Yes, the information helps the website identify your likes and interests, but most often the information is simply used as a tool to help advertisers.)

So, using our above Facebook Step 2 as an example, you don't need to put in (say) your high school or current employer.

Again, just because the website wants information doesn't mean you have to give it.

You'll discover that mandatory information on a website is usually denoted by an asterisk ("*"); any additional information is optional!

---

7. The final piece of the sign-up process (Step 3) is to provide Facebook with your picture.

   Facebook is assuming you already have taken a picture of yourself or have a webcam hooked up to your computer. You can find out more by revisiting our chapters on Digital Cameras (Chapter 13) or Webcams (Chapter 2).

   Again Facebook allows you to "Skip" this step.

   We do recommend that you add a picture of yourself – if not now, at some point in the near future. A picture of yourself can help friends identify and recognize you. (Once you become comfortable with Facebook, you'll also want to post pictures for your friends and family to see. You may as well start here with your personal picture.)

   If you have privacy concerns, you can post a picture of something that has meaning to you – for example, your pet.

8. Facebook then takes you to your basic profile page, which offers a summary of who you are. In short, much of what you've just inputted into Facebook.

   (You're tantalizingly close to completing your Facebook sign-in. All that's needed is go your e-mail account – the e-mail account you used to register in Step 1 – and verify your e-mail address.)

9. Go into your own personal e-mail account. You'll find an e-mail from Facebook.

Hey, where's the e-mail?

Sometimes your e-mail service provider directs any 'automated' e-mails to your "spam" folder. (Handy most of the time, but in situations like this that can prove annoying.)

Simply locate the "spam" or "junk mail" folder – usually one of the folders located below the inbox – then "move" the e-mail back into your inbox for easy access (by holding down your left mouse button and "dragging" the e-mail from your spam folder into your inbox).

Just follow the information in the e-mail which will (essentially) ask you to click on the "Complete Sign-up" button.

Once you've clicked on the button, you'll be directed back to your Facebook page, along with a note that your account has been activated.

Identifying some basic Facebook terms

Friends / "Like"

"Friends" are just that – these are the people you've befriended. These are the people you connect and share with on Facebook. You can send Friend requests to any other member on Facebook. Conversely, other members on Facebook can send you a Friend request (which you can accept, decline or even ignore).

When you click the "like" button on any update, you're showing your approval of the content. In essence, you're giving positive feedback about some content, company, group and so forth.

News Feed

We'll start here. When you log into Facebook, the News Feed dominates your home page. Located in the center column, your News Feed contains an ongoing stream of status updates posted by your Facebook friends (and any Facebook pages you might follow).

The Wall

Your Facebook Wall is where you can write and publish snippets about your day-to-day activities (as well detailed information via a timeline about your personal history and background).

All this information can be viewed by your friends whom, in turn, can post updates and comments directly to you. The ability to write ("**post**") or add photos can be located on the left column of the Facebook page. In many ways, the distinction between the News Feed and the Wall is minimal. They're both nuances of the front page of your Facebook page.

You can also post items of interest on the Walls of friends and family. For example, if you know a friend loves cats, you can post something relevant to his or her Wall.

Profile / Timeline

Your profile page is a complete picture of yourself on Facebook. Depending on what you choose to add, your profile would generally include your picture, biography and assorted bits of personal information.

Facebook has structured this page to form a "timeline" which shows your updates in reverse chronological order. (For example, any information you might choose to add about your birth – say, place of birth or a baby picture – would be located at the bottom of your timeline, with current information appearing at the top of the page / timeline.)

How to get started on Facebook

Once you've sign-up on Facebook, you can log into your account at any time, using your e-mail and password.

Once you log in, you'll come to the **main page**:

> If, when you signed up, you allowed Facebook to access your address book and provided high school, college and employer information, you may actually already find your Facebook page populated with people knocking on your (online) door, waiting to befriend you.

You should note the main page isn't necessarily what your friends and family will see. Depending on how your privacy settings are configured, they will only see what you allow them to see.

This main page actually serves as your internal account. From here, you'll be able to edit your profile, navigate around Facebook and much more.

If you ever get lost, there are two easy ways to return to this screen. Either click on the name "Facebook" on the upper left side of the any page; or click on the title "Home" on the upper right side of the screen.

Adjusting your profile

There are two ways to access your profile:

- Either click on your name on the upper left part of the screen (directly below the name "Facebook); or

- Click on your name on the upper right side of the screen.

By clicking on the icon marked "Wall" – this will show you what your friends and family will see. There's probably not much to see at the moment… but you still should get the general idea.

If you haven't done so already, probably the first thing you might want to do is add a photo; add some general information about yourself; and add some friends.

- You can add a picture by clicking on "Upload a Photo" or "Take a Photo" under the blank picture at the upper left corner.

  If you select "Upload a Photo", Facebook will allow you to browse your computer in order to select a picture of yourself (which we're assuming you've already saved onto your computer). If not, take a picture of yourself – via your digital camera or cell phone – then save to your computer (see Chapter 13 on Digital Cameras for specifics) and "upload" that photo.

  If you have a webcam on your computer (see Chapter 2 for specifics), you can also select "Take a Photo". Facebook will then allow you to take a picture of yourself directly from that camera.

- You'll also want to add information about yourself. In this case, click the button / label which says "Edit Profile".

While we won't walk you through every choice, you can see that the information – **while highly personal** – can be easily filled in.

> **Remember**: While Facebook asks for a host of information, you're not obliged to fill in every last detail.
>
> Only fill in those items you're comfortable telling about yourself.

Once you add the information you want, just click the "Save Changes" button.

From there, click on the menu options on the far left where you can add information about your Philosophy, Activities and Interests, Friends and Family and much more.

> **Remember to fill in your Facebook profile responsibly…**
>
> We've advised a level of caution throughout the set-up of your Facebook account and profile.
>
> For example, one item in the "Edit Profile" section above is for Contact Information. This section asks for your e-mail address, phone numbers and address.
>
> While you might feel that your friends and family should have that information, what about the "<u>friends</u> of your friends"?
>
> Facebook is an open community and, unless you keep reins on your privacy settings, anyone can see this information. Are you sure you want everyone to have access to your home telephone number and address?
>
> We can't answer that question for you, but we do want to stress that you think carefully before posting personal information online.

What are all these names and buttons?

Since you can spend hours checking out Facebook – and many people do – we'll simply provide you with some information highlights.

Let's circle back to our opening Facebook page and look at some of the names and buttons:

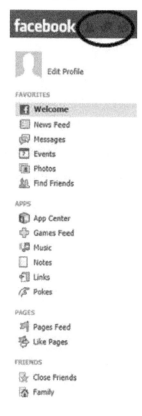

Three icons (on the top, faint but slightly to the right of the word "Facebook", which we've circled in the above graphic). In order from left to right:

Friends Request

The first icon is for "Friends Request". If someone wants to become your friend, you'll find that request here.

Messages

The second icon is for "Messages" when someone sends you a personal message that no one else can see. An "internal" message, if you will.

Notifications

Finally, the third icon is for "Notifications" when you receive a notification from Facebook.

As mentioned, these icons certainly aren't the most pronounced and tend to fade into the background. You'll be able to identify them once you receive a request for friends, messages or notifications for a red number will appear, advising you of the number of pending messages or requests.

Just click on the icon and you'll be taken to the appropriate area to handle the request or message.

Also in our graphic above, you'll see four areas under "Favorites", which include:

Welcome

This will give you access to the first three steps that you had available during the initial sign-in. You again have access here to find people from your address book; enter items for your profile (high school, college and employment); and the ability to add a picture of yourself.

News Feed

Don't expect a summary of the day's current news events. In News Feed, you type whatever is on your mind (which your friends can see on their News Feeds). Additionally, you can see what is on the minds of your friends, since their **"ramblings"** will also be available for you to look at.

> Or "pertinent information", depending
> on your point of view.

Messages, Events, and Find Friends

These last three are self-explanatory. Here, you'll be able to check for any messages, set up or view an event announcement, or find friends.

Adding / Deleting your Favorites:

You can add, rearrange or delete any item from this "Favorites" section.

- Go to the left of any item (and hover your mouse for a moment). For example, go to the left of the Welcome in our Favorites.

- You'll find a pencil icon with the word "edit" alongside.

- Click on the icon or the word "edit" and you'll be able to delete or rearrange.

You can add an item to your favorites using the same procedures:

- Go to the left of any item you'd like to add (and hover your mouse for a moment). For example in our above graphic, go to the left of the "Music" in the Apps section.

- You'll find a pencil icon with the word "edit" alongside.

- Click on the icon or the word "edit" and you'll be given the opportunity to "Add to Favorites".

Apps

- Apps Center

- Games Feed

- Music

- Notes

- Links

- Pokes

Like a number of the other buttons, many of these should be self-explanatory. "Apps Center" and "Games Feed" allow you to access applications and games. "Music" should be obvious. "Notes and Links" allow you to share notes and links to favorite or personal websites or online articles.

"Pokes" is one button that is unique to Facebook.

In Facebook, "poke" is synonymous with "nudge". You could "poke" a friend to say 'hello / I've been thinking of you'.

A poke puts a "poke" alert icon onto a friend or family member's home page. You can "poke" back – essentially replying that you're thinking of them, too.

(Since a poke has no specific purpose other than to poke, we'll just leave it at that and let you figure out the nuances of how you want to use it.)

If you hover over the "Apps" link itself, a "MORE" button will appear to the right. When you click on MORE, it will take you to a page which will offer up some additional games and applications.

Pages

These choices allow you follow and "like" (in essence, give your support to) pages created by everything (and anyone) from companies, organizations, celebrities, musicians, communities organized around a particular interest (i.e. magicians or cat fanciers) and on and on.

Want to know more about your favorite rock groups or comedian; interested in finding out what's new regarding your favorite charity or special interest group; or want to know about any promotions for your favorite products? Well, this is the place to click, search and find.

Friends

Close Friends / Family

Again, these items are self-explanatory. Here, you can have access to your close friends or family members and can easily see which of them are online.

Facebook's invisible menus

Facebook has the annoying tendency of hiding its menu buttons.

Take, for example, the case of "Friends."

Suppose you want to add or restrict people from your Close Friends or Family. Where to begin?

Well, if you hover over the word "Friends", you'll find a "More" button magically appearing on the right. (To be fair, you can also click on the word "Friends" and you'll be taken there.)

This holds true for the "Apps" section as well.

As a rule of thumb for Facebook:

- Hover or click. Chances are that one of those two actions will take you somewhere.

- If you get hopelessly lost, remember …just click on the word "Facebook" or the word "Home" on the far left or right of the top of the page. That will take you back to your home page.

Finally, on the far upper right corner, you'll find three additional buttons / links and a down arrow:

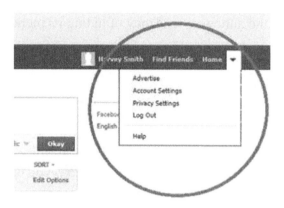

1. You'll see a button / link with your name and an icon with your picture (if you've uploaded one).

   By clicking on your name, you'll be taken directly to your profile. From there, you can add information about yourself; post pictures for your friends and family; write notes and much more.

2. The "Find Friends" button / link is a quick way to, well, find friends.

3. The "Home" button / link will take you to your Home page.

   You might want to click back and forth between the Home button and the button with your name (which takes you to your profile).

   By clicking back and forth, you'll see the two main areas on Facebook and will be able to familiarize yourself with them both.

4. By clicking the "Down" arrow (as seen circled in the graphic above), you can check out your account and privacy settings as well as the **ability to log out**.

Logging out is important, especially if you're trying to access Facebook via a friend's computer (or any public computer).

As long as the computer is logged in, anyone with access can view your Facebook account – hence the need to log out.

Privacy and Facebook

Throughout the book, we've encouraged **caution** regarding the type of information you provide to any online website.

That said, there's a difference between providing information that a website might need to conduct business with you; versus random information that – quite frankly – isn't any of the website's business.

Walking between what's needed and what's random is a fine line. To that end, we recommend you lean on the side of caution.

Facebook is no exception.

Remember, while Facebook doesn't charge any fee, the website isn't a non-profit organization. Facebook derives much of its income from selling personal information to advertisers. Who's personal information? Why <u>yours</u> naturally.

When you click on the "Privacy Settings" button – see our graphic above, circled for details on where to find the "Privacy Settings" button – you'll be taken to the main Privacy Settings page.

Facebook, unfortunately, doesn't make it easy. For example, checking "Friends" as your Default Privacy setting is certainly wise, but what if you've allowed permission for "Friend of your Friend" (who may be a complete stranger to you, but who now would be able to access your information)?

There's no two ways around it. No matter what your Default Privacy Setting, you'll still need to "Edit Settings" on each of the five sections underneath.

Yes, it takes time…although usually not more than five minutes. Just review these settings and decide what's right for your comfort level. Those five minutes will go a long way towards your personal security and peace of mind.

Remember the first steps regarding privacy

While Facebook privacy settings can help curtail the people and organizations that can view your information, the first place to start is the data you provide in your Profile page.

We want you to feel comfortable sharing with family and friends, but you can take steps to protect your privacy by not posting any information that a third-party could take advantage of.

Just as you wouldn't post your credit card number for the entire world to see, is it wise to post the specific dates you'll be traveling on vacation (and leaving the house empty)?

As a rule of thumb: pretend there is a stranger looking over your shoulder when you post something online. And ask yourself the question: would I be comfortable sharing this information with that stranger?

If the answer is "yes", post away. If the answer is "no", perhaps you might reconsider.

Facebook etiquette

While etiquette is often personal, here's just a handful of basic Facebook dos" and "don'ts":

- Be mindful of what you "**post**", especially when it concerns personal or private matters.

  (Do you really want everyone to know that you're feuding with your Aunt Helen? And you certainly don't want to post your travel itinerary for the world to see!)

- Avoid posting "**comments**" on every single post you receive. (Do you really need to post "you're welcome" every time someone posts their "thanks"?)

- Don't vent about work. (You never know what a friend from the office might decide to share about you.)

- For that matter, avoid chronic complaining.

- Don't "**tag**" (identify) the names of your friends in unglamorous photographs.

- Avoid sending "friends" requests to strangers. (Your Facebook popularity shouldn't be judged by the total number of friends you have. Besides, do you really want strangers to know all about you?)

- Avoid meaningless "calls to action". Fighting world hunger is a noble cause. Asking people to show their support for world hunger by updating what they're watching on television is just plain silly.

- Don't "**post**" too frequently. Do we really need to know what you're doing every five minutes?

As we said, "just a handful". You'll find tons of etiquette tips on the Internet as well as on the Facebook site itself.

Facebook: At a glance

The Pros

- With nearly 1 billion users, you'll undoubtedly find most of your friends and family already connected.

- Once you understand Facebook's terminology and 'what's where', the social networking site gets easier and easier to use.

- Many businesses list themselves on Facebook, offering sweepstakes, coupons and more.

The Cons

- On occasion, you may find you've written a post with glaring errors for all your friends and family to see. Unfortunately, **you cannot edit your post**. Instead, you'll need to **delete the post** and start all over.

> **To remove a Wall post:**
>
> 1. Hover your mouse over the post.
>
> 2. Click the "x" button that appears to the right of your post.
>
> 3. Select "Remove Post" from the dropdown menu.
>
> 4. Click "Remove Post".

- Chances are – whether knowingly or not – you'll befriend people you don't know well; or you'll change your mind about how close you want to remain to a particular friend or relative.

  Consequently, you'll need to periodically monitor your Facebook friends and settings…all of which can take time (to say nothing of the annoyance factor).

The Hidden Costs

- For every good photo you receive or worthwhile news feed you read, dozens upon dozens are less-so. Facebook can become a large drain of your time and energy.

- Facebook's membership is an advertiser's dream. As our digital society becomes a haven for consumerism, don't be surprised at how easily you can purchase an array of items, all tailored to your specific needs.

Chapter 20

LinkedIn

Who should read this section

If you're engaged in business on any level or would like to connect with like-minded business associates, having a LinkedIn profile is an absolute must.

If you're currently employed and are considering switching jobs or even careers, LinkedIn is the number one site that companies use to recruit and hire new employees.

LinkedIn allows you to reach out to like-minded business groups. You can also find key contacts within most companies (and how these contacts connect via your friends and associates).

Who should skip this section

If you're retired and know you can reach out to former business associates via other social networking sites such as Facebook, then a site like LinkedIn probably offers no inherent value.

LinkedIn: What you need to begin

As with Facebook, you will need these before you can sign up for a Linked account:

1. A computer (see Chapter 1 for specifics)

> You can use **LinkedIn** via an "**app**" on your smartphone, iPad or tablet. You can also access it using any digital device that allows you an Internet connection.

2. Internet access (see Chapter 4 for specifics).

3. A valid e-mail account (see Chapter 6 for specifics).

How to sign up for LinkedIn

Just follow these simple steps:

1. Go to the LinkedIn website. www.linkedin.com

2. You'll be taken to the LinkedIn sign-up page (similar to the graphic below):

Reminds you of the sign-up pages such as Facebook and others? It should. You'll find that most sign-up pages require much of the same information and will look remarkably familiar.

3. Fill in the content under "Get started – it's free": Your first name, last name, e-mail address, and password.

4. Click "Join".

5. You'll then be asked to fill in some **specific information about yourself**.

> Naturally – since LinkedIn is a business-centric social networking site – most of what you'll be asked to provide will concern your career and vocation.

6. You'll be asked a series of questions, which will take you through a number of pages. At any point, you can choose to skip or ignore a particular step.

These questions and steps include:

- You'll be asked to provide your e-mail address and the password you decided upon. (Yes, again).

- Much like Facebook, LinkedIn will send a confirmation letter to your e-mail account. This is to verify that you have a legitimate e-mail address.

  Open the confirmation e-mail in your e-mail account, then just click on the "Click Here" link. This will confirm your identify and return you to your profile on LinkedIn.

- Once you've confirmed your identity and you're sent back to LinkedIn, you'll be asked whether you want to share your information with people on Facebook and Twitter. You can choose to click on either link or just "Skip this step".

- The next step is pure advertisement. LinkedIn wants you to sign up for their "Premium" account (at a cost, naturally).

  For most people, the free LinkedIn is more-than-enough – so just "Skip this step". (If you happen to be job hunting, you might want to assess whether there is any value for you.)

7. Once you've completed these steps, you'll then be taken to your profile page. Granted, it is still a shell of what it will eventually become, but now the fill-in-the-blanks are up to you.

8. Just begin to fill in information about yourself.

    LinkedIn will walk you through all the steps. You'll start with your business experience, your education, personal information and skills.

    As you complete each section, LinkedIn will keep you posted on your progress. You'll see a yellow highlighter under the "To Do" list on the right which will automatically move downward as you move through each section.

9. Once you complete this section, your profile is **set** and you're ready to go.

Don't fret. LinkedIn makes it easy for you to change, tweak or edit any of this information. We'll show you ways below.

Getting started on LinkedIn

Once you've signed-up for LinkedIn, you can log back into your account at any time, using your e-mail and password.

As you log in, you'll come to the main profile page:

If you're familiar with Facebook – or have just read the previous chapter on Facebook (Chapter 19) – you might recall that the navigating menu is located along the left hand size of the screen, running down the screen vertically.

With LinkedIn, the navigating menu is located at the top of the screen, running horizontally across the screen (see below):

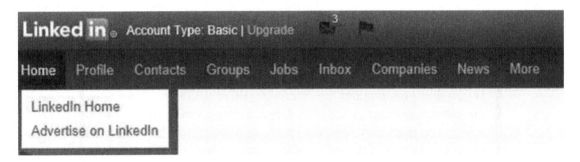

As you can see, the navigating menu includes nine categories. When you hover over each of the menu names, you'll see a drop-down menu that gives you additional choices.

As in our example (above) when you hover or click on the Home button, you'll be able to connect to LinkedIn Home page or a page that can let you advertise on LinkedIn.

Here's information for the additional eight categories:

Profile

In this drop-down menu, you can view and edit your profile; seek and provide recommendations; and **review statistics about visitors to your profile**.

The last two item on the drop-down menu are actually part of LinkedIn's upgrade package and aren't really necessary (unless you run a large company and are trying to assess who's visiting your profile).

Contacts

Under "Contacts", you can "Add Connections" – which is just another way to say 'find friends or contacts'. Clicking on "Connections" will take you to friends or associates you've already made. Selecting "Network Statistics" will give you some basic statistics: for example, how many connections you have (called "**first degree**"); and how many connections are **second** or **third degree** away.

If you don't understand the reference: there was a quasi-popular game years ago called "Six Degrees from Kevin Bacon" in which you tried to tie together pairs of films (or actors) using reference to Kevin Bacon (and his filmography).

Trust us, you don't need to know about this.

Suffice it to say, LinkedIn uses first degree, second degree, third degree and so forth to see how close you can be to a particular connection.

Groups

Within Groups, you can find LinkedIn business groups that revolve around your areas of interest. These links will take you to groups you sign up for; groups you might enjoy; a "Groups" directory; and you also have the opportunity to create (and moderate) your own group.

Jobs

Under Jobs, you can look for jobs; post a job; manage your job applications; or get recruiting tips via hiring solutions. (Job Seeker Premium and Find Talent are both costly upgrades and this isn't the right forum to elaborate upon their pros and cons. By clicking on those links, however, you can find more information about what they offer.)

Inbox

The Inbox is just that: a way to send and receive messages; track invitations; archive and more.

Companies

The Companies link allows you to search for a company. If it exists; chances are LinkedIn is tracking it. Additionally, LinkedIn provides a great deal of data on the company (including company statistics, employees who are members of LinkedIn and more). Once you find a company you're interested in, you can "follow" the company.

News

With the drop-down menus you can **check the news** and save articles.

> That is, the "**news**" as provided by LinkedIn. Sometimes helpful; most of the time not what you think of as news. Still, you might be interested in the information from a business perspective.

More

The "More" tab provides a healthy dose of valuable resources. You can ask questions (and get answers from like-minded members); consult a learning center, and add a myriad of applications that might suit your business needs.

We recommend you play with some of these links to see whether or not they work for you.

Privacy settings and LinkedIn

As you can see on the upper right next to your name – circled in our graphic image example below – there's a drop-down arrow that allows you to access your **"Settings"**.

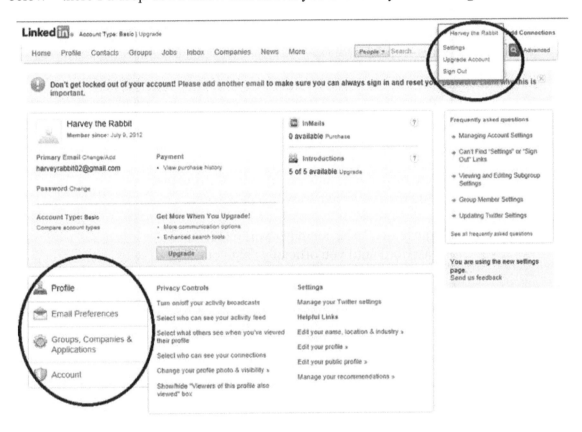

The drop-down menu also allows you to "**Sign Out**" from LinkedIn.

As we've mentioned throughout the book, make sure you sign out – another term is "log out" – when you're using the Internet on any open computer.

By "**open**" we mean any computer that isn't yours – yes, including friends' computers.

If you're using an "open" computer, make sure to sign out from any Internet website that requires you to sign in with a password.

The reason? The computer will retain that password until you officially "sign out / log out".

You don't want strangers gaining access to your personal information nor the ability to purchase from a site you've signed into (say, Amazon or Apple's iTunes Store).

Here, you'll be able to add an e-mail address, change your password, and – more importantly – adjust your privacy settings.

At the bottom left – circled in the above graphic – you'll see the four areas in which you can control your various settings.

We wish we had better news for you about LinkedIn's privacy policy. Unfortunately you'll need to check each of the four areas – which, in turn, all have a number of additional settings.

For example, if you click on "Profile" (circled in our above graphic), you'll see just to the right six additional links to control your settings. You should check each of these links to make sure you're not 'broadcasting' all of your business history to people you might not want to access this information.

These settings are annoying and time consuming, but if you stick with it and make sure your settings are properly secure, you'll find that LinkedIn can be a valuable business tool.

LinkedIn: At a glance

The Pros

- LinkedIn is the #1 business social networking site used by professionals, business associates, corporations and more.

- As a business network, LinkedIn is chock-full with statistics, business resources, and ways of staying in touch with people within your industry or professional interests.

The Cons

- LinkedIn's settings – including their all-important privacy settings – are very cumbersome and can be extremely time consuming to adjust properly.

- As with all social networking sites, LinkedIn requires a fair amount of time to fill in the profile properly and to monitor on a frequent basis.

  (Truth is, if you have no pressing need to stay in touch with your business friends and colleagues, you probably will let this site atrophy.)

The Hidden Costs

- LinkedIn tries to entice you at every turn into upgrading from their basic free service to their variety of premium services.

  While we suggest you closely examine these premium services to see if they're truly needed and wanted for your specific situation, our experience has been that most of what you might be looking for can be found as part of their free service.

Chapter 21

Twitter

Who should read this section

If you enjoy being on the cutting edge of new technology or social phenomena, you will probably find Twitter interesting (if not downright amusing).

Twitter allows you to express your thoughts and opinions to a global audience.

If you are facile with words and brevity, Twitter might be the right social networking site for you.

Who should skip this section

If you prefer a more thorough examination of your ideas and opinions – and aren't enamored with off-the-cuff remarks and popular culture trends – then Twitter might not offer you any value.

Twitter: An overview

A few **bits of statistics** to whet your appetite about Twitter:

> You know our feelings about the ever-changing landscape of **statistics**. These were gleaned over the last year.

- There are over half-a-billion registered profiles on Twitter (over 100 million in the US alone).

- Twitter users send out over 175 million tweets per day.

- The last few minutes of the recent SuperBowl generated 10,245 tweets per second. In fact, most popular events generate over ten thousand tweets per second.

- 69% of Twitter users follow others based on recommendations of friends.

Getting started on Twitter: What you need to begin

If you've been reading along diligently about Facebook and LinkedIn, this is familiar territory. If you jumped to Twitter first – and can't wait to get started – this is what you'll need before you can sign up for a Twitter account:

1. A computer (see Chapter 1 for specifics)

> By the way, you can use **Twitter** via an "**app**" on your smartphone, iPad or tablet. You can also access it on any digital device that allows you an Internet connection.

2. Internet access (see Chapter 4 for specifics).

3. A valid e-mail account (see Chapter 6 for specifics).

How to sign up for Twitter

Just follow these simple steps:

1. Go to the Twitter website. www.twitter.com.

2. You'll be taken to the **Twitter sign-up page.**

> Twitter's **sign-up page** is similar to the sign-up pages for Facebook and LinkedIn.
>
> If in doubt, see the graphic images for those earlier sign-up pages (Chapter 19 for Facebook and Chapter 20 for LinkedIn).
>
> Twitter can be easily identified by its blue bird icon / logo. (Birds "twittering" – you get the idea.)

3. Fill in the content under "New to Twitter? Sign Up": Your full name, E-mail address and a password.

4. Click "Sign Up for Twitter".

    You'll be taken to a page that confirms your name, e-mail address and password. Twitter automatically selects a user name for you, which you can try to change on the spot or at a later time.

    Twitter also asks whether to keep you signed-in on this particular computer and whether to tailor Twitter to your recent website visits – handy, if this is the primary computer you'll be using for your Twitter tweets; not so handy, if this is an outside computer.

    You then click the "Create my account" button – which also says you're agreeing to their terms and conditions – and away you go.

Two-Step Verification

Twitter offers additional protection with what is known as "**Two-Step Verification**". (This protection is being offered by more and more websites these days and is worth noting.)

Essentially, when you sign onto Twitter from a device you're using for the first time – whether a computer, smartphone, iPad or tablet, or the like – in addition to your user name and password, you would also need to register a "**code**".

The "code" is a string of numbers that Twitter sends to your phone via a text message or an automated phone call.

This two-step verification – user name and password and special code – offers added security for all your digital devices.

Some websites automatically establish a two-step verification when you first register. Other sites, like Twitter, require that you 'enable' that protection (by clicking a "Require a Verification Code when I Sign In" box in the account settings area).

You'll be asked to enter your mobile phone number and to click the "Active Phone Button". From there, you'll be given simple instructions on how to activate the code for your account.

5. Twitter then starts you off with a Welcome page.

You'll notice on the right a preview that includes "The Twitter Teacher" message (or "tweet").

The tweet explains that any **Twitter message** is called a **Tweet**. Tweets are short messages – in fact cannot contain more than 140 characters – fortunately, Tweets can contain links to websites, blogs or articles (with no restriction on the linked word count).

6. As you click "Next", you'll be asked whether you want to follow any of the popular Twitter accounts. You can also search for a particular individual, or – at the bottom of the page – you can opt to "Skip this step":

7. The next step is similar to the one above. Except, instead of naming personalities, you'll be able to find and follow Tweets based on categories. You can opt to "Skip this step".

Am I really receiving "tweets" from my favorite celebrity?

On occasion "yes", but the more likely answer is "no".

Unfortunately, many celebrities hire people to maintain their Twitter accounts.

---

8. **Ever redundant**, on the next page Twitter than asks if you want to search through your e-mail account to see if there are Twitter accounts that match with the people in your address book. Again, you can "Skip this step" if you choose.

Redundant but understandable. Twitter can only succeed if you follow people (and people follow you). They make every effort to connect you.

---

9. On the next page, Twitter starts to ask you about information about yourself. Much like Facebook and LinkedIn, you're asked to upload a picture of yourself and to fill in a brief bio. Again, your choice – you can also skip this step.

10. That's it. Once you complete the information or skip the step, you'll be taken to your main Twitter page.

Understanding your Twitter home page

Once you complete the information or sign into your Twitter account, you'll be taken to your home page (see graphic image below). Note that our Twitter home page image is simply a **shell**. Your home page may differ, but much of the configuration should resemble our graphic:

> Once you've sent tweets; followed individuals or personalities; and have people follow you, your Twitter page will become populated and highly active.

A few items of note which we've boxed off in the above graphic:

- You'll see in the top box that Twitter has sent a confirmation to your e-mail account. You'll need to check your e-mail account and click the link contained within the e-mail message. This will allow you to fully access all of Twitter's features.

When you click on the confirmation link, you'll be asked to sign into your Twitter account using the e-mail account and password you've already created. Once you sign in, you're good-to-go.

- Slightly below, in the box with your name – created for "Harvey the Rabbit" in our example – you'll can access your profile and settings. Just click on your name and you'll be taken to a page where you can organize your tweets and edit your profile.

- Finally, under your name, is a blank white box where you can type and send your Tweets. Just type inside the Tweet box, then click "Tweet" when you're ready to send.

Ready to "tweet"?

As we've mentioned, you can use Twitter to reach millions of users on a myriad of topics. You can discuss news developments as they occur (real-time); you can editorialize or express your opinion on any topic; you can solicit feedback on issues; and much more.

The steps to getting started are simple:

1. Decide what you want to say. By in large, most tweets deal with the questions: what's on your mind? or what are you doing (or thinking) right now?

2. Type your message in the appropriate blank white box on the Home Page.

3. Express your message in a short, cohesive sentence or two. Remember, you can also add a link inside your tweet (which will allow you to flush out the topic you're discussing).

   For example, you could be attending a sports or music event; make a comment about the event; and then add a link to a website about the particular musical group or sports team.

4. Although you're limited to 140 characters, Twitter keeps track of the number of characters you have available.

> When you start typing, you'll see the number of characters still available on the button of the message screen.

5. That's all there is to it – just click on the "Tweet" button and your message will be sent for users to view.

Organizing your Tweets

As mentioned, you can easily access your profile and settings. Just click on your name and you'll be taken to the following page where you can organize your tweets and edit your profile:

Just click on the "more" arrow (>) – circled in the above graphic – next to your Tweets, Following (those personalities and organizations you're following), Followers (friends or people who are following you), Favorites and Lists.

Editing your Twitter profile and Privacy Settings

To access and edit your Twitter profile, just click on the "Edit your profile" button (also circled to the upper-right in the above graphic). You'll then come to the Profile Page:

In this Profile page, you'll be able add your picture, a location (where you're from), describe yourself in a short bio; and so forth. You'll also be able to save your Tweets directly to your Facebook account.

More importantly, this page will allow you to made adjustments to your Preferences and Settings.

We urge you to review **two of Twitter's most important settings** – Account and Notifications – in which many of these preferences are stored. (Although not directly labeled "Privacy Settings", your preferences, nonetheless, allow you to tweak what is displayed and to whom.)

> These settings are slightly buried within Twitter; but at least the content isn't as overwhelming as the privacy settings in Facebook and LinkedIn.

Twitter: At a glance

The Pros

- Enables you to express your thoughts and opinions to millions of users.

- Teaches you brevity. You need to express your point-of-view concisely (all within 140 characters).

The Cons

- While you can make reference to thought-provoking articles that can be found on the Internet, a Twitter tweet does not allow enough space to express yourself in any depth.

  As a result, the majority of tweets are shallow and lack substance.

- You can easily become addicted to Twitter.

The Hidden Costs

- Time and attention.

  Even a short composition of 140 characters requires your time and attention.

  The more people you follow (tweets you receive) and the more tweets you send, the more cluttered your in-box becomes.

  Wading through these tweets can be exhausting. Imagine how much energy it would take if you read all your spam (junk) mail and you've a pretty good idea of how draining keeping track of all those tweets can be.

Chapter 22

Additional Social Networking Sites

Who should read this section

Facebook, LinkedIn and Twitter are the most obvious social networking sites. If you'd like to learn more about sites that are on the periphery – but pushing hard to compete – read on.

Who should skip this section

If you'd had your fill with social networking sites – and certainly have no interest in adding still more to the mix – you probably should skip this section.

Why 'additional social networking sites'?

Remember the social networking site "MySpace"?

For years, MySpace was <u>the</u> social networking site. Millions of users and climbing. And then, seemingly overnight, Facebook appeared and MySpace practically dropped from sight.

Most of us think: "Facebook is too large – it will never vanish."

Variations of those same words were actually used in connection with MySpace.

In this fast-paced digital age, technology and its applications change practically overnight. What's more, much of the success (and failure) of this fast-paced / ever-changing world is dictated by the whims of people like you and me.

Consequently, we thought we'd take a look at a few of the social networking sites (and off-shoots) that are knocking on Facebook's door.

Pinterest

One of the fastest climbing social networking sites – at least "today" – is "**Pinterest**".

Pinterest is a visual pinboard. In other words, the site allows you to organize and share all the beautiful things you find – or stumble upon – on the Internet.

Whether you're planning a wedding; decorating your home; or organizing and sharing your recipes (or clothes or every Broadway musical you've ever attended), Pinterest allows you to create visual pinboards on any subject imaginable.

What's more, you can browse pinboards created by other people to discover new things and get inspiration and ideas. Since this is a very visual site, you'll find an abundance of new concepts.

Getting started on Pinterest

1. First, go to the website: www.pinterest.com. When you reach their home page – similar to the sign-up pages for Facebook (Chapter 19) or LinkedIn (Chapter 20), select the "Join Pinterest" button.

2. Once you click the "Join" button, notice that Pinterest works seamlessly with Facebook and Twitter. If you've already signed up for either of these social networking sites, just click the link "log in to our Facebook or Twitter account"; and you're immediately connected with Pinterest.

    Otherwise, you can register using your personal e-mail account.

3. When you click the link to 'sign up with your e-mail account', you're taken to the "Create Your Account" page.

    If you've been following along through these last few chapters, you'll see that Pinterest's sign up page is fairly basic and, at the moment, they don't collect intrusive information. (That said, you still might want review their "Terms of Service" and "Privacy Policy" near the bottom).

    After you've filled in the information – and adding your photo, by the way, is optional – just click the "Create Account" button at the bottom.

4. Once you've clicked "Create Account", Pinterest will send a verification to the e-mail address you've provided.

    Make sure to visit your e-mail account; open the e-mail; and click the "Verify E-mail" button in the body of the Pinterest e-mail message.

    Once you've verified your e-mail, your Pinterest account is active.

5. That's really all that's needed. Once you sign in, you'll be asked to personalize your interests by clicking on the images you like (which Pinterest provides).

    You'll find dozens upon dozens of images to choose from.

Once you've selected the images, you click "Continue" at the bottom of the page and Pinterest takes you to their main page.

6. A few final tips before we leave you to prowl Pinterest.

When you reach the Pinterest Home Page, you'll see three buttons on the upper right hand side of the page:

Click the "Add" button and you'll be able to "start a board" which is the Pinterest way of defining their pinboard. You can also add friends to help "pin" your board.

Select the "About" button and you'll find two valuable resources. The "Help" button which provides instructions on how to best use Pinterest. We recommend you review the "Help" categories before you actually begin – they're not complicated and will only take a moment.

You'll also see the "Pin It Button" (which we'll discuss in a moment).

Finally, you'll see the down arrow alongside your name at the very far right. When you click the down arrow, you'll find "Settings", the ability to "Logout", ways of adding friends, and more.

By the way, if you wander the site (and find yourself lost and want to make your way back to the main page), just click the red "Pinterest" name and logo at the top of every screen and you'll be taken back to their home page.

7. "Pin It Button".

When you select "Pin It Button" – a subset of the "About" button – you'll be taken to a "Goodies" screen.

You'll find instructions – including a step-by-step video – on how to add a "Pin It" button to **your browser's toolbar**.

When you open your **browser** – say,
Window's Internet Explorer – you'll
find the "Pin It" button (by the top left
portion of the screen).

Once you've added the "Pin It" button on your toolbar, you can click on any image
you might find on the Internet and it will add the image to your Pinterest Board.

In addition to the "**Pin It**" button, you will also
discover that many websites now have Facebook,
Twitter and Pinterest icons for easy sharing.

A personal disclaimer

While I don't consider myself visually-challenged – close, but not quite – I've never been a fan of "collages" and "pinboards".

Consequently, I personally find Pinterest an 'acquired taste' and one that I haven't quite mastered. I'm also a little unsettled by the easy way in which pictures can be "captured" by Pinterest users (and its potential copyright violations).

Yet, that said:

I understand that Pinterest – with millions of registered users (and climbing) – has a loyal group of followers; and I can appreciate the visual / graphic components to the site.

Rather than be guided by my personal bias, I recommend you take a look at the site first and decide whether this is a social networking site that is right for you.

Instagram & Vine

By all rights, Instagram and Vine should not even be included in the social networking section as they…

- Both are stand-alone mobile "apps" not unique websites (although they do have a website 'presence').

- Instagram was recently acquired by Facebook; while Vine was acquired by Twitter, making them both subsidiaries of larger social networking sites.

Still, hundreds of millions of members can't be wrong, so we decided to include a brief description.

So what are they?

Vine is a video "app" which allows you to upload six-second videos clips to Twitter and Facebook.

Instagram is both a photo and video "app", allowing you to post photos and 3-15 second videos to Facebook, Twitter, email and several other social media sites.

Both "apps" allow you to make adjustments and post the results onto their respective social networking sites.

So why are Instagram and Vine important? A look into the future

We realize that many of you are still getting used to taking pictures on your mobile phones, never mind figuring out how the video settings work.

So even with their millions of users, why did we single out Instagram and Vine?

The digital revolution – or should we say "evolution" – is upon us and its impact is profound.

Already studies, articles and books have shown that the Internet is affecting the way we read, even the way we think. (Jakob Nielsen's *How Users Read on the Web* and Nicholas Carr's book *The Shallows: What the Internet is Doing to Our Brains* being among our favorites.)

Looking out into the future from these premises, one could make a strong case that we will soon become (perhaps are already) a society that relies on visual imagery and stimulus as its communicator of knowledge – rather than the spoken word or written word in eras past.

We'll leave this conversation to the philosophers and sociologists. Still, if this supposition is accurate, one should be able to point to "apps" such as Instagram and Vine as part of the launching point.

We shall see.

Buying Sites: Coupons / Special Offers

While technically not social networking, there are a number of sites that offer coupons and special deals (with deep discounts).

These sites focus on local stores and outlets – 'local' usually based on your area code – and offer deals on products and services, with discounts often more than 50% off.

Among the top '**social group buying sites**' are GroupOn.com, LivingSocial.com, Dealster. com, Coupons.com, SmartSource.com and more, all coming (and going) on a regular basis.

You search the site for deals within your local area or even register to receive daily e-mails about new deals. Some deals are ongoing – usually with a limit per customer – while other deals must be purchased within a specific time period.

The discount trend is contagious and even **review sites such as Yelp!** sometimes offer deep discounts from the businesses listed or reviewed there.

Yelp! is a '**review**' site by which consumers (you and I) can offer (post) our opinions about restaurants and services for everyone to see.

The site places its emphasis on local / regional goods and services.

Yelp! is very handy if you're looking for a good place to eat; or want to know other people's opinions about which doctor or dentist is best in your area.

Obviously, you'll need to give these sites your e-mail address in order to access coupons and discounts, but this might be a small price to pay for huge savings.

Keep an eye on: Google +, Amazon Fresh and EBay Local

We'd be remiss without mentioning three sites and services that are poised to dominate the scene.

Google +: A 500 pound gorilla?

One such site – already with hundreds of millions of loyal followers – is "**Google +**" (pronounced "**Google Plus**").

Google + is a social networking site that is housed within the behemoth corporation, Google.

You'll find that registering for Google + is similar to the registration process for the myriad of other social networking sites we've covered.

In many ways, Google + is very reminiscent of Facebook. Perhaps the major difference is that Facebook has "friends", while Google +'s friends are called "circles".

We're recommending Google + for several reasons:

- Google + is already making a competitive run against Facebook.

   While Google +'s 100 million subscribers (only months into its launch) is certainly impressive, the site has a ways to go to catch up with the billion Facebook users. Nevertheless, Google certainly has a lot of money to make that happen.

   Google has already acquired the Frommer's Travel Guides brand to enhance its travel offerings. Other staples like Google Maps are already heads above the competition. Factor in the billions of users who use Google's search engine and you can understand why Google + might be poised to give Facebook a competitive run.

- Another reason to recommend Google + is the way the social networking site works seamlessly with the various Google array of functions…Google's search engine, YouTube, **Picasa**, Google Maps and Gmail being just several prime examples.

> If you're not familiar: **Picasa** is Google's free, highly-rated service that allows you to view, organize and edit your digital pictures.

If you're frustrated with Facebook and are looking for a viable alternative, Google + is certainly a social networking site worth considering.

Same-Day Delivery: Amazon and EBay

One of the more interesting website trends – with Amazon and EBay leading the way – involves same-day delivery.

Yes, that sentence wasn't a mistake. You will shortly be able to order products from Amazon and EBay and receive your item within a matter of hours.

Amazon and EBay have launched test sites: primarily the Seattle area (for Amazon) and the San Francisco area (for EBay).

What makes the Amazon experiment interesting is they have launched Amazon Fresh as part of their same-day delivery. "Amazon Fresh" delivers groceries, produce, health and beauty, frozen foods and much more **fresh to your door**.

> Again, the test model is being conducted to a limited number of neighborhoods in the Seattle area.

Will these website-driven same-day delivery services catch on?

The verdict isn't in yet, but certainly large companies are experimenting in that direction.

We're guessing that, if feasible, rollouts would occur in major metropolitan areas first. After that, we'll have to see what additional modifications can be made.

If successful, you will no longer have to call your spouse to remind them to pick up milk on the way home. Just type your request on an applicable website and – presto! – **milk is on its way**.

In fairness, groceries stores have been providing local delivery service via the Internet for years.

Unfortunately, grocery stores don't have the online clout of a site like Amazon – which just might tip the balance in its favor.

Chapter 23

YouTube / Video Calls

Who should read this section

Tired of your plain-old telephone? We'll show you how to connect with friends and family using voice <u>and</u> video.

If you have a video camera and would like to maximize its potential, we'll show you how to launch and host your videos on the Internet.

Videos are *de rigueur* in today's digital world. We'll open your mind to the possibilities of how you can participate in this new form of visual communication.

Who should skip this section

If you have neither interest in videos on any level, nor any inclination in communicating with friends or family via a camera (webcam), then you probably should skip this section.

(On the other hand, if you're interested in the direction digital technology is taking, you might at least skim through this chapter.)

YouTube / Video access: What you need to begin

In order to host your videos on the Internet (**YouTube**) or to connect face-to-face in video-telephone calls (**Skype** or **FaceTime**), you'll need to make sure you have the following:

1. A computer (see Chapter 1 for specifics)

> By the way, you can also post your videos and connect face-to-face with video calls from your smartphone, iPad or tablet.

2. Internet access (see Chapter 4 for specifics).

3. A digital video camera or webcam for your computer (see Chapter 13 and Chapter 2, respectively, for specifics).

4. A microphone.

   Digital video cameras contain a built-in microphone, so there's no need to purchase a separate microphone unless you're planning to produce high-quality videos and the sound from the built-in microphone is too feeble for your needs.

   On the other hand – excluding newer smartphones, iPads and tablets – for many face-to-face video calls you'll need a microphone. We recommend that you find a microphone that also includes a headset. That way, you'll be able to talk and listen from the same device.

   You'll find a wide range of microphone-headset devices. Most will do the job properly and the costs should be reasonable (from \$20 – 75, with the middle range figure providing a more-than-adequate quality). Logitech produces good quality microphone-headsets, but you can certainly find recommendations from stores like Best Buy, Costco, Walmart and others.

Once you've obtained these necessities, you're ready to go:

About YouTube

YouTube is the world's largest **video-sharing website** and, as such, qualifies as one of the key social networking sites (along with Facebook, LinkedIn and Twitter).

> The name "**YouTube**" is shortened from the words "your tube". The implication is that this is your video site (true, since just about anyone can post their videos to the site).
>
> You should know that YouTube was purchased by Google in 2006.

A few statistics (and increasing exponentially):

- YouTube has over 800 million users each month.

- Over 3 billion hours of video are watched each month.

- 72 hours of video are uploaded to YouTube every minute.

- YouTube has more than 1 trillion views. (Yes, folks, that's trillion with a "t").

These statistics were courtesy of the YouTube website. Even if the figures were inflated to fluff up its image, reduce the numbers by half and these statistics are still staggering.

First things first

If you haven't done so already, our first recommendation is browse the YouTube website. Just type in the site name: www.youtube.com and take a look around.

You do not need to register for YouTube in order to view most of its videos. If all you ever want to do is browse the **YouTube site**, mission accomplished – you're done.

> We've covered the basics of YouTube in Chapter 10, so if you want an additional overview, you might want to check out that section.

Assuming, however, that you want to upload your own videos onto YouTube, you still need to take one more step: record a video you'd like to share.

We'll assume that you've read our chapter on Digital Cameras (Chapter 13) and understand **how to record** from your digital camera (or cell phone or tablet).

> **Recording** is usually as simple as pressing the "red" record button. To be on the safe side since video cameras and cell phones vary, we also suggest you check your camera or phone's user guide.

Record what you'd like to share, and then make sure to **save and download the video onto your computer**.

Again, a simple process, but since devices vary, we suggest you double-check with the appropriate user guide / manual.

A few guidelines for your YouTube videos

- There's no limit to the number of videos you can post onto YouTube.

- The length of the video can be no longer than 15 minutes.

  YouTube will occasionally allow select users to upload videos that exceed 15 minutes, but you'll have to request permission. We suggest you try uploading videos less than 15 minutes for a while to get the hang of things.

- Your videos will remain on YouTube until you remove them.

- Your video cannot contain copyrighted material or content used without the permission of the owner.

  (What this means is you can't decide to include a short video clip from some television show or some video you've seen on the Internet without permission.)

- Finally, YouTube accepts most video formats, including the most popular ones. Chances are your video camera will automatically save into one of these acceptable formats.

With that, you're ready to go…

How to sign up for YouTube

Just follow these simple steps:

1. Go to the YouTube website. www.youtube.com.

2. You'll be taken to the YouTube page:

3. Click on "Create Account", located in the upper right hand corner of the page.

4. If you don't already have a **Google account** (for example, a Google Gmail account), you'll be asked to create one. See our graphic below:

> **Why a Google account?**
>
> As we mentioned earlier, YouTube was purchased by Google and is now one of their subsidiaries. (As a result, everything in a way goes through Google.)

5. Just fill in the information on the screen (in the graphic we've offered above). Name, Google user name, password and so forth.

A few tips:

- In signing up for a Google account (even on YouTube), you are – in essence – also signing up for a Google Gmail (e-mail) account. You might want to safely store or remember your Gmail user name (for example, JohnDoe@gmail.com) and password. An extra e-mail account occasionally comes in handy.

- Near the bottom, you're asked to type in two random words (usually a series of letters, numbers and symbols) to prove you're a person not a robot.

  Sometimes these "words" are blurred or the letters run together and are too difficult for any sane person to figure out. If you're not sure what the letters and symbols are, you can always click the "refresh" or "audio" symbol (circled in red in our graphic above) and you'll be given a fresh set of letters and symbols.

- Finally, Google asks to use your information and send you ads, etc. (see our above graphic, circled near the very bottom). Remember, you're under no obligation to agree, so you can easily uncheck that box by clicking on it.

6. Once you've completed all this information, Google and YouTube consider you a legitimate user. As a legitimate user, you will be given a designated place to **upload** all your videos.

Let's clarify the terms "**download**" and "**upload**" as the Internet defines it.

When you "**download**" something – it could be a web page or article or music file – you are taking something that currently resides on the Internet and bringing it 'down' into your computer. (Hence: <u>Down</u>load)

When you "**upload**" something – and for our purposes here let's talk about videos onto YouTube – you are taking something from your computer and bringing it "up" into the Internet. (Hence: <u>Up</u>load)

7. This space where you can upload your video – in YouTube vernacular—is known as a "**channel**".

Channels, in theory, are very much like your television channels (except instead of a Channel 2 or 4, your channel is assigned to your designated YouTube user name).

How to upload your video onto YouTube

1. Just log into your account and the home page – similar to other home pages which you should be familiar with by now – will appear.

2. From here, it's just a matter of clicking on the right buttons and following the instructions.

3. To start, click on the "**upload**" button (located as a text /button along the upper-middle portion at the top of the page).

4. The first time you click on the button and attempt to upload a video, YouTube explains what "activities" you can share on your channel. These activities are standard (and benign) – such as 'like a video', 'comment on a video' and so forth – but you can uncheck any of those boxes if you want.

   Also, you can learn more about your new channel (and its settings) by clicking on the "Learn more" link (at the end of the first paragraph on the left portion of the screen). You can also edit your profile by clicking on "Edit" (the link alongside your name on the right portion of the screen).

   After that, just click "OK, I'm ready to upload".

5. From here, YouTube makes uploading very easy.

   You just upload your video by clicking on "Select files from your computer".

   You'll be brought to a directory of the files on your computer. (We've probably already saved your video in your "**Video Library**", so just select the right one and YouTube will automatically upload your video onto their site.)

See Chapter 6 on Saving an Attachment for some basic guidelines on how to save (and therefore find) your files.

It's as easy as that!

6. Notice that YouTube enables you to "Upload multiple files" from your computer and even to "Record from webcam" directly onto YouTube. The process is similar to the one above: just click and follow the instructions.

A (general) word of caution...

On the upper right hand corner of the YouTube "upload video files" page, you'll notice a "Get Started" button on the far right.

You might think that YouTube is giving you more options on how to get started uploading your videos. On a closer examination, you'll see that the "Get Started" button actually refers to (and is part of) the "Monetize your video...Become a YouTube Partner today!"

Clicking on the "Get Started" will actually take you to a screen you might have absolutely no interest in.

In this case, clicking "Get Started" does no harm and is just a 'promotion' as part of YouTube.

On the other hand, you are likely to encounter similar buttons such as "Click Here" or "For More Information" or even more dire warnings such as "Is Your Computer at Risk" while navigating the Internet.

As a general practice: Before you click anything, make sure you know where the button or link is coming from.

Don't randomly click on buttons or links:

At the best, you'll be taken to ads or promotional sites in which you have no interest; at the worst, these buttons or links can download viruses or malicious software or advertising (known as "malware") which can infect your computer.

As a general rule: the more well-known and well-used the site, the less likelihood of hazardous risks.

Additionally, most web browsers and search engines (See Chapter 5) offer built-in tracking protection when surfing the Internet.

No need to be paranoid about clicking buttons, but certainly be cautious.

YouTube: At a glance

The Pros

- As an 'entertainment' website, YouTube offers a myriad of short videos that can satisfy even the most discriminating viewer's tastes and interests. (As the videos are free to watch, you certainly can't beat the price.)

- Videos have become our society's newest form of communication. By recording and uploading your videos onto YouTube, your views and interests can be seen shared (and seen) all around the world.

The Cons

- For every single enjoyable or informative video, you'll often have to wade through dozens (sometimes hundreds) of poor videos.

  We're not suggesting that every video needs to be a Steven Spielberg movie, but we do recommend that you give some thought to the quality (and focus) of your video before you post onto YouTube. (Otherwise, yours will become one of those "poor" videos people will have to wade through!)

- Quite often, YouTube entries will have 15 or 30 second ads which precede the actual video. Occasionally, you're given the opportunity to skip the ad after 5 seconds, but most of the time, unfortunately not. Most annoying.

The Hidden Costs

- The hidden costs should be apparent. While the site is free and there is no charge to upload your video, to engage in this world of videos you will need **video capabilities** (plus the 'costs' of time and effort in making your videos).

Fortunately, these **capabilities** are already built-into most digital camera, cellphones and tablets.

- In addition, YouTube is expanding its channels. You can now access films, television shows and unique programming. As you might imagine, however, these channels require subscription and, hence, added costs.

Video calls: An Overview

Another practical way to utilize video is via telecommunication. In essence, you hook up a camera (also known as a "webcam") and microphone to your computer (or utilize an app on the newer iPads, tablets or smartphones – see Chapters 14 and 15 for specifics) and, presto, you can **video chat** with friends and family literally face-to-face anywhere around the world.

> Yes, you can talk face-to-face from your computer, smartphone, iPad or tablet. What was science fiction only a decade or two ago has now gained momentum in our daily lives.

While there are several video communication programs on the market, the two most popular are Skype and Facetime.

Skype, which has recently been purchased by Microsoft, allows you to make audio and video telephone calls around the world via your **computer or mobile device**.

> **Skype** can be used on any Windows computer as well as an app within most Android and Apple devices, such as smartphones, iPads and so forth.

Facetime, which is unique to Apple, is a video telephone application that allows you to place and receive video calls on the latest Macs, iPads, iPhones and iPod Touch.

If you're planning to make calls from your computer, you'll need:

1. A computer.

2. Internet access.

3. A webcam.

4. A microphone.

Webcams and microphones are simple plug-and-play devices that hook in effortlessly using your USB port (see Chapter 1 for an explanation and visual example). Note that several webcam models offer built-in microphones.

If you're planning to make video calls from your mobile device, all you need is:

1. The mobile device.

2. Internet access.

The good news...

Since a camera and microphone are already built into mobile devices – such as an iPad, tablet, iPhone, smartphone and some computers – you don't need to purchase them as separate items.

Skype

You'll find that signing up for Skype is **similar to most online sign-ups.**

> Actually, the **similarity** is there for good reasons. Websites want to make the signing up process as easy as possible.
>
> Some websites get greedy, trying to pull as much personal information as they can get away with; but, by-in-large, most website sign ups are simple and familiar.

1. First, go to the website: www.skype.com. Remember, ads on a website change frequently, so today's home page for a website might not quite resemble tomorrow's home page.

    There are two areas worth noting. On the upper right hand corner of the screen, you'll find a 'Join Skype' button which you'll click in order to join Skype.

    You'll also see several links and buttons – "Learn About Skype" and "Support" – which offers an introduction to Skype…and step-by-step instructions how to use its various functions.

2. Once you're ready to begin, click the 'Join Skype' button.

    You'll be taken to the usual "Create an account" page (which in many ways resembles the "Create Account" graphic we used in the YouTube section, several pages above).

3. The "Create an Account" page is straight-forward. Just fill in the information; review their terms of use and privacy statement near the bottom of the page; then click "I Agree – Continue" at the very bottom when you're done.

4. You'll next be taken to a page where you can sign up for Skype Credit.

In English, this means you can **purchase "time"** to use Skype.

Wait a minute, wait a minute – didn't you say said that Skype was free?!

It is free – at least for most of the basic features:

1. You can Skype computer-to-computer for free.

2. You can Skype for free to someone's smartphone, assuming they've downloaded the Skype application to their phone.

You can also use Skype to call any non-Skype member's *telephone* around the world – those calls are not for free; however, the cost for this feature is minimal and is actually handy if you're prone to call all over.

This page, however, is optional and, for the moment, we recommend you check the "Not now, thanks" button and then click "Continue".

We suggest you first get use to Skype and all its features. See if you enjoy the site and plan to use it before you start to shell out money.

Notice at the bottom of this page, Skype puts in a disclaimer that you cannot make any emergency calls with Skype. Our understanding – at least at this moment in time – is that emergency centers (911) cannot track calls made from your computer. Consequently, while Skype has its advantages, don't get rid of your landline or cell phone just yet.

5. You'll next be taken to a page where Skype will download its program to your computer. No fears, Skype asks you first.

   You can either "Run" the program or "Save" the program (and then "run" it from the saved file). Since there's no particular reason to save the program, we simply suggest that you click "Run".

   Note also that Skype provides instructions on "How to Install Skype". Skype tries to make it as easy as possible.

6. You'll be taken through a series of screens.

   Just follow the prompts – in this case, "I Agree – next" and Skype will automatically download the program for you.

7. Once the program downloads – you'll then be asked to sign in again using your user name and password – Skype will take you to a screen that will allow you to test your microphone (audio) and webcam (video). See graphic below:

Just make sure to plug in your microphone and webcam (unless your computer has a built-in microphone and camera) in order to perform the tests. The rest is simple!

8. Once you've tested your system and everything is working properly, just continue to click on the prompts. Eventually, Skype will take you back to its main page.

9. From here, you're good-to-go. Just track down friends and associates with Skype or video access; connect with them; and enjoy one of the Internet's wonderful perks.

FaceTime

Although designed for Apple products, the beauty of FaceTime – which operates in much the same way as Skype – is that the program comes pre-installed on devices that can support it, In other words, Facetime is pre-installed on devices like the newest iPhones and iPads, both of which have cameras built inside.

If you have such a device, all you need to do is click on the program and you're set to go.

Okay, maybe not quite.

- You still need to find friends and family who also have the recent models of the iPhone or iPad and access to FaceTime. (You can't Facetime someone who only has Skype, for example). Sounds easy, but chances are the number of friends and acquaintances that currently have these devices might be limited.

- And although the program is pre-installed (hence: free), FaceTime is only available through a 3G network – and, in the near future 4G network – which means you'll have to pay your telephone carrier for the time and bandwidth necessary to use this program (see our Chapter 15 on Cell Phones for specifics). The costs tend to mount up.

Skype and FaceTime: At a glance

The Pros

- Imagine not just talking to your friends and family, but being able to see them as well. (In particular, this is a great boon to grandparents!)

- There's something fun about being on the 'cutting edge' of digital technology.

- Comparatively, the cost to use Skype – either to make calls or connect via video – is far less than other telecommunication services. In other words, Skype is much cheaper than your phone company.

- If you have a new Apple product – iPhone or iPad – and know a friend or family member who also has one, you can connect instantly using FaceTime.

  And, by reversing the device to capture the outside world around you, you can also show them exactly what you're seeing.

The Cons

- Finding friends and family members who have video capability – a webcam for Skype or one of the newest Apple devices – may not be as easy as it sounds.

  You might find one or two friends, maybe even a small handful, but, easy as it may be to set up, video calls haven't quite caught on with the general population.

- While video calls can be 'cool', technology hasn't quite caught up with the notion. You'll discover small audio lags and the video images can sometimes be a little choppy.

- Chances are, you'll need to some spend time "looking good" for the call – a little make-up for women; a shave for men; to say nothing of what you'll need to wear.

The Hidden Costs

- As you've undoubtedly seen from the very beginning of this chapter, equipping your-self – whether to upload videos on YouTube or video calls via Skype or Facetime – often requires an outlay of cash to purchase the necessary items, such as a camera, webcam and microphone.

  Even the 'free' built-in FaceTime still necessitates buying an iPhone or iPad – with 3G capability or better – which tends to be expensive.

Section 4: Glimpsing the Future

Chapter 24

Beyond the Basics

Who should read this section

If you're ready for more – or if you'd like to see what else current technology can do for you – the next few chapters should prove interesting.

While we might not turn you into a techno-wizard, we'll nonetheless show you how easy seemingly complex issues can be.

If you'd like to understand – and banter around – state-of-the-technical-art phrases and terminology, these chapters will let you hold your own through most digital conversations.

Who should skip this section

If you've already absorbed the chapters that interest you and aren't quite ready to move beyond the basics, then just set the book aside for now. Perhaps you can pick up these chapters later on when you feel more at ease with the technology around you.

Beyond the basics: An overview

If you've reached this far into the book, consider yourself a "graduate".

Over the next few chapters, we'd like to offer up some subjects that are a step or two more advanced than the digital basics.

> We'll keep these upcoming chapters short – just enough to give you a taste; and, in case you're interested, we'll send you down the right road.

Unlike previous chapters, we won't be walking you step-by-step through each segment. Instead, we'll give you an overview, then trust that what you've learned in our earlier chapters – searching on the Internet; viewing instructions on YouTube and so forth – will help you navigate your way deeper into these new arenas.

Remember: Despite evidence to the contrary, technology is supposed to be fun. Experiment with these new advances. If any of the upcoming chapters seem too complicated (or not to your liking), just put it aside and pick up some other topic that you'd enjoy instead.

Chapter 25

Blogs

Who should read this section

If you're curious about "**blogs**", in essence, a website "**journal**", you might find this chapter worthwhile. We'll even show you how you're probably already a "**blogger**" (without even knowing it).

We'll show you how – and where – you can set up your own blog at no cost.

Who should skip this section

The upkeep of a blog takes time and a little bit of effort. If you are already over-extended on your commitments, maybe you should avoid this chapter.

Blogs

So what is a blog?

A **blog** is essentially a website "**journal**" wherein individuals or group of users record their opinions and pass along information on a regular basis.

Each entry into this website journal is called a "**post**" and the person who keeps a blog is referred to as a "**blogger**". Although the numbers frequently vary, current estimates indicate there are about 450 million active English language blogs.

Generally, new blog entries are **created** daily – or, at a minimum, once or twice a week – and are displayed in reverse chronological order, with the most recent "post" at the top.

> These new entries are referred to as "**updates**" (which is a bit of a misnomer, but the language of technology isn't exactly noted for its grammatical exactness).

Does any of this sound familiar? It should.

If you've signed up for a Facebook or Twitter account and have created (**posted**) any entry – for example, a picture of your Aunt Helen or a description of your last vacation – congratulations, you're officially a blogger.

You might also have "surfed" the Internet; found a website with some articles that sparked your interest; then responded with a "comment" of your own. By posting your comment, you can now officially consider yourself part of the world of blogging.

See? Not complicated at all.

If you want to elevate yourself from a mini-blogger to a full-fledged blogger, you should post frequent entries. Ideally, you should also try to focus your blog around key ideas. As an example, if you're fond of animals or enjoy sharing your thoughts about your favorite sports team, you might want to focus your blog entries with one of those subjects in mind.

You could also, as some bloggers do, simply keep a personal online 'diary' of events, thoughts and opinions. One of the more noted motion picture films born from a blogging site was "Julie and Julia" (starring Meryl Streep and Amy Adams) about one blogger's exploits to cook 524 Julia Child recipes in 365 days.

Although not a must, most blog sites are interactive in nature – allowing people to leave comments or messages about what you've written. As we've pointed out, these could be people you've befriended on Facebook or Twitter or, as we'll show you in our next segment, you can easily create your own website and have people from all over the world respond to your entries.

The most popular free blogging "**platforms**" – essentially websites that will "**host**" your blog for free – include:

> To find any (or all) of the sites listed below, just add "**www.**" to the beginning; and "**.com**" to the end.
>
> For example: **www.blogger.com.**

Blogger   www.blogger.com. Highly rated. Owned and operated by Google.

WordPress   www.wordpress.com. Like Blogger, also very highly rated.

Tumblr   www.tumblr.com. Popular among "visual" bloggers (who like to post artwork and photography. Very light on written text.

Other notable blogging sites include:

Weebly
Blog
Medium
LiveJournal
Wix

With an eye on the downside

One of the major downsides to these "free" sites – in other words, not having to pay to "**host**" your blog – is that you don't exactly own your blog.

As a result, if the "**provider**" (the owner of the site you've created your blog on) decides, for whatever reason, that something isn't quite right with your site, it can shut your blog down without any warning. (What's more, the provider doesn't even have to tell you why, nor even give you access to any of the content you've already created / written.)

The chances of that ever happening are slim, but it's something worth considering.

As an alternative, in our next chapter, we'll show you how to create and build a website that is uniquely your own.

Blogs: At a glance

The Pros

- An easy-yet-unique form of communication.

- Whether on Facebook, Twitter or on a blogging website – your own or someone else's – just type your thought; publish your post; and, presto, you're a blogger.

The Cons

- Time, time, time. Posting a single blog isn't difficult, but creating and posting 365 blogs a year can be exhausting. Blogging can be very time consuming. Assess what's most comfortable for your lifestyle before you begin full-time or even part-time blogging.

The Hidden Costs

- Time considerations aside, there are very few hidden costs to bloggers.

  If we had to pick one hidden cost, it would probably be emotional. When you put your ideas and thoughts out into the Internet for everyone to see and comment upon, you might encounter critical or negative feedback.

Chapter 26

Building your own Website

Who should read this section

If you think that building your own website is something that should be left to nerds and techno-geeks, think again.

If you're interested in creating your own website, we'll show you the way in four easy steps.

Even if you're not interested in our 'do-it-yourself' model, this chapter will nonetheless give you an overview on how a website can be set up (in case you want to leave that to others, but would still like to understand 'how' it all works.)

Who should skip this section

If you have no interest in a website of your own – only in websites that you peruse on the Internet – this chapter probably isn't for you. (Still, if you want to know the basic set-up for the sites you visit, you might give this chapter a glance.)

Building your own website (honest, it's easier than you might think)

We can already hear some of you muttering: "Build your own website? You've got to be kidding me!"

In truth, the procedure is a lot easier than you might think.

There are four simple steps to building your own website:

1. **Pick a domain name**.

   Okay, what's a "**domain name**"? That's just computer-talk for the actual name for your website (in other words, the name which follows "www.").

   The domain name consists of the actual name you plan to call your website; followed by a period (called a "dot"); then followed by the extension. The extension could be .com (the most popular) or .org (for organization) or .edu (for education) or .biz (indicating a business) and so forth.

   Examples abound: Google.com; Facebook.com; Pepsi.com; AARP.org; Wikipedia.com; Harvard.edu. You can even register your own name (i.e. JohnDoe.com or MarySmith.com).

2. **Check the availability of (and then purchase) your domain name.**

   > The ability to pick and purchase a website name is what's known as "**registering**" your domain name.

   Once you've picked the name for your website, you need to check whether the name is actually available.

519

> There are a number of websites that will let you check available **domain names** for free. Among the most popular:
>
> - NetworkSolutions.com
>
> - Hostmonster.com
>
> - GoDaddy.com.

Say, for example, you're starting a shoe business. Well, your first choice might be "shoes.com". A quick search and you'll realize that the name "shoes" with all the various extensions has already been snatched up. Same goes for "Cheap Shoes".

On the other hand, playing around with various combinations, you might decide to go with Cheap New York Shoes" which is available.

Same goes for names. If your name is John Doe, there is no JohnDoe.com, but there is a JohnDoe.us. There might also be a website available that includes your middle initial, say, JohnTDoe.com. You get the idea.

Just go to any of these websites and type in the name (or names) you have in mind. These sites will let you know whether the name is available and with what extension. For example, a name with .com might not be available; but a name with a .net or .org might be available and might suit your needs perfectly.

Finally, once you've selected a name and discovered that the name is available, you can then purchase that domain name.

Prices for domain names are reasonably inexpensive. Believe it or not, many of these sites have "sales", so you could purchase a domain name for $19.95 on one site or $9.95 (for the same name) on another sites.

You can purchase the domain name for one year or for a number of years. Domain names can be renewed on a yearly or multi-year basis. For example, you can renew every year until you're tired of the name or have no more use for it.

3. **Build an actual website (using templates).**

   There are quite a number of websites that will allow you to build your website, many for free.

   You might want to check out some of these sites (or perform an Internet search to narrow down the best or most popular web building sites for your needs):

   NetworkSolutions.com
   Hostmonster.com
   WordPress.com

   SquareSpace.com
   Web.com
   Webs.com
   Google's Blogger.com
   SquareSpace.com
   JimDo.com

   What makes these sites so attractive is their **do-it-yourself** approach to websites. They each provide a large assortment of templates for you to choose from. The templates are easy to use and navigate, each with a distinct design. All you need to do is insert information about yourself and your website, and you're all set.

   Many of these sites will also offer their own internal services, in that they will build the website for you.

   There's usually a fee involved. Sometimes hefty.

Most of these websites provide tutorials and have good customer / technical support should any questions arise. Chances are, you can also even find 'how-to' videos on YouTube.

4. **Host your website online.**

Once you've selected and purchased your domain name (Step 1 and 2) and created your web design (Step 3), the final piece of the puzzle is to have your website "**hosted**" or "**launched**" online.

What this means in English: you'll need a website hosting service that will allow you to make your website accessible on the Internet.

These 'hosting' companies provide space on their **servers** and provide the Internet connection necessary for you (and others) to access your website.

> "**Servers**" are much like the hard drive on your computer. They're gigantic and can hold tons of data – including your website (and any changes you might want to make to it).

These website hosting companies traditionally charge a monthly fee in order to "host" your website. Shop around a little and you should find some affordable deals with reputable companies.

As a rule of thumb, we suggest you utilize the hosting services on the site where you purchased your domain name and/or the website on which you created your website design. While this isn't necessary, using one single company often makes things a lot easier – which is why we suggest 'shopping' ahead of time for a good deal and reputable company.

Building your own website: At a glance

The Pros

- As you can see from the four steps (above), building your own website is surprisingly easy.

- Having your own website puts you on the leading edge of digital technology.

- Having your own website allows you to create the design (and content) that is unique to your life and experience. It is the digital age equivalent of your calling card (plus some). You can build followers and increase the visibility of your website to people from all around the world.

The Cons

- While by-in-large an easy process, building a website can sometimes challenge your understanding of digital technology. Fortunately, the companies you will be interacting with all have online tutorials (and helpful telephone technical support).

- The costs. You'll need to purchase your domain name as well as purchasing monthly hosting services. The annual cost isn't too bad. Multiply it out by years, however, and the cost begins to mount up.

The Hidden Costs

- Time and money. We've discussed the costs in our "Cons" section above. There is also a great deal of time involved: Time to search for a domain name; time to build the website; and time to maintain your website – especially if you're planning to use your website to host your daily or weekly blogs.

Chapter 27

The Cloud

Who should read this section

We've touched on "**The Cloud**" in other chapters of this book. In this chapter, however, we'll offer a more detailed explanation – including some basic questions and answers about the Cloud.

The Cloud is the (current) wave of the future. Much of what you'll digitally access over the next number of years will probably be "**Cloud-based**". If you want to know what The Cloud is all about, you might want to read through this chapter.

Who should skip this section

If you're the kind of person who's only interested in results – for example, you're just want to get water from a faucet, and have no curiosity about how the water got there in the first place – this chapter probably isn't right for you.

The Cloud

What is "**The Cloud**" and why should I bother understanding it?

> Also known as "**Cloud Computing**".

The Cloud is a new way of delivering products and services directly to your computer (as well as to any digital device you may own).

We'll try to explain it in this fashion:

- In the very early days of computer online shopping, if you wanted a DVD movie, a CD album or some software, you'd make your purchase, and then the company would send you the product via the mails.

  The product – let's say for our example, a DVD movie – could be used on any DVD player you owned.

  Not bad for the early days, but as new digital devices became more mobile, your original DVD wouldn't work on these new devices and eventually just took up space (and collected dust) in the closet.

- As times progressed, online shopping evolved so that you could download the product as a digital file.

  A slight improvement as you could now download your movie directly to your computer or digital device. But what if you wanted a hard copy of your movie for your DVD player? Do-able, but complex (and, again, you were still stuck with a product that took up space and collected dust).

- As technology continued to evolve, formerly 'stationary' devices (such as televisions and DVD players) were manufactured with Internet capabilities. Suddenly, all of your entertainment devices had the ability to receive digital files. The only drawback: each device needed a "unique" digital file in order to work.

- Fast forward to the present. Manufacturers of digital product – whether movies or books or music or software – realized that if <u>they</u> stored the product for you, they could deliver a pristine digital file to <u>any</u> digital device you might own.

  If you own three devices – say, a television, smartphone, and an iPad or tablet – your product would be stored in the company's large storage facility, and they could deliver the product to your devices wirelessly.

  Since you can access the product – but can no longer really 'touch' the product – the zippy phrase "**in the cloud**" was coined. The underlying implication was that you didn't have to worry, since the product was always there (on their servers) and always available for use on any device you might own.

  What's more, if you started to catch a movie on your iPad or tablet, then came home and turned on your television set, this new capability would allow the movie to be "**synched**" (synchronized) to your other devices, so you'd just continue watching right where you left off.

In theory, not bad.

In reality, however, we're still a culture that likes to "touch and feel" our products to know that they're real (and that they're <u>ours</u>).

Accessing products "in the Cloud" requires a new way of thinking about what we own.

Adjusting to products in the Cloud might take some time getting used to (and will require a new way of acclimating to the products we've purchased).

A few "Cloud" questions that might have popped to mind

Is "The Cloud" similar to streaming music and video? (See Chapter 10 for an overview).

Absolutely. Same concept. Clearly, from the **manufacturer's point of view**, the advantage is you can now stream anything to any device.

The advantages are all from the manufacturer's point of view.

While Cloud storage is an expense, manufacturers would no longer have to absorb major production and shipping costs.

Also, since manufacturers control the content, any outside attempt to "pirate" these films would be greatly reduced.

Is it safe?

Should be. Purchasing something and storing it in The Cloud is as safe as the protocols that the manufacturer provides. If you felt safe purchasing a movie from (say) Amazon or Apple in the past, there should be no concerns purchasing the same product which they will now store on their own servers (in short, in The Cloud).

Is it practical?

Ah, there's the rub!

As long as technology remains constant, there should be no problem. But if this book has shown you anything, it is how rapidly technology is evolving.

As devices like the iPad and tablets continue to improve and evolve, will access from The Cloud keep pace? Probably. But what will happen when an entirely new device suddenly reaches the consumer…requiring a new set of parameters for your products in The Cloud? Well, we'll probably have to wait and see.

More problematic from a consumer's point of view: Suppose in a few years 90% of your entertainment is stored in The Cloud, when suddenly the company's (again, say, a company such as Amazon or Apple) server crashes or its online system is "hacked".

Well, in the short term, you wouldn't be able to access your products until the glitch is re-solved. In the long term, if a hack-attack is successful, your products might vanish entirely from that company's system. Fortunately, most of these companies have enormous backups as well, so this shouldn't be a long-term issue.

Obviously, companies are aware of the potential for these problems and are taking every precaution to make sure this doesn't happen.

We're not trying to be harbingers of gloom-and-doom; rather we're simply advising you that "The Cloud" still needs some work before it becomes fully integrated into our mainstream culture.

Is it inevitable?

Yes – it's already here. Six of the largest film and television studios are supporting a service called **UltraViolet**. UltraViolet is a Cloud service; and – to purchase, manage and watch movies in the near future – you'll probably need sign up for an UltraViolet account. Are the bugs and kinks worked out? No. Does it matter to the studios? Not really.

Backing up your computer onto the Cloud

A number of online services have recently sprung up which allow you to (safely) back up the contents in your computer onto Cloud-based servers.

These services – for example, www.backupify.com. www.crashplan.com or www.carbonite.com – provide very powerful backup and storage tools and are far more reliable than backing up on traditional USB drives.

Cloud-based backup of your computer data offers protection in case your computer crashes (and your data is irretrievable); or in case of disasters such as fire, flood or earthquake.

You'll also find Cloud-based servers available for free with your e-mail. SkyDrive (Microsoft), GDrive (Google), iCloud (Apple) among them. You can also store and move your files on Cloud-based programs such as Dropbox and Box.

So, while we remain cautious about services on "The Cloud", we would be remiss if we didn't suggest this alternative to backing up your computer.

The Cloud: At a glance

The Pros

- Unclutters your home. Storing your movies, books music, even backing up your computer 'in the Cloud" means you can save the space that these products might normally take up.

- The Cloud allows you to access all your entertainment and computer services on every digital device you own.

- The Cloud will also allow you to sync your product to every device. In this way, you could watch a movie on your television, iPad or tablet, or even on your smartphone without missing a beat (or having to hunt down the place you left off).

- No more concerns about damaged or defective discs. The Cloud retains a pristine copy for you all the time.

The Cons

- How do you, as a consumer, keep track of all your products on the Cloud? If you've purchased a few movies from (say) Amazon; other movies from Apple; and still others from Company X, how can you keep track of everything?

- In addition to the challenge of keeping track of all your product, will products streamed from the Cloud from reputable Company A be the same quality as products streamed from less-reputable companies?

The Hidden Costs

- The verdict is still not in regarding The Cloud. Companies are clearly pushing in that direction and we, as consumers, might not have a choice in the matter. Still, there are potential pitfalls that aren't immediately apparent – and, as such, they could represent a hidden cost.

Chapter 28

Online shopping / PayPal

Who should read this section

If you've already been on the Internet – and one time is usually enough – chances are, you've gone online shopping (or certainly have been tempted over the prospect).

This chapter will guide you through online shopping; and we'll even offer you a peek at a payment service called "**PayPal**" (which can help make your online purchases safe and secure).

Who should skip this section

If you're been on the Internet, but vow never to go online shopping, this chapter isn't for you. (We sincerely hope that's not the case, since that would mean we didn't do our job in making you feel more comfortable and secure about technology.)

Online shopping

"**Online shopping**" has become an extremely popular and easy way to purchase goods and services.

> "**Online shopping**" – also known as "**electronic commerce**" or "**E-Commerce**" – allows you to purchase products or services directly from a seller (anywhere in the world) over the Internet.

Online shopping has grown in popularity over the years, mainly because consumers find it convenient to shop from the comfort of their home. Among the advantages:

- You're more-than-likely to find bargains when shopping online. This is especially true since most "online" stores don't have many of the same expenses as brick-and-mortar retailers or their shopping centers counterparts.

  Additionally – depending on the location of the consumer – many "online" stores do not charge state tax and offer shipping discounts.

  Among the largest online retailing corporations are eBay, Amazon.com and Apple.com.

- Certainly during the holiday season, online shopping alleviates the need to wait in long lines or search from store to store for a particular item.

Normally, the way you purchase an item online is to input your name, address and credit card information.

While most sites are secure, you nevertheless run the risk of your financial information being "**hacked**".

We've mentioned earlier in this book that **"hacked"** refers to someone's malicious ability to tap into a computer (and retrieve information and personal data).

It's one thing if someone hacks into your computer – you can take precautions (see Chapter 3). It's quite another thing if someone hacks into a third-party computer which might be holding your credit card information (since, obviously, that scenario is out of your control.)

PayPal

PayPal – which is a wholly owned subsidiary of eBay – is a service which offers a (secure) financial alternative.

PayPal is a global e-commerce service which allows payments and money transfers to be made across the Internet. You sign up for the PayPal service, giving your credit card information just once; then PayPal performs the payment processing for online vendors on your behalf.

If the website you're shopping on allows for PayPal – and more and more sites now offer this service – you simply provide your PayPal user name and password and nothing else: PayPal takes care of the rest.

(Your user name and password is provided to the PayPal site, not the third-party website. Further, the charge you'll see on your credit card statement is for PayPal, not the third-party vendor).

Certainly, the advantage to PayPal is that you no longer have to enter your credit card information every time you decide to shop.

PayPal: At a glance

The Pros

- Ease of use. You only need to enter your credit card information once (when you initially sign up for a PayPal account).

- Much like other financial institutions, PayPal is secure and protects your credit card information.

- When purchasing from an online vendor using PayPal, you only need to enter your PayPal user name and password (onto the PayPal site, not the third-party site).

The Cons

- Not all websites take PayPal.

- Currently, risks are there – however slim – that your information can be accessed. The potential risk is as unlikely as if your bank or financial institution would be hacked.

The Hidden Costs

- PayPal is likely to inundate you with offers for additional services. These services are often unnecessary and tend to be a mild nuisance.

Chapter 29

Mobile Payments / Google Wallet

Who should read this section

While this chapter talks about mobile payments and deals specifically with "Google Wallet" – what is it and how it works – in truth, what we're saying should provide you with insights into where (and how) digital financing is evolving.

Who should skip this section

If you're fiercely loyal to your checkbook and are opposed to anything "digital" when it comes to your finances, you might skip this chapter. (You can close your eyes all you want, but welcome to one of the waves of the future.)

Mobile Payments / Google Wallet

The **Google Wallet** is a payment system developed by (naturally) Google. This "**mobile payment system**" allows a consumer to store their debit and credit cards onto their mobile smartphone and purchase products by simply tapping or swiping the phone onto any compatible terminal at any store's counter or checkout.

Launched late in 2011, the Google Wallet is still in its infancy, although the system operates with major credit cards, gift cards, sales promotions and so forth at over 300,000 (and growing) locations. Not bad for a start.

The risks? Obviously, a few. If your mobile phone is lost or stolen, you need to cancel access to your cards immediately. (Of course, the same case could be made if you happened to lose your wallet).

Currently, Google is storing your credit card information in the Cloud (on their servers). Google insists that their servers (and, therefore, your credit card information) are secure. Quite possibly. Yet more and more companies are being "hacked". We'd like to believe Google, but the risks are there nonetheless.

Additionally, as technology expands, the ability to "lift" your credit card information from the wireless airwaves is potentially a problem.

So with all these potential risks, why are we even bothering to talk about Google Wallet and the mobile payment system?

Well, let's remind you of an earlier statistic we mentioned in our chapter on cell phones: Over 90% of all Americans own a mobile phone. Over **60% of these phones are smartphones** – in other words, they have the capability to utilize Google Wallet.

> And this percentage is increasing rapidly as inexpensive smartphones continue to flood the market.

The ease for you to go shopping, then simply "**tap**" your smartphone on a reader and 'away you go with your purchase' is tremendously appealing both for consumers and businesses. One only needs to think about long holiday shopping lines to realize its value.

We're not professing to have a crystal ball about the digital future. We do suspect the mobile payment system is an idea that will continue to be tweaked – especially regarding the security of your financial information – and could one-day-soon find itself an integral part of our consumer culture.

Google Wallet – or some variation on the mobile payment system's functions and abilities – is definitely worth keeping an eye out for.

Mobile Payments / Google Wallet: At a glance

The Pros

- Ease of use. One stop (one "tap") shopping.

- Potentially, the end of waiting on long lines. Google Wallet gets you in and out in a flash.

- No need to fumble for cards…your information is automatically retained on your smartphone and is therefore available for instant use.

The Cons

- Since your smartphone would contain your financial credit card information, you need to take extra precautions in safeguarding your phone.

- Currently, risks are there – however slim – that your credit card information can be accessed by smartphone "hackers".

The Hidden Costs

- As we mentioned earlier in connection with The Cloud, the verdict is still not in regarding Google Wallet and mobile payments. You'll need to walk that fine line between ease-of-use versus potential pitfalls (some of which might not be immediately apparent).

Chapter 30

Smart cars, apparel and homes

Who should read this section

Digital technology is gradually being assimilated into your car, your home, even the clothes you wear.

If you'd like to understand how this technology is being embraced – and whether it's right for you (or if you even have a choice in the matter) – then this chapter should prove interesting.

Who should skip this section

Chapters, like this one and the one to follow, are taking you very close to the precipice of the digital future. If you've had enough – or just want to be surprised by what the future holds in store – then you can probably skip the rest of the book.

Cars, clothes and appliances that think for themselves...

As technology evolves, its impact can also be seen in commonly used products from our everyday lives.

Let's start with automobiles...

Smart Cars

By now, many of you are familiar with **GPS (Global Positioning System)** systems within our car – those miraculous devices that give us seamless street and highway directions to our destinations with, quite frequently, voice-activated systems.

Well, the next round of technology has already begun to show up inside new automobiles: **apps**.

You remember "**apps**" – those nifty applications that add fun and information and entertainment to your smartphones, iPads and tablets, even your televisions? Now automobiles have gotten on the "apps" bandwagon.

We certainly hope you remember as we've covered "**apps**" throughout the book.

If you're drawing a blank, you might want to check out the chapters on iPads and Tablets (Chapter 14) and cell phones (Chapter 15) as a refresher.

With new cars on the market today, you can find models with built-in music "apps" such as Pandora; search engines such as Google; social network connections such as Facebook and Twitter; and much (much) more.

Sounds hazardous? Probably. As a society, we're still arguing the use of cell phones and texting in automobiles. Adding "apps" into the mix will only add fuel to the fire.

Automobile manufacturers have designed (and will argue) that these apps can only be accessed when the car is in a stopped or parked position. Possibly – although there are always ways around this.

For the moment – assuming safety precautions are installed and adhered to – the addition of apps into automobiles will undoubtedly become the latest trend for cars (and drivers).

Smart Apparel

The first wave of smart apparel actually appeared below the marketplace radar. This first wave of apparel consisted of devices that were woven into clothing and took on the name of **wearable technology**. They included:

- Headphones that seamlessly emerge from shirts or caps so you can listen to music or talk on your cell phone while moving about.

- Clothing with built-in iPods.

- A ring that tells time.

- Smart fabric that can monitor your pulse or heart rate.

- "Apps" woven into clothing or via a bracelet that can measure your running or walking stride; even oversee your entire exercise program.

Interesting, but none of this first wave of smart apparel ever caught on with the public.

The same cannot be said about the second wave of smart apparel, which includes 'watches' that serve as phone, camera, music player and Internet connection, all-in-one.

What makes this second wave of smart apparel more likely to succeed is that these 'watches' are being manufactured and led by communication and technology giants Samsung ("Galaxy Gear Smartwatch") and Apple ("iWatch") with many others to follow in their wake.

Whether this second wave of smart apparel will catch the public's fancy remains to be seen; but we're certain the public will have to endure a barrage of ads before the final vote is counted.

Our vote? We vote in favor of these new items and apparel.

There's a very good chance this second wave of smart apparel will succeed. Even more, we suspect the success of items such as the smartwatch will lead to a resurgence of other smart apparel items (and might signal a new wave of how we access technology).

Smart Homes

Another – much safer – way in which technology is beginning to interface with our lives, can be seen within the home.

All of what we're about to describe is available – to a greater or lesser degree – and much can be programmed or controlled by remote devices, including your smartphone, iPad and tablet, and more.

- Imagine starting off on a trip with a nagging feeling that you forgot to turn off the coffee machine or set the security system. With a "smart home", you can assuage these fears by checking online to make sure your systems are on (or off).

- Imagine coming home from a hard day of work and having your "smart home" play your favorite songs the minute you walk through the door (and follow you through the house no matter which room you enter).

- Imagine your sprinkler system connected to the Internet with the ability to translate the current weather report to your lawn or garden's needs. If a thunderstorm has just passed (or is due to arrive), your sprinkler system will automatically adjust accordingly.

- Imagine your lighting system with the ability **to illuminate (or shut off) lights** the minute you walk in or out of a room. (Some of you might even work in an office or facilities in which such a system is already in full operation.)

> Actually, not much imagination is needed here. These lighting systems are prevalent in Europe and in many businesses and hotels around the United States.

- Imagine a smart washer or dryer that can adjust your wash or stop your dryer as soon as the load is complete.

- Imagine an air conditioning system that you can program while away from home. Hot out? You can shut down the system for most of the day, then, as you head home, start it up by accessing the Internet via your smartphone or iPad and tablet.

- Imagine a smart house where all commands are voice activated. "Preheat the oven"; "Turn on the television"; "Shut the upstairs lights". All activations are available on your command.

- Imagine video doorbells that can let you see who is at the door.

- Imagine door locks that can be opened or closed with your fingerprint.

- Imagine refrigerators that separately adjust their temperature for milk, vegetables and left-overs.

- Imagine programming your television so your children can only watch television at certain times.

We think you get the idea. And remember: When we say "imagine…" in our examples above, we're simply describing technology that exists and is already available.

Smart Cars / Smart Apparel / Smart Homes: At a glance

The Pros

- Smart cars…smart apparel…smart homes…technology continues to expand into our daily lives.

- What was looked upon as science fiction years ago is now on the marketplace.

- New technology within our cars, clothes and homes provides a never-before-experienced level of ease and access.

The Cons

- As with all new technology, the current price for many of these devices or features is quite expensive.

  Still: wait a few years until this technology becomes more prevalent and mainstream. Once that's accomplished, the costs will drop dramatically.

- Like much of today's technology, the fancy features will undoubtedly become obsolete year-after-year / model-after-model. Nevertheless, as technology expands – and the marketplace understands what consumers need and want – the improvements will be worth the wait.

The Hidden Costs

- Keeping up with the Jones. As technology expands into our daily lifestyle, the temptation might be to purchase the latest gadget that your neighbor or friend or family member own.

- How often do you need to really buy a refrigerator or replace your lighting system and so forth? The realistic answer is 'not that often'. Remember that 'keeping up with the Jones' can become quite costly and addictive.

Chapter 31

A Peek into the Future

Who should read this section

If you'd like to take a look into the digital 'crystal ball', we'll show where technology is heading over the next 5-10 years.

Who should skip this section

If you're a person who hates 'spoiler alerts' for your books, movies and television shows; and want to be surprised by what the future has to offer, then just put the book aside for now. Come back in 5-10 years to see how accurate we were..

Here are some additional trends – which we'd like to think are "cutting-edge" – that you might want to keep an eye on:

Second Screen / T-Commerce

"**Second Screen**" is the term used to identify **an additional electronic device** that allows the television viewer to interact with the content they are watching – whether the content is a television show, sports event, movie, music, video games or more.

> Think of **second screen** as an interactive remote. At the moment, devices such as iPads, tablets and smartphones can serve as second screens.

The way "second screen" works is that extra content is displayed on the additional (second) device and is synchronized with the content being watched.

As examples:

- You're watching a sporting event – let's use baseball for illustration – and your television is showing the game-winning home run. Your additional device – your "second screen" – can provide you with the player's statistics and the team's current standings; and let you see the winning home run from a number of different (and unique) camera angles.

- You're watching a television show when an actor (or actress) appears on the screen. You know you've seen this actor before, but can't remember his or her name. By shifting to your second screen, you can find that person's name (and credits).

- You're watching a music event on live television. One click on the "like" button on your "second screen" and all your friends on Facebook can be alerted (even linked) to the concert, along with your personal take on the band or musical group.

We mentioned a variation of "Second Screen" earlier in our chapter on Television. This variation is known as **T-Commerce** (short for **Television Commerce**).

> If you missed it, take a look at Chapter 7's final section ("Television: A Glimpse into the Future").

What T-Commerce allows you do is interact with your favorite television programs or events via a "Second Screen" in order to purchase items of interest.

Using our prior examples, you could purchase the hat or sweatshirt of your favorite baseball team with just a click of a button on your "Second Screen". Additionally, if you like what a character is wearing on your favorite television show, again, just select the item on your "Second Screen" and the product can be instantly purchased and sent to you.

"Second Screen" is a new phenomenon known as "social television" by which the user – you! – can become an active participant in the broadcast content (without having to interrupt the flow of the program). Definitely an upcoming trend worth noting.

Going Mobile

Another trend that should be fairly obvious to anyone paying attention is that much of our digital technology has gone mobile.

Most of the new digital devices reaching today's marketplace have certain criteria in common.

They're…

- Small.

- Affordable.

- Portable (mobile, obviously).

- Able to access the Internet (and other media airwaves).

- Can "synch" up with other digital devices.

Such mobility can open new technology doorways. We'll cover some trends and services in a moment:

Geolocation

"**Geolocation**" is the term used to identify where an object – such as a mobile phone or any Internet connected device – can be "located" and "tracked" anywhere on our planet.

In English: Say you're walking in New York City with your tablet or smartphone. Mobile applications – such as Foursquare, Gowalla, Facebook Places and others – can target which street you're on (and can let your friends know <u>exactly</u> where you can be found).

In addition to serving as a "locator" for family or friends, Geolocation may soon become an advertiser's (or shopper's) paradise.

A practical example: If you happen to be passing a restaurant or retail store, applications on your mobile devices can forward or "**push**" (to use the digital expression) coupons or discounts unique for these specific establishments.

Geolocation is the stuff science-fiction films are made of:

Imagine driving down the highway or walking city streets and having every digital billboard you pass post up advertisements that are unique to your personal profile.

Equally, imagine pointing your smartphone or tablet at a retail store to see whether any coupons are available (or what sales are happening).

Wireless Television

Another mobile trend worth noting is "**Wireless Television**" that has now begun to roll out onto the marketplace.

As the name implies, much like their small, mobile counterparts large screen television sets are now going wireless. Not wireless <u>capability</u> (that's been out for a while and which we've covered in Chapter 7 on Television.)

No, power cord aside, we're talking about is a completely wire-free television set. No more cable cords. More interestingly – especially as television sets become more-and-more light-weight – you can actually take your television set from your living room and just bring it into your backyard or roll it into any room in your house.

Practical?

Aside from the lack of clutter from cords? Not really. We don't care how lightweight your flat-screen television might be, the novelty of lugging your television set from room to room would grow old, fast.

Yet like all trends, there's something about the portability of our devices – especially our large, previously immobile devices – that might have merit in the near future.

Context-Aware Services

The more personal information you provide to companies, the more companies can target ads and services designed specifically to your interests.

We tend to think the only information that's gathered about us is the information we enter ourselves into our computer or mobile devices. Not true. Every time you perform a search; every time you call directory assistance; every time your phone or GPS system is tracked from location to location, **all of this data is added to your personal profile**.

> All this data is retained by companies and, quite often, sold to other companies. Facebook is a notorious (but legal) offender.
>
> After a while, this data becomes readily available – which is why you receive so much spam and targeted advertising.

Once the topic for government conspiracy theories, this enriched – and ever-enlarging – **"information data gathering"** is now coveted by corporations and advertisers around the world.

And the more information these companies are able to acquire, the more specific their profile of you: your likes, your dislikes, your political or religious leanings, your spending habits, what (or whom) you trust or distrust, where exactly you travel (and how often), what restaurants you frequent, where you gas up your car…the list go on and on.

Object Recognition

You may have seen the ads on television: Motion sensing video games. In other words, the game console's controller picks up your movement and then moves the action on the screen accordingly. (Microsoft's X-Box Kinect and Nintendo's Wii Motion Plus are two current examples).

The ability to pick up your surroundings and movement is now coming to your mobile devices.

As examples:

- The latest Galaxy smartphone touts that you can transfer a picture or music from one Galaxy smartphone to another, just by tapping the two phones together.

- Applications for your smartphone and tablet are now sophisticated enough to recognize your surroundings and specific places of interest (to you).

- Brand-new safety features on automobiles can recognize and alert you to moving objects – cars, bicycles, young children and more – that might be just outside your normal range.

Projecting the future slightly: imagine these visual recognition sensors within our computers and mobile devices, recognizing our smile or frown – in other words, track our 'social gestures' – and offering mobile suggestions and advice accordingly?

Like so many of the systems and services we've mentioned within this chapter, the future is already here (or very nearly so) and offers a wide new array of technical innovations and opportunities to bring ease and comfort to our lives.

Augmented Reality

"**Augmented Reality**" – also referred to "**AR Technology**" or '**virtual reality**' – is a live view of your physical environment wherein elements are "**augmented**" (enhanced) with computer-generated data (such as sound, video, graphics and more) to enrich your real-world experience.

By using AR Technology – via head-mounted devices (enhanced glasses) or hand-held devices (smartphones or tablets) – this augmented reality replaces real world events with simulated ones.

In English: By wearing augmented glasses, jewelry or clothing; scanning your augmented smartphone or tablet; or even waving your watch around your surroundings, computer-generated data could…

- Let you know what friends might be in the area.

- Give you virtual menus and reviews of restaurants in your area.

- As a tourist, AR could highlight key sites and would light up a (virtual) path from point to point.

These tasks might seem simplistic at the moment, but realize that AR Technology is currently in its infancy.

Google has already completed testing its **augmented-reality glasses** – you may have heard them touted as "Google Glasses". Other companies are jumping on the bandwagon; and these glasses are gradually populating the marketplace.

Even now, with a further nod towards the future, researchers are in the process of developing **augmented-reality contact lenses!**

As augmented reality evolves, don't be surprised if we begin to enter new realms of technology that might push digital media aside (and begin a whole new chapter in the ways in which we receive and access information).

If so…don't worry. **Just Tell Me How It Works** will be there to help you naviate that world, too!

Some final words

Hopefully, you've read (or at least skimmed) the book and have traveled the journey with us to better understand the current digital universe that's available to you.

If we were successful, you should have a more well-rounded acceptance (and appreciation) of digital technology. Perhaps you're a little less apprehensive about technology. Perhaps you're more willing to experiment with some of the devices currently out on the marketplace. Perhaps you've begun to anticipate future digital advances.

Technology, as we've mentioned time and time again, is ever-expanding…and digital technology is no exception.

By now – possibly by the time it's taken you to finish the book – several of the devices we've talked about have already added new features. Some of these devices may already be on the road to obsolescence; while other devices stand poised as new inventions, ready to be released to an otherwise unsuspecting world.

Enjoy the technology. Enjoy the change.

Life is meant to be an adventure; and – for better or worse – digital technology is a major part of that adventure.

As a "graduate" of this book, we wish you much success with your new-found relationship to technology.

Remember, technology exists to make your life easier, happier. Have fun with it all.

Keep us posted on your successes and adventures. Feel free to write to us at Paul.Lance@ JustTellMeHowItWorks.com or even the old fashioned way at

Paul Lance
Just Tell Me How It Works
13930 Old Harbor Lane
Marina del Rey, CA 90292

We wish you our (digital) best!

Let us know…

Mistakes happen. If you've noticed any mistakes – whether a technology tweak or grammatical gaff – please let us know.

If there's something you would like us to cover – which we might have omitted or which you might have a special interest in – again, just let us know.

As we promised at the very beginning, we plan to keep this material up-to-date; and, certainly, your help is needed and wanted.

And finally, if our book has inspired a personal 'success story', jot us a note and tell us all about it!

CPSIA information can be obtained at www.ICGtesting.com
Printed in the USA
LVOW03s1916020714

392719LV00009B/526/P